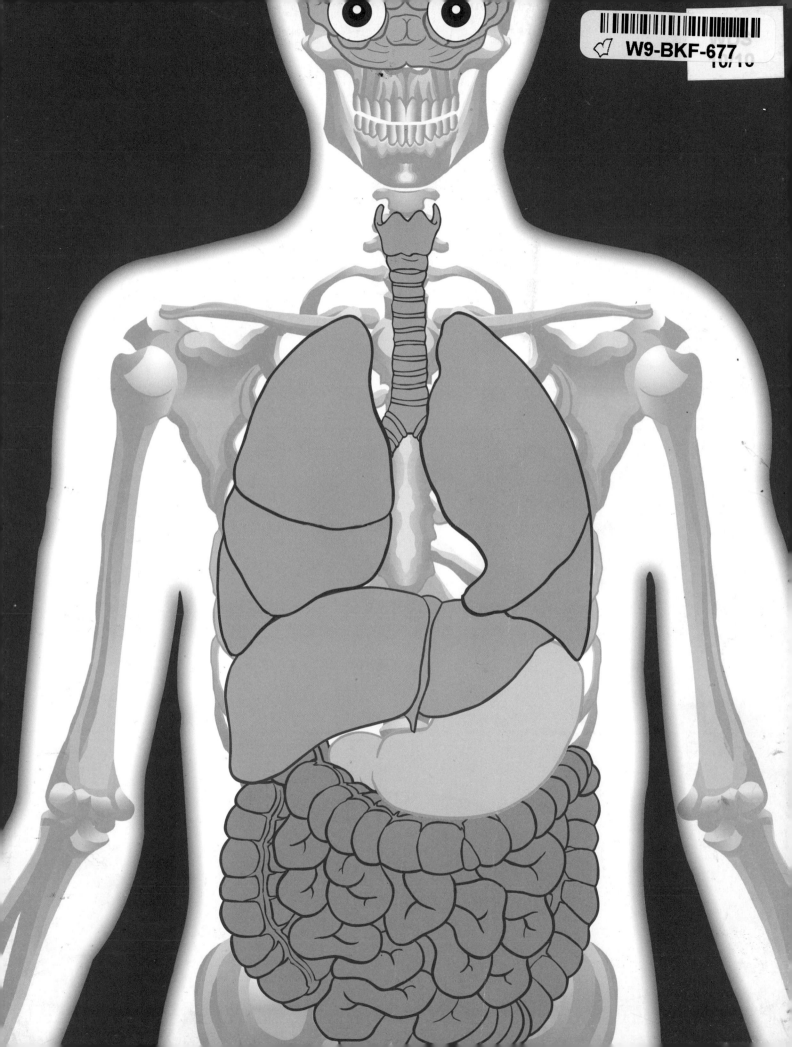

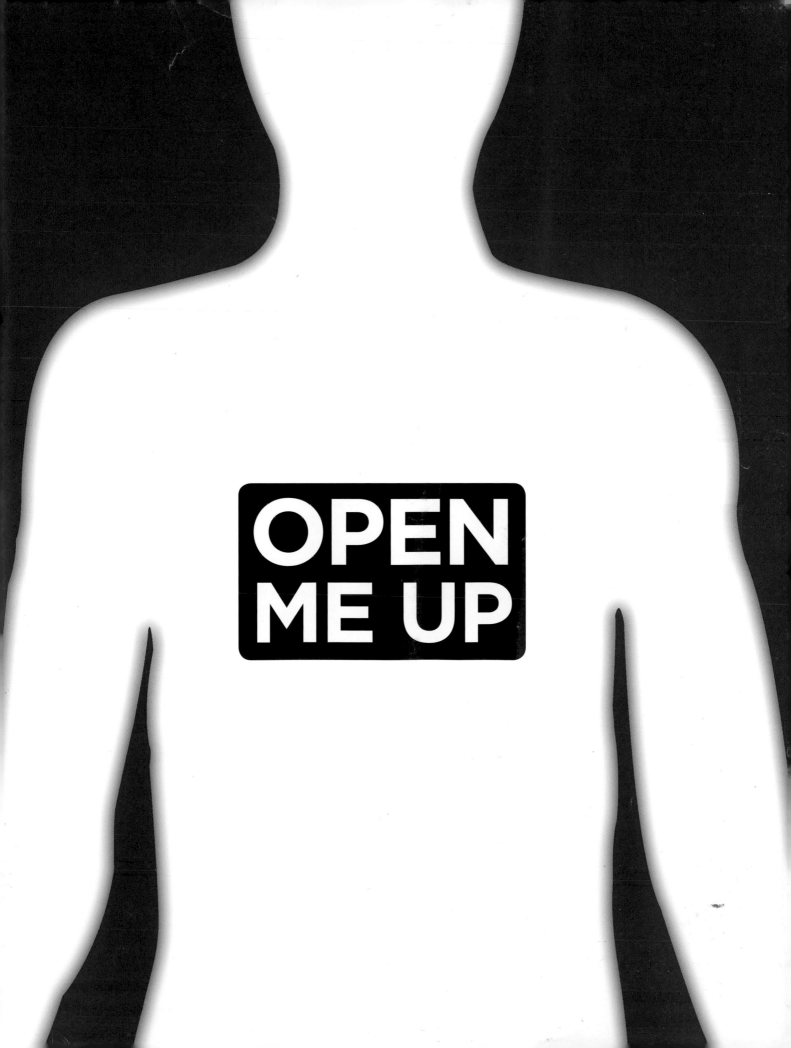

LONDON, NEW YORK, MELBOURNE, MUNICH, AND DELHI

Senior editor Julie Ferris
Senior art editor Philip Letsu

Project editors Niki Foreman, Fran Jones
Designers Jim Green, Spencer Holbrook, Katie Knutton, Hoa Luc, Rebecca Painter, Marilou Prokopiou

Editor Ashwin Khurana
Additional design Johnny Pau, Owen Peyton Jones, Stefan Podhorodecki, Jacqui Swan

Managing editor Linda Esposito
Managing art editor Diane Thistlethwaite

U.S. editor Stephanie Pliakas
Creative retouching Steve Willis
Picture research Nic Dean

Publishing manager Andrew Macintyre
Category publisher Laura Buller

DK picture researchers Rose Horridge, Emma Shepherd
Production editor Hitesh Patel
Senior production controller Angela Graef

Jacket design Yumiko Tahata
Jacket editor Mariza O'Keeffe
Design development manager Sophia M. Tampakopoulos Turner

This edition published in the United States in 2009
by DK Publishing, Inc., 375 Hudson Street
New York, New York 10014

09 10 11 12 13 10 9 8 7 6 5 4 3 2

Copyright © 2009 Dorling Kindersley Limited
OD052 – 07/09

DK books are available at special discounts when purchased in bulk for
sales promotions, premiums, fundraising, or educational use. For details, contact:
DK Publishing Special Markets, 375 Hudson Street, New York, New York 10014
SpecialSales@dk.com

A catalog record for this book is
available from the Library of Congress

ISBN: 978-0-7566-5532-7

Colour reproduction by MDP, United Kingdom
Printed and bound by L-Rex, China

Discover more at
www.dk.com

Written by:
Laura Buller, Julie Ferris,
Niki Foreman, Fran Jones,
Susan Kennedy, Ashwin
Khurana, and Richard Walker

Editorial consultant:
Richard Walker

OPEN ME UP

CONTENTS

SECTION 3: MOVING FRAMEWORK

SECTION 4: IN CONTROL

SECTION 7: MALFUNCTIONS AND MEDICINE

SECTION 8: LIFE STORY

10–11 THE HUMAN RACE
Introduces the ancient relatives of modern humans

20–21 MEASURE ME UP
Throughout history, humans have used body parts as units of measurement

12–13 IN TOUCH
How humans are social animals that live in groups

22–23 LOOKING INSIDE
Modern scanning techniques enable us to see the body's organs and systems in action

What are humans, how are we unique, and how has our knowledge of the body developed since ancient times?

16–17 ANCIENT WISDOM
Looking at ancient theories about the body, some of which remained unchallenged for thousands of years

24–25 NOWHERE TO HIDE
How DNA analysis, biometic scans, and body sensors can be used in criminal detection

18–19 ART INSIDE OUT
Portrays how human anatomy in art has developed with (and been influenced by) our knowledge of the body

14–15 LIVING ANYWHERE
The way humans can adapt to survive and thrive in exlreme environments

BEING HUMAN

THE HUMAN RACE

Around six million years ago in Africa, the earliest humans evolved from apelike ancestors, leaving their forest homes to walk upright on two legs. Since then, different human species have appeared and disappeared, although the precise family tree is not certain. Follow this evolutionary story and find out more about the competitors in the Human Race. On your mark, get set, GO!

HOMO ERECTUS
▶ *1.8 million to 300,000 years ago*
Trailing in fourth place, sturdy *H. erectus*, or "upright man," is the first human to have spread from Africa to Asia and Europe. *H. erectus* specializes in stone tools, including axes, and uses fire for cooking and warmth.

HOMO HABILIS
▶ *2 to 1.8 million years ago*
In fifth place is another contender from the East African grasslands. *H. habilis*, or "handy man," has a bigger brain than *A. afarensis* and is smart enough to make stone tools and use them to cut up meat.

AUSTRALOPITHECUS AFARENSIS
▶ *4 to 3 million years ago*
Bringing up the rear, apelike *A. afarensis* has long arms and short legs and a small brain. He and his much smaller female partner live in the grasslands of East Africa, eating mostly fruit and leaves.

◀ DINOSAURS 61 million years THIS WAY   PRESENT DAY 4 million years THIS WAY ▶

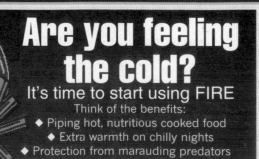

♥ U HEIDE

BEST OF LUCK SAPIEN!

Try bipedalism. It's the way forward!
☛ Hands freed to gather food, make tools, and throw weapons
☛ Look over tall grasses to watch out for enemies and prey
☛ Save energy by not walking on your knuckles

A CHANGE OF SCENE

◆ Tired of endless hot weather? ◆ Prepared to step out of your comfort zone? ◆ Then it's time for you to get out of Africa ◆ Explore exotic Europe ◆ Aspire to the Asian dream

Get your FREE travel guide from: www.homoerectus.com

HOMO NEANDERTHALENSIS
▶ *200,000 to 30,000 years ago*
In second place, burly, big-brained *H. neanderthalensis* lives in Europe and western Asia. He can survive cold conditions by using fire for warmth and cooking, living in caves, and wearing animal furs. He also cares for the sick and elderly.

HOMO SAPIENS
▶ *150,000 years ago to present*
The winner and only finisher is *H. sapiens*. Modern humans started out in Africa but are now found almost everywhere. Big-brained and intelligent, he wears clothes, lives in houses, and has sophisticated cultures, technologies, and languages.

HOMO HEIDELBERGENSIS
▶ *600,000 to 100,000 years ago*
Just behind the front-runners, *H. heidelbergensis* lives in Africa, Asia, and Europe. He is a skilled hunter and uses teamwork to pursue larger prey, such as deer and rhinos, with stone-tipped spears.

✔ **Must be team players**
✔ **Good interpersonal skills essential**
✔ **Previous experience an advantage**
✔ **Must supply own spear**
NO TIME WASTERS

MISSING FOR 30,000 YEARS

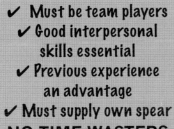

Neanderthal Man
Last seen in a limestone cave in the Rock of Gibraltar
Features:
● Height 5.5 ft (1.7 m)
● Bulbous nose
● Prominent brow ridge
● Deep-set eyes
● Muscular body
● Strong arms, with a powerful grip
● Wears animal skins
● Enjoys meat

May be armed and dangerous; approach with caution

IN TOUCH

Like their closest relatives, the apes, humans are social animals, living in large groups, or communities. They depend on one another for survival and will use touch, sound, gestures, and facial expressions to convey messages of warning, affection, approval, or anger, and to interact with one another.

Humans have developed one vital communication skill that other primates haven't—language.

LIVING TOGETHER

Inside this apartment building, a community of humans is going about its daily life and work. The humans live in separate cells, or "homes," and share facilities such as heating, lighting, and garbage disposal.

FAMILIES

The smallest social group among humans, the family, consists usually (but not always) of two parents and children. It may be connected to the larger community by a network of relations—grandmothers, grandfathers, aunts, and uncles—sometimes called the extended family.

HELPING ONE ANOTHER

Here we see one human, a doctor, helping another human, who is sick. The doctor is using touch to gently explore the cause of the pain, and language to ask where it hurts.

PAY ATTENTION!

Human offspring go to "schools" where adult "teachers" instruct them in the skills they will need later in life. Humans are unique among animals in using spoken and written language as a means of handing on information from one generation to the next.

TO THE RESCUE

Fire has broken out in part of the apartment building, putting the community at risk. Firefighters, humans who have been specially trained to tackle blazes, are on hand to defend the lives and property of the whole group.

IT'S GOOD TO TALK

See how this young couple is bonding in a one-to-one conversation. Through direct eye contact, smiles, a relaxed posture, and an intimate tone of voice, they are sending each other a message—"I like you and want to get to know you better."

TEAMWORK

Humans are good at working together to solve problems or carry out difficult tasks. They give one another helpful advice and will try not to shout when the person helping ignores their instructions, allowing the heavy box to fall on their foot. . . .

FAR AND WIDE

Working from his desk at home, this man is able to send information instantly around the world. With the development of radios, phones, and the Internet, the human community has become a global community.

AT PLAY

Young humans love to play together. It teaches them useful skills such as getting along with their pals and responding quickly to challenges. For some reason, many of their games involve throwing or striking a ball.

LIVING ANYWHERE

Visit the Human Biodome Project and find out for yourself how humans have adapted over thousands of years to living in a wide range of environments. First stop is the Visitors' Welcome Pod to select the clothing and equipment you'll need before traveling to the first of your chosen biodomes. Absorb the total experience, and then move on to the next destination. You will marvel at the ingenious tools, shelters, and ways of life that humans have developed to thrive in different extremes.

CITIES AND TOWNS

In the Modern City Biodome, everything that humans need in order to live is provided on tap. Central heating and air conditioning regulate the temperature in high-rise apartment buildings equipped with devices for easy living, food is trucked in from the countryside, and people travel to work by car, bus, or subway.

HIGH ALTITUDE

You'll find it difficult to breathe in the oxygen-thin atmosphere of the High Andes Biodome. Over time, the people who farm these terraced slopes have developed large lungs so that they can absorb greater amounts of oxygen, and they produce more oxygen-carrying red blood cells than people living at lower altitudes.

HOT AND DRY

Experts believe the San people of the Kalahari Desert are descended from the world's earliest humans. In the Southern African Biodome, you will experience their nomadic way of life—moving frequently from one place to another in search of food in the harsh, dry environment. Go on trips into the bush to hunt and trap animals with the men or gather wild fruit, berries, and leaves with the women.

HUMID RAINFORESTS

The Brazilian Rainforest Biodome will make you sweat! Here you'll visit a riverside village of the Yanomami people. They tend small gardens in the forest, which they prepare by burning the vegetation to make the ground more fertile. When the nutrients of the soil are used up, they move on to another patch, giving the forest time to recover.

FROZEN WASTELANDS

Don't forget to collect your warm parka and snow boots for the Arctic Biodome. The Inuit inhabitants cope with the extreme cold by eating a diet of seal meat and fish, high in protein and fat. On hunting trips they build igloos from blocks of snow, which act as insulators to conserve heat.

ANCIENT WISDOM

Claudius Galen was a doctor, and a highly influential one at that. Born in Pergamum, in what is now Turkey, about A.D. 129, Galen was ambitious and arrogant. His ideas, often wrong, about the body's anatomy and its workings were based on the teachings of the ancient Greeks and his own research. No one, from East or West, dared challenge them for 1,400 years after his death. Then a few brave people queried Galen's work and suggested it was flawed. Time for the great debate.

GLADIATOR

I'm right behind Dr. Galen. Back around A.D. 160 we were entertaining the residents of Pergamum with bloody fights at the town arena. Dr. Galen was the gladiators' doctor, and what a star he was. Whenever we got stabbed, bashed, or slashed, he looked after us. Mind you, he did spend a lot of time poking around inside our wounds. Said it helped him understand how the body works.

GALEN

How dare you question my work? I have described the body's anatomy based on my treatment of gladiators and dissection of animals. I have proved that diseases are caused by imbalances in the body's "humors" (blood, yellow bile, black bile, and phlegm) that can be cured by bleeding and purging. I know that blood is made daily in the liver. There is nothing further to learn about the body.

MARCUS AURELIUS

I'm the emperor of Rome, by the way. When Galen came to Rome in A.D. 163 he soon made a name for himself—and lots of enemies too. Other doctors didn't appreciate the fact that he could cure patients! He left Rome for a while, but I summoned him back to be my personal physician. That gave him time to write and experiment.

AVICENNA

I owe a lot to Galen. Eight hundred years after his death, he's still a major influence on medicine here in Persia. I've taken on his teachings and added a dash of Islamic medicine along with my experiences as a doctor. You can read all about it in my *Canon of Medicine*. It's predicted to be a bestseller for the next 500 years.

ANDREAS VESALIUS
Facts, please, not fiction! My 1543 bestseller, *On the Structure of the Human Body*, shocked doctors everywhere by exposing Galen's mistakes. To discover the truth about human anatomy, I cut up dead people, not animals. That's something Galen never did. And I recorded precisely what I saw, not what ancient Greeks told me I should see.

APE
I'm not a big fan of Galen. He wasn't allowed to find out about bodies by dissecting humans. So what did he do? He cut up apes, like me, along with pigs, dogs, and goats, to see what makes them tick. And they weren't always dead!

PARACELSUS
What nonsense! Such is my contempt for Galen and Avicenna that I have burned their books. This is the 16th century, for goodness sake. Medicine must reinvent itself. We doctors should not be bloodletting and purging; we should use commonsense treatments based on our experiences. My travels and research have taught me that we must learn how the body works before we treat it.

21ST-CENTURY DOCTOR
Let's be fair. Modern medicine owes a debt to all of you. Making mistakes and challenging long-held ideas are all part of how we make discoveries about medicine and patient care. There's still more to learn, though. And one more thing. These days we have female doctors, something all these men would have found outrageous!

OINK! OINK!

ANCIENT THEORIES

ART INSIDE OUT

So you want to make an exhibition of yourself? Enter this gallery and find out how art and anatomy evolved together.

Flat-out wrong (figure 1)
Ancient scholars and early Muslim scientists learned about the body's inner workings through studying cadavers (dead people) and animals. However, a lot was based on guesswork and imagination, as this 13th-century drawing of flattened-out blood vessels shows.

Early realism (figure 2)
During the Renaissance, Italian anatomists cut up cadavers to identify major organs, and depictions of the human body became more realistic. In the 1500s, Leonardo da Vinci dissected 30 corpses to create very accurate drawings.

A cut above (figure 3)
In the 1530s, Belgian-born anatomist Andreas Vesalius was given access to the bodies of executed criminals. In 1543, with the help of talented artists, he published a book called *On the Fabric of the Human Body*. It caused a sensation, revealing human anatomy in incredible detail.

Art school (figure 4)
Attending a dissection became a must do in the 1600s and 1700s. Some cities even charged admission to see a dead body being cut open. Fascinated observers are captured here in Rembrandt van Rijn's painting *The Anatomy Lesson of Dr. Nicolaes Tulp* (1632).

Classic poses (figure 5)
In 1747, German anatomist Bernhard Siegfried Albinus published the landmark book *Tables of the Skeleton and Muscles of the Human Body*. The images of dissected humans were posed against bizarre backgrounds.

Wax models (figure 6)
There were not always enough cadavers to go around, so intricate wax models were made to help anatomy students learn. They showed body structures in complex and realistic detail.

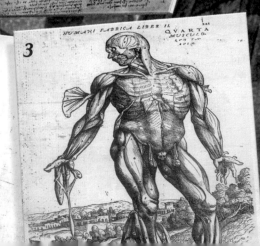

Mass appeal (figure 7)

New printing techniques in the 1800s meant that high-quality anatomy images could be widely reproduced. Classic tomes like the complete *Treatise of the Anatomy of Man* (1831–1854) provided a comprehensive guide to every part of the body. Dissections were no longer open to the public, but held only in medical schools.

Body as art (figure 8)

In recent times, MRI (magnetic resonance imaging) scans and computer imagery enable us to appreciate and understand the art of the human body as never before. German doctor Gunther von Hagens uses actual human bodies as art in his Body Worlds exhibitions. Using a technique called plastination, the liquids and fats in a cadaver are replaced with plastic, so the body does not smell or decay and is pliable enough to pose.

yard

YARD

No one can quite put their finger on the true origin of the yard. It may have developed as a double cubit. Other theories say it is the length of a man's stride, or the distance around his waist. Some say English King Henry I determined that a yard was the distance between his fingertips and his nose. It's impossible to choose.

The ancient Greeks used the breadth of a finger as a basic unit of measurement. A Greek cubit consisted of 24 fingers.

Greek cubit

cubit

MEASURE ME UP

In many ancient civilizations, units of measurement were based on human body parts. Although these measures weren't exactly accurate, as they vary from one person to the next, they were handy (people had their measuring tools built in) and gave a good estimate of length. Here's a heads-up.

CUBIT

The pyramid builders of ancient Egypt measured things in cubits. A cubit was the length of a man's forearm from the elbow to the tip of the middle finger. One of the first recorded (written down) units of measurement, the cubit was used until the Middle Ages.

span

SPAN

Once ancient people started using their arms to measure in cubits, they put their heads together and devised even more ways to use body parts for measurement. The unit of measurement based on the width of a hand, stretched out as far as it could go, from thumb tip to pinkie, was called a span.

fathom

FATHOM

Dating back to the ancient Greeks, the fathom was two yards, or the distance between the fingertips of a man's outstretched arms. Fathoms measured distance on land, but sometime around the 1600s, fathoms became the unit to measure the depth of water. It's difficult to fathom why.

HAND

The width of the four fingers where they meet at the palm is known as the handbreadth, or hand. Used as a unit of length in the ancient world, the size of a hand is now set at 4 in (10 cm) and used to give the height of horses and ponies.

hand

foot

FOOT

People who think this unit of measurement represents the simple length of a man's foot may be putting a foot wrong. In ancient Greece, 16 fingers confusingly made up a foot. The Romans kicked this idea around and adapted the foot as the basis of measurement. One foot was divided into 12 units and measured 12 in (29.6 cm).

The Romans did a lot of marching, so they measured distance by counting their steps. A pace, for example, was the distance between one foot hitting the ground and the same foot landing two steps later.

 6 feet

LOOKING INSIDE

In the past, doctors had to cut bodies open to reveal the organs inside. Modern scanning techniques are a cut above, getting under your skin without . . . well . . . actually getting under your skin. Doctors can check out your internal body parts and watch your organs in action, helping them understand how the body functions and to diagnose diseases. Time to take a sneaky peek for ourselves.

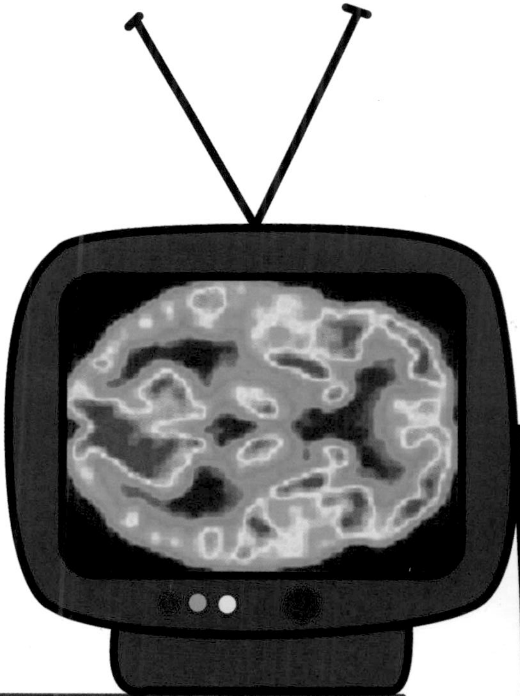

▼ PET SCAN

Positron emission tomography (PET) scans are used to observe activity in body tissue. Radioactive glucose is injected into the part of the body to be scanned (for example, the brain) and the scanner takes pictures of the cells that metabolize (convert into energy) the glucose.

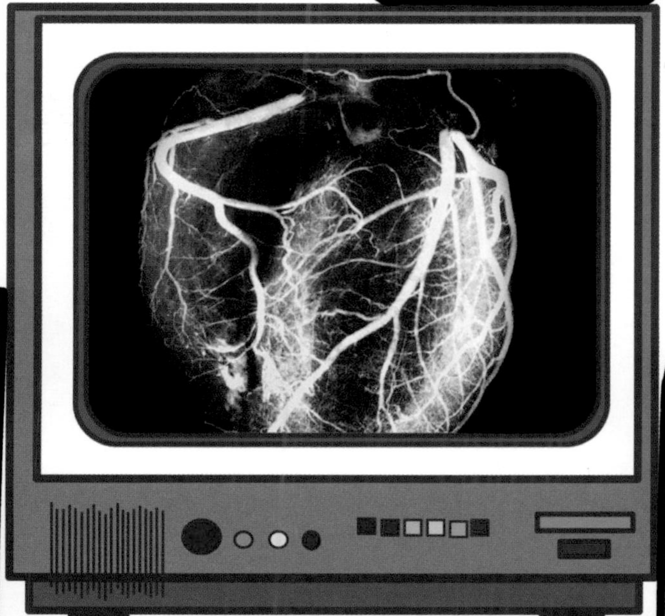

ANGIOGRAM ▶

A special dye is injected into the blood vessels around the heart. The dye shows up on an x-ray, revealing the blood vessels so that doctors can spot any blockages that could prevent the heart from pumping blood.

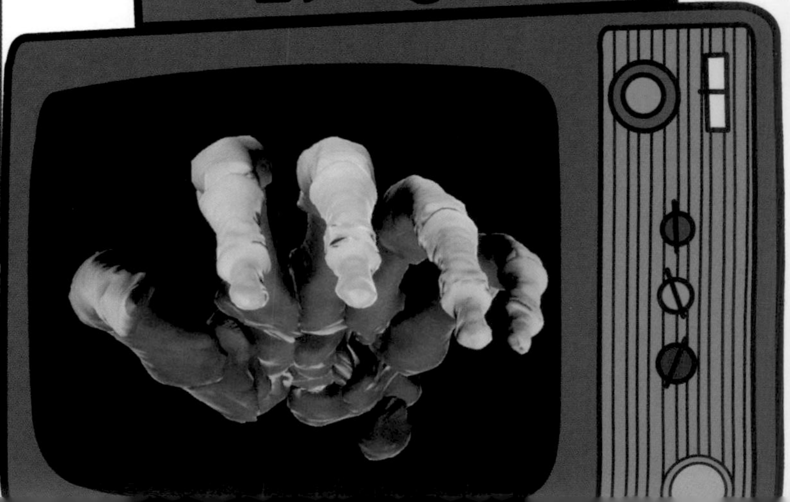

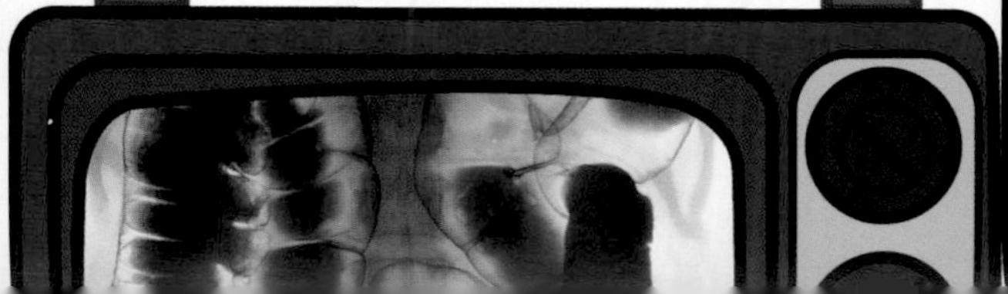

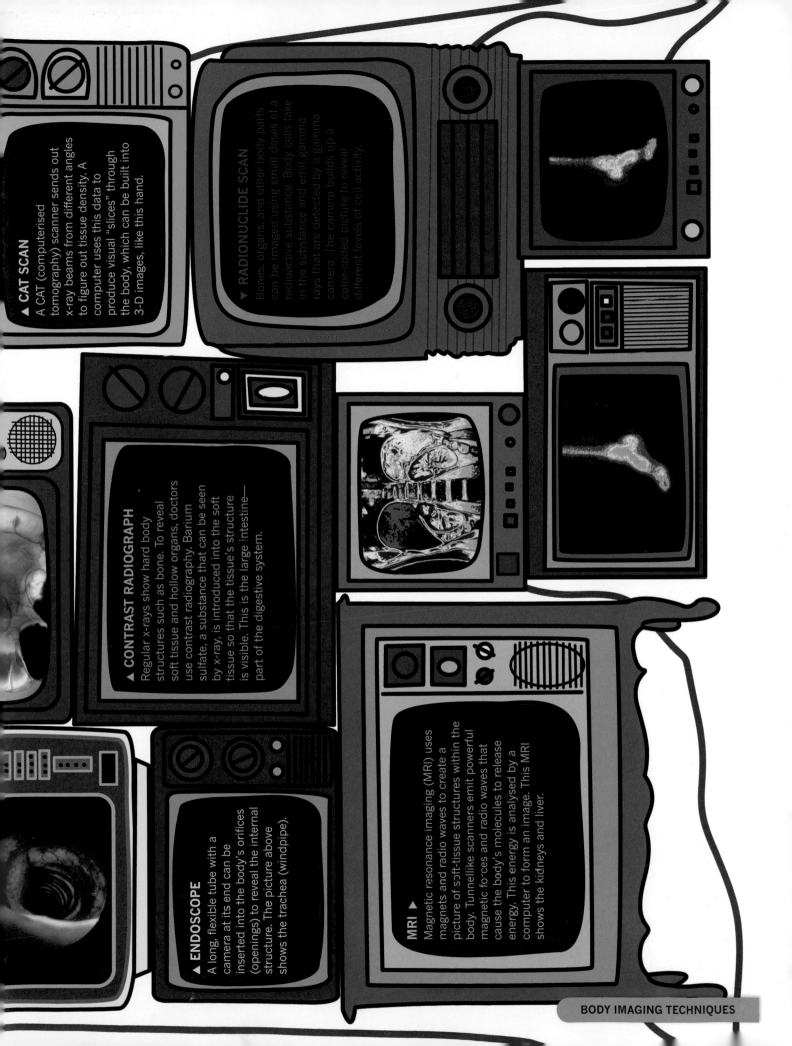

◄ CAT SCAN
A CAT (computerised tomography) scanner sends out x-ray beams from different angles to figure out tissue density. A computer uses this data to produce visual "slices" through the body, which can be built into 3-D images, like this hand.

▼ RADIONUCLIDE SCAN
Bones, organs, and other body parts can be imaged using small doses of a radioactive substance. Body cells take in the substance and emit gamma rays that are detected by a gamma camera. The camera builds up a color-coded picture to reveal different levels of cell activity.

◄ CONTRAST RADIOGRAPH
Regular x-rays show hard body structures such as bone. To reveal soft tissue and hollow organs, doctors use contrast radiography. Barium sulfate, a substance that can be seen by x-ray, is introduced into the soft tissue so that the tissue's structure is visible. This is the large intestine— part of the digestive system.

◄ ENDOSCOPE
A long, flexible tube with a camera at its end can be inserted into the body's orifices (openings) to reveal the internal structure. The picture above shows the trachea (windpipe).

MRI ►
Magnetic resonance imaging (MRI) uses magnets and radio waves to create a picture of soft-tissue structures within the body. Tunnellike scanners emit powerful magnetic forces and radio waves that cause the body's molecules to release energy. This energy is analysed by a computer to form an image. This MRI shows the kidneys and liver.

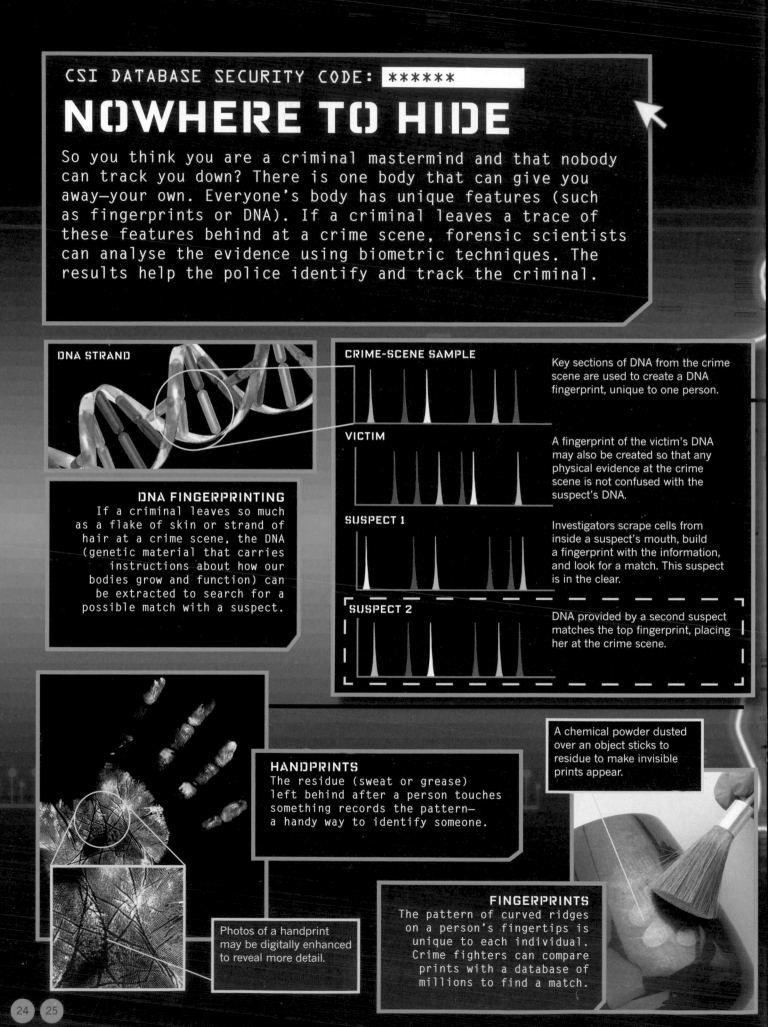

CSI DATABASE SECURITY CODE: ******

NOWHERE TO HIDE

So you think you are a criminal mastermind and that nobody can track you down? There is one body that can give you away—your own. Everyone's body has unique features (such as fingerprints or DNA). If a criminal leaves a trace of these features behind at a crime scene, forensic scientists can analyse the evidence using biometric techniques. The results help the police identify and track the criminal.

DNA STRAND

DNA FINGERPRINTING

If a criminal leaves so much as a flake of skin or strand of hair at a crime scene, the DNA (genetic material that carries instructions about how our bodies grow and function) can be extracted to search for a possible match with a suspect.

CRIME-SCENE SAMPLE

Key sections of DNA from the crime scene are used to create a DNA fingerprint, unique to one person.

VICTIM

A fingerprint of the victim's DNA may also be created so that any physical evidence at the crime scene is not confused with the suspect's DNA.

SUSPECT 1

Investigators scrape cells from inside a suspect's mouth, build a fingerprint with the information, and look for a match. This suspect is in the clear.

SUSPECT 2

DNA provided by a second suspect matches the top fingerprint, placing her at the crime scene.

HANDPRINTS

The residue (sweat or grease) left behind after a person touches something records the pattern—a handy way to identify someone.

A chemical powder dusted over an object sticks to residue to make invisible prints appear.

Photos of a handprint may be digitally enhanced to reveal more detail.

FINGERPRINTS

The pattern of curved ridges on a person's fingertips is unique to each individual. Crime fighters can compare prints with a database of millions to find a match.

FACIAL-RECOGNITION SOFTWARE

Think you're just another face in the crowd? This computer application maps up to 100 facial features and then compares the results against a database to "recognize" you. It can confirm that you are who you say you are, or may be used with CCTV footage to spot people wanted by the law.

The measurements of facial landmarks are converted into data known as a faceprint.

IRIS RECOGNITION

The pattern of the iris (the colored ring around the pupil) in each person's eye is unique. Iris-recognition software converts an iris pattern into a digital code that is compared with others stored in a database.

Each eye, left and right, has its own unique pattern that remains unchanged from a very young age.

FORENSIC DENTISTRY

The shape and size of a person's teeth, as well as evidence of dental work such as fillings and crowns, help identify an individual. Bite marks on a victim or in an object left at a crime scene can be compared against the dental records of a criminal suspect.

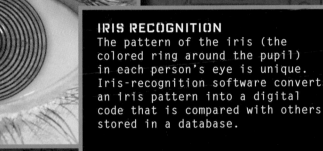

THERMAL IMAGING

We keep ourselves at a constant temperature by generating heat, some of which is given off by our bodies. Thermal-imaging cameras create pictures of this radiated heat, so people can be seen even in complete darkness or through pitch-black smoke.

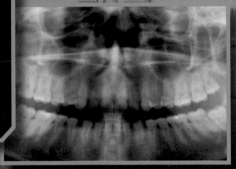

Border-patrol agents use heartbeat and carbon-dioxide detectors to find stowaways.

CARBON-DIOXIDE DETECTION

Detection equipment helps reveal people who are hiding to avoid immigration checks. Carbon-dioxide detectors pick up traces of carbon dioxide in exhaled air, without needing to open containers or doors. When this technology is used, there is no way to stow away.

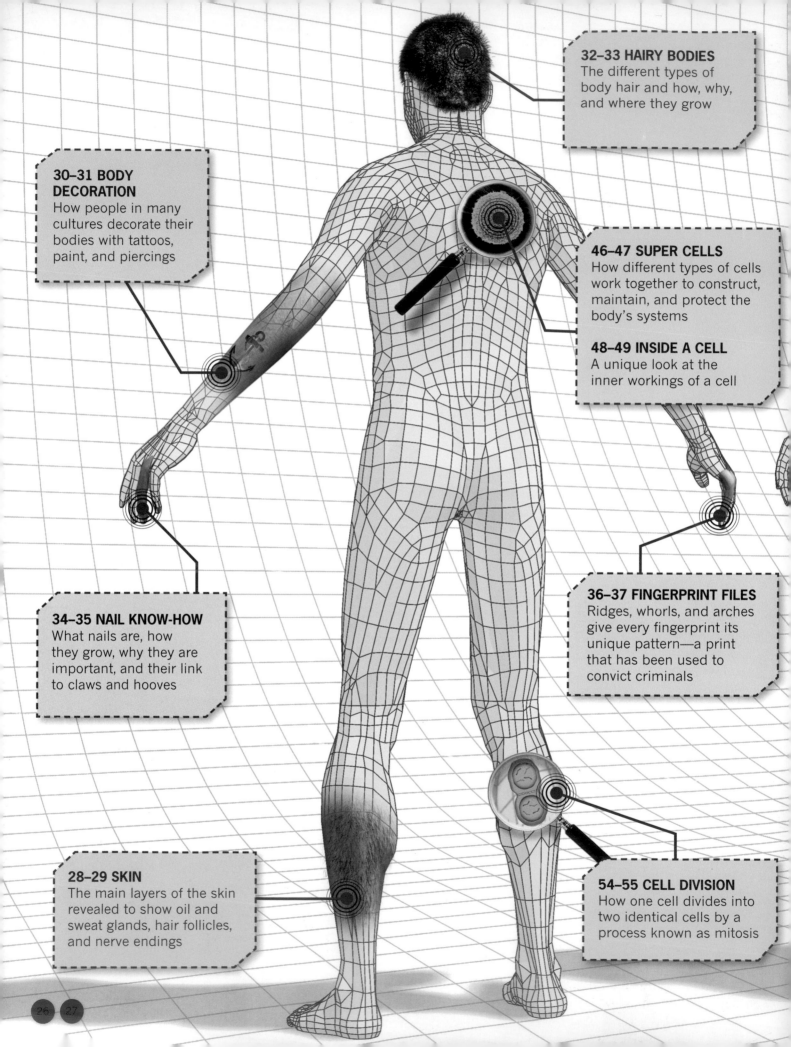

32–33 HAIRY BODIES
The different types of body hair and how, why, and where they grow

30–31 BODY DECORATION
How people in many cultures decorate their bodies with tattoos, paint, and piercings

46–47 SUPER CELLS
How different types of cells work together to construct, maintain, and protect the body's systems

48–49 INSIDE A CELL
A unique look at the inner workings of a cell

34–35 NAIL KNOW-HOW
What nails are, how they grow, why they are important, and their link to claws and hooves

36–37 FINGERPRINT FILES
Ridges, whorls, and arches give every fingerprint its unique pattern—a print that has been used to convict criminals

28–29 SKIN
The main layers of the skin revealed to show oil and sweat glands, hair follicles, and nerve endings

54–55 CELL DIVISION
How one cell divides into two identical cells by a process known as mitosis

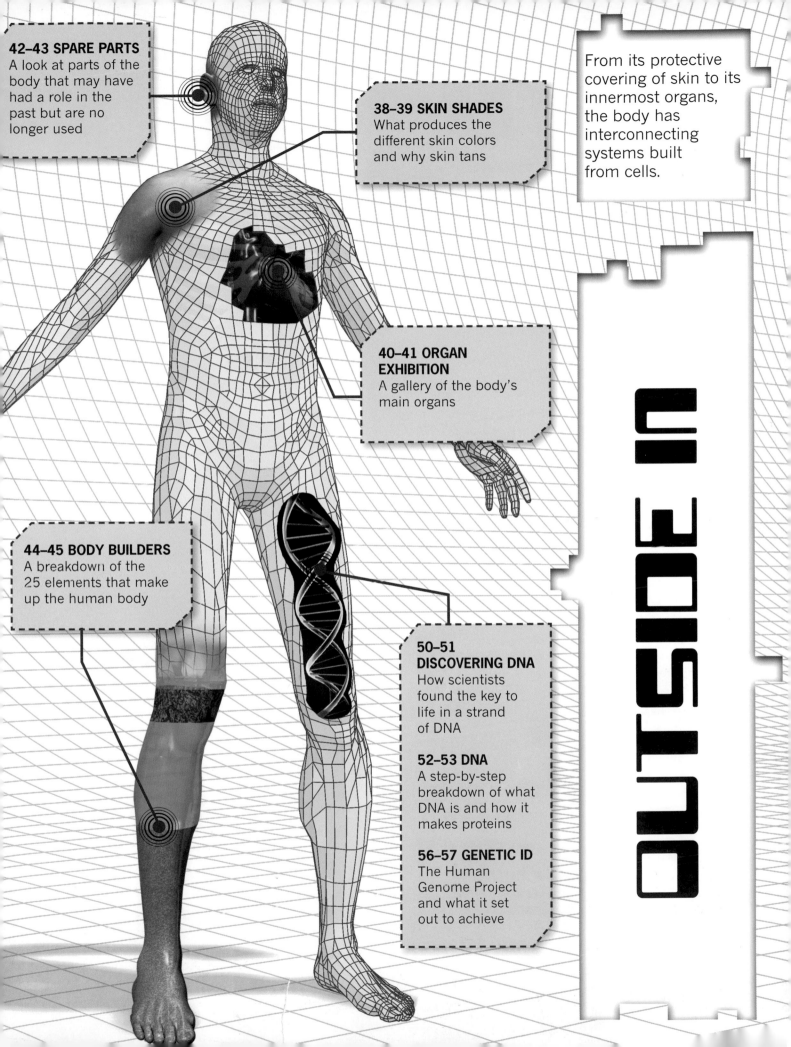

42–43 SPARE PARTS
A look at parts of the body that may have had a role in the past but are no longer used

38–39 SKIN SHADES
What produces the different skin colors and why skin tans

From its protective covering of skin to its innermost organs, the body has interconnecting systems built from cells.

40–41 ORGAN EXHIBITION
A gallery of the body's main organs

44–45 BODY BUILDERS
A breakdown of the 25 elements that make up the human body

50–51 DISCOVERING DNA
How scientists found the key to life in a strand of DNA

52–53 DNA
A step-by-step breakdown of what DNA is and how it makes proteins

56–57 GENETIC ID
The Human Genome Project and what it set out to achieve

OUTSIDE IN

Skin™
the ultimate in body coverings

✔ **Revolutionary design features:**
Fully elasticated to fit all shapes and sizes.
Protects your body from damage, infection,
and dehydration.

✔ **High performance:**
Surface cells flake off and are continually
replaced with new ones, ensuring a completely
new epidermis every 30 days—guaranteed!

✔ **Tough barrier:**
Keratin protein in epidermis surface cells
forms durable overcoat, protecting the body
from harmful bacteria.

✔ **Temperature control:**
Feeling hot under the collar? Skin has the
solution. Sweat glands deep in the dermis
release sweat to the surface. The sweat takes
heat from the skin as it dries. Cool!
Feeling the chill? Blood vessels in the skin
narrow, so they lose less heat to the outside.

CUSTOMIZE YOUR SKIN
extensive range of colors

all levels of hairiness
available, from bald
to super hirsute

**Supersensitive
pressure receptor**
picks up pushes, pulls,
and vibrations

Oily sebum released
by sebaceous gland ensures
smooth skin surface

**Rapid response
by erector muscle**
pulls hair upright to make
goose bumps when it's cold

**Heat-releasing network
of blood vessels** helps
keep body temperature steady

**Quick-as-a-flash
nerve** carries
signals from
receptors to brain

Lifetime warranty

Product care

Wash regularly
with warm water
and mild soap

Prevent infection
by keeping cuts and
scrapes clean

Use sunscreen to
prevent sunburn,
which can damage
the skin cells

**Disposable layer
of skin** releases
dead cells
as skin flakes

Tough keratin
fills the newly flattened
skin cells

Basal layer
produces new cells

epidermis

Sensitive receptor
detects light touch

Nerve endings
work hard to detect
pain and temperature
changes

dermis

Hair follicle
surrounds the root
of each hair

fat layer

Dermis design

Oil glands lubricate
the skin, keeping it
soft and supple

★

Fibrous collagen
protein provides
strength and resilience

★

Touch, pressure, and
pain sensors give
maximum
sensitivity

Stay-cool sweat gland
releases cooling sweat onto skin's
surface when it's hot

Supercells in hair bulb
divide to make the hair grow

Fully waterproof!

SKIN

Home | Videos | Channels | Community | Search

Search | Body decoration

Your Body

Broadcast Yourself
Worldwide/English

BODY DECORATION

Share videos with friends, family, and the world on Your Body—the website that celebrates the ancient and not-so-ancient art of body decoration. See the weird and wonderful ways that people modify, or change, their bodies, by painting, tattooing, or piercing them. Check out examples of patterns and styles, share tips on techniques and equipment, or simply browse some of the zanier aspects of body art. Some of these methods are permanent so remember to "deliberate before you decorate."

0:00 / 0:00

1,946 views

Subscribe

PAINTING

0:00 / 5:35

11,855 views

It took this Kathakali performer from Kerala in south India almost ten hours to paint his face for his part in a traditional dance-drama that enacts popular stories from ancient Hindu myths. The green base color of his make-up indicates instantly to audiences that he is playing a noble or divine character, in this case Lord Rama.

▼ **Playlist**
For Kabuki enthusiasts!

Factoid 1
Face makeup plays a vital part in Kabuki (Japanese theater). Red means anger!

Factoid 2
The bold lines of color highlight the eyes, cheekbones, and jaw line.

Factoid 3
All colors are important. Indigo means sadness or gloominess.

Related videos

Military mask
This video compares the way that soldiers paint their faces to blend in to their surroundings with the natural camouflage patterns of jungle, sand, and wildlife.

2,568 views

Read my face
Face paintings at dance ceremonies in Papua New Guinea send a message to others about the wearer's age, sex, and social status. See more . . . .

859 views

Soccer fan
I'm Erik. I painted my face with the colors of the national flag when I went to see the Swedish soccer team play. It made me feel happy to be part of the crowd supporting my team.

16,422 views

TATTOOS

Most popular designs

Anchor
Popular with sailors, this stands for hope and loyalty.

Fancy fern
Motifs drawing on nature are traditional in many different cultures.

Heart
Representing love, this design never goes out of fashion.

Rose
Another symbol of love and romance, especially if it's red.

Scorpion
This is good luck for anyone born under the Scorpio zodiac sign.

1.25 / 2:56

26,604 views

A bride displays her hands covered with elaborate tattoos made from a natural henna dye that stains the epidermis (outer layer of skin). The tattoos, called mehndi, will last for several weeks until the layers of skin have worn away. Mehndi is a traditional body art in South Asia and the Middle East. Follow our instructional video.

Related videos

Maori markings
Warriors of New Zealand tattoo their faces to make themselves look fierce and intimidating. Watch a Maori apply traditional markings.

491 views

Total tattoo
Check out this impressive tattoo from Tahiti. It will never disappear because the colored dye has penetrated the cells of the dermis (inner layer of skin).

468 views

PIERCING

Share

Replay

PIERCING TRIBES/....
3:59
From: 349856
Views: 2965

PIERCING TRIBES/....
3:30
From: 345077
Views: 115,432

3:30 / 3:30

115,432 views

So you think body piercing is a new craze? Think again—people have been doing it for centuries. Some of the objects they insert through holes made in their bodies (mostly ears or lips) can seem very bizarre to us—twigs, feathers, or pottery disks, for example. Visit our gallery of crazy body piercings from around the world.

▶ **Text comments (3)**
Show: average ▶

Goldilocks (1 hour ago)
Wow—those mehndi tattoos are really cool. Can't wait to try tnem out for myself.

Doctor Bob (5 hours ago)
Thinking of having a piercing done? Tell your parents first and make sure the equipment is sterile and the piercer is wearing gloves—you don't want to get an infection as well as a tattoo!

Big Bird (1 week ago)
Wondered who had stolen my feathers—that's scme getup, dude.

Related videos

In the pink
Not many people take body art this far. Piercing has become a form of self-expression, something that makes an individual style statement.

89,778 views

Say it with feathers
In Papua New Guinea, birds of paradise are highly valued for their colorful plumage. Two feathers thrust through the nose completes this man's ceremonial garb— now he's ready to party.

36,005 views

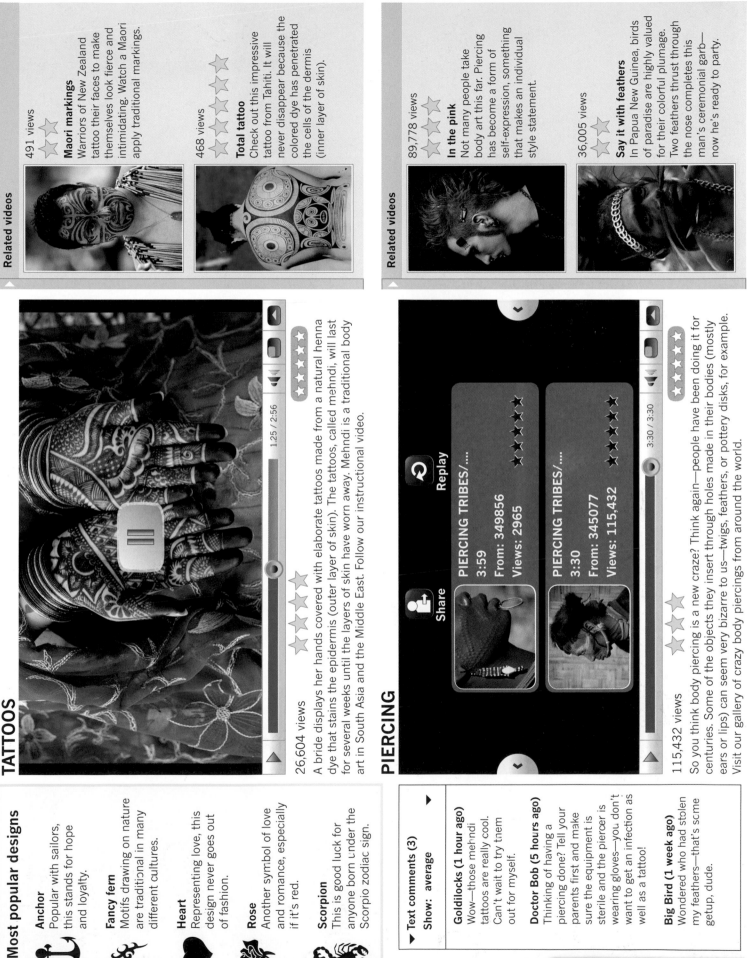

HAIRY BODIES

As mammals, we humans are naturally hairy—with the same number of hairs per area of skin as gorillas and chimps. Hairs cover almost every part of the body besides palms, soles, and lips. Fine, short vellus hairs cover most of the skin, especially in children. Longer, thicker terminal hairs are found in all ages on the scalp, eyebrows, eyelashes, and nostrils. People devote the most attention to the hair on their heads.

STRAIGHT TALKING

Each human head carries roughly 100,000 hair follicles, and every follicle can grow around 20 new hairs over a lifetime. At any one time, about 90 percent of scalp hairs are growing and ten per cent are resting. It is normal to lose around 100 hairs per day from the scalp.

WHAT IS HAIR?

Our hair is made of a tough protein called keratin. A single hair consists of a hair shaft (the part that shows), a root deep in the skin, and a follicle, from which the hair grows. The hair's color pigment, called melanin, is produced at the lower end of the follicle.

SKIN

HAIR SHAFT

OIL GLAND

ROOT

HAIR FOLLICLE

OLD, DEAD HAIR IS PUSHED OUT

OLD HAIR IN REST PHASE

NEW HAIR FORMS TO REPLACE OLD HAIR

STOP AND GROW

Most hairs grow in cycles of three or four years and then rest for a few weeks. Not all hairs rest at the same time of course! While growing, cells in the hair root at the bottom of the follicle divide to form the new hair. Once the hair is at the skin's surface, cells within the strand of hair are no longer alive. That's why a haircut is painless!

HAIR COLOR

Melanin, the pigment that colors the skin, also colors hair. There are two color variants of melanin (darker and lighter), and the color of hair depends on how much of each is present. The mix of the two produces shades of color that are limited to yellow, brown, red, and black. White hairs have no melanin at all—the whiteness is a result of the way they reflect light.

HAIR ELSEWHERE

During puberty, terminal hairs start to grow on the faces and chests of males. If left uncut, beard hair—like head hair—can grow up to 35 in (90 cm) long. Terminal hair also grows in the armpits and pubic areas of both males and females. This hair does not always match the color of the person's head hair.

HEALTHY SHEEN

Oil glands—also known as sebaceous glands—are attached to hair follicles. They produce oil, which they pump into the follicles to make the hair shiny and healthy looking. Sometimes these glands can secrete too much oil and a person's hair may look greasy. Time to grab the shampoo!

SHAPE SHIFTER

Whether hairs are straight or curly depends on the shape of the hair follicles. Straight-haired people have circular follicles, while curly-haired people have flatter follicles. This shape also affects whether hair is thick or thin. Straight, fine hair, for example, will grow from small circular follicles.

FOLLICLE SHAPE

STRAIGHT   WAVY   CURLY   SPIRAL, COILED

FOLLICLE SIZE

THICK   THIN   THICK   THIN

BALDNESS

Male pattern baldness is caused by oversensitivity of the hair follicles to the male sex hormone testosterone. This reduces the growth phase of the hair from years to weeks, meaning that a hair has barely emerged from a follicle before it is pushed out by the next hair in line.

GOING . . .   GOING . . .   ALMOST GONE

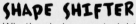

HAIR

What are nails?

NICE NAILS

Nail know-how

Polish up your nail knowledge

All the facts about nails at your fingertips

* NATURAL PROTECTION *

These hard plates at the tips of your fingers and toes will protect the nerve-packed sensitive upper surfaces of your fingers and toes.

* SUPERB HANDLING *

Guaranteed to improve dexterity (coordination) and enable you to pick things up.

* TOUGH AND DURABLE *

Made of layers of a tough protein called keratin, the same substance that makes your hair and the scaly skin of the upper epidermis.

Go to great lengths to learn about nails

Contents: keratin, an extremely strong protein that is also part of skin and hair and animal claws, hooves, and horns

Warning! Fingernails may be sharp. Use extreme caution when scratching an itch.

Nail anatomy

NICE NAILS

Inside info

What's inside your fingertips (and tippy toes)

cuticle
lunula
nail matrix
body of nail
nail bed
nail root
bone
fat

In the pink? Healthy nails have a rosy tint

Healthy nails, healthy you!

The BODY OF THE NAIL is the hard translucent part you see when you look at your finger or toe.

Cells in the NAIL MATRIX divide to produce nail cells that fill with keratin and push forward over the nail bed so that the nail grows.

The CUTICLE is one of three folds of skin that overlaps the edge of the nail. At the base of the body of the nail is a white crescent called the LUNULA (little moon).

Free gift of colored emery boards

How nails grow

NICE NAILS

Polish up on how nails grow

Fast facts

★ As cells form in the nail matrix, the older ones are pushed out of the way toward the fingertips.

★ The cells fill with keratin, become harder, and die (which is why cutting the free edge of your nails doesn't hurt).

★ Nails grow faster in the summer months than during the winter.

★ Fingernails grow between three and four times faster than toenails.

Protect your nails and they'll protect you

WHY YOU NEED NAILS

★ They protect the sensitive skin of your extremities. Anyone who's stubbed their toe knows that there are lots of nerve endings in those fingers and toes.

★ Nails help us better use our fingers for picking up and handling things.

★ Some nail conditions signal health problems elsewhere in the body.

Toenails

Top to toe

NICE NAILS

Foot notes

Compared to fingernails, toenails have some catching up to do—growing a new toenail can take 12–18 months. Your toes are enclosed in sweaty shoes for most of the day, so they are vulnerable to fungal infections. Give your toes fresh air and keep them dry!

Bare feet are happy feet!

Claws and hooves

NICE NAILS

Feet first

The same toughened keratin that tops your toes makes the various claws, talons, hooves, and horns that appear in the animal kingdom. Animal "nails" have adapted for specific tasks. Predators such as eagles and bears have strong claws to help them grasp their prey. Hooves in horses and elephants aid movement.

Tired of your toenails? Try these natural alternatives

eagle

horse

bear

elephant

NAILS

BLOODY PRINT SOLVES MURDER

FORENSIC FIRST: Expert Juan Vucetich matches fingerprint to killer

Buenos Aires, Argentina: June 1892

A bloody thumbprint has brought a killer to justice in a landmark case for forensic science. After brutally murdering her two young sons, Francisca Rojas finally confessed to the hideous crime.

Police investigation of the crime scene led to the discovery of a bloodstained print, so fingerprint expert Juan Vucetich was called in to examine it. He compared it to prints taken from possible suspects and discovered it was a perfect match to Rojas's. This is the first time that a fingerprint has led to a conviction.

The bloodstained print that betrayed the heartless mother.

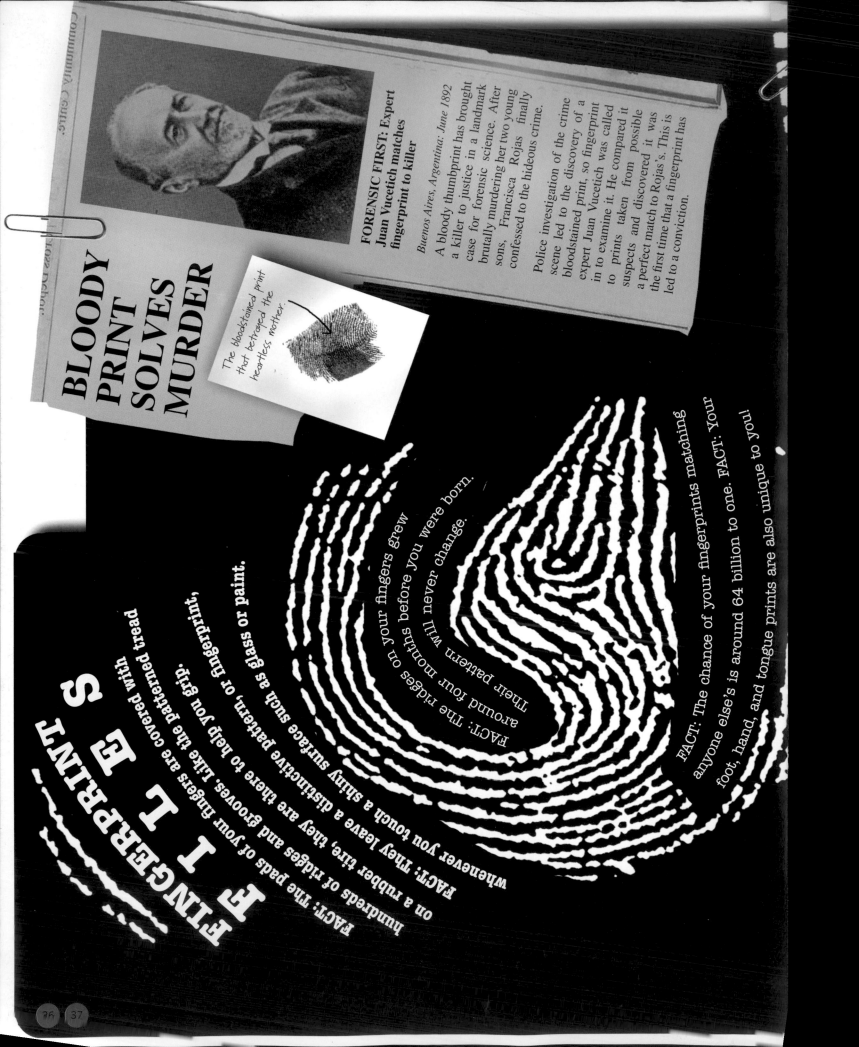

FINGERPRINTS

FACT: The pads of ridges of your fingers are covered with hundreds of grooves. Like the patterned tread on a rubber tire, they leave a distinctive pattern, or fingerprint, to help you grip.

FACT: They leave a distinctive pattern such as glass or paint.

FACT: Whenever you touch a shiny surface such as glass or paint.

FACT: The ridges on your fingers grew around four months before you were born. Their pattern will never change.

FACT: The chance of your fingerprints matching anyone else's is around 64 billion to one. **FACT:** Your foot, hand, and tongue prints are also unique to you!

The man with no fingerprints

American bank robber John Dillinger earned the title Public Enemy No. 1 after killing a cop in 1934. He eluded the FBI for months—and even burned off his fingertips with corrosive acid in an attempt to avoid detection. The pain drove him crazy, but it wasn't worth the effort—the prints grew back in exactly the same pattern as before! He was later arrested and jailed for a range of crimes.

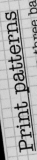

Close-up on this magnified fingerprint
The ridges on this magnified fingerprint look like coils of rope. The skin releases tiny pores (openings) along the ridges, and when the finger touches an object, it leaves a sweat pattern.

Identical twins, identical fingerprints?

No. Identical twins form when a single fertilized egg splits in two. This means they share identical DNA (genes). However, fingerprint development begins three months into a pregnancy. Although activated by genes, it is also affected by specific factors in the womb, such as the position of the unborn baby, nutrition, and growth rate. Ridge patterns are similar, but there will always be some small differences.

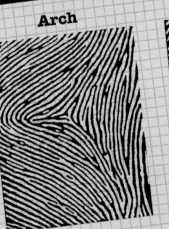

Print patterns

Fingerprints have three basic shapes—arches, loops, and whorls—all with variable features. Forensic scientists compare a scanned image of the print they want to match to a computer database of fingerprints. The Federal Bureau of Investigation (FBI) currently has 70 million fingerprints on file.

Arch

Loop

Whorl

SKIN SHADES

People can't check a shade chart to choose a color for their skin. Not yet, anyway! The color is inherited from their parents and depends on the amounts of three substances in the skin. People with ancestors in tropical areas have darker skin than those with ancestors from cooler regions. Here's the mix.

MELANIN
This protein is an essential ingredient. Its colors range from yellow to reddish-brown to black. People with dark skin have more melanin than light-skinned people. This acts as a natural defense against the Sun's ultraviolet (UV) rays.

CAROTENE
Now push the button for some yellow-orange tones from the carotene that collects in the uppermost part of the skin. This color is most noticeable on the soles of feet, especially the heels, where the skin is thickest.

HEMOGLOBIN
Finally add a dash of hemoglobin— a pigment found in red blood cells. Blood flowing near the skin's surface gives it a pinkish tinge. This is most obvious in light-skinned people, where blood beneath the skin is easier to see.

SKIN PIGMENTATION

LIGHT

MEDIUM

DARK

melanin

melanosome

melanocyte

Skin color is determined mostly by the amount and type of melanin produced by melanocytes. These branching cells produce tiny granules of melanin inside organelles called melanosomes. These make their way to surrounding cells, where they release the melanin granules closer to the surface of the skin.

Darker skin
❶ Larger melanocytes
❷ Many melanosomes are released into the surrounding cells
❸ Many melanin granules are released
❹ Melanin is evenly spread throughout the upper layer of the skin

Lighter skin
❶ Smaller, less active melanocytes
❷ Only a few melanosomes are taken into the surrounding cells
❸ Melanosomes stay intact
❹ The upper layer contains very little spread-out melanin

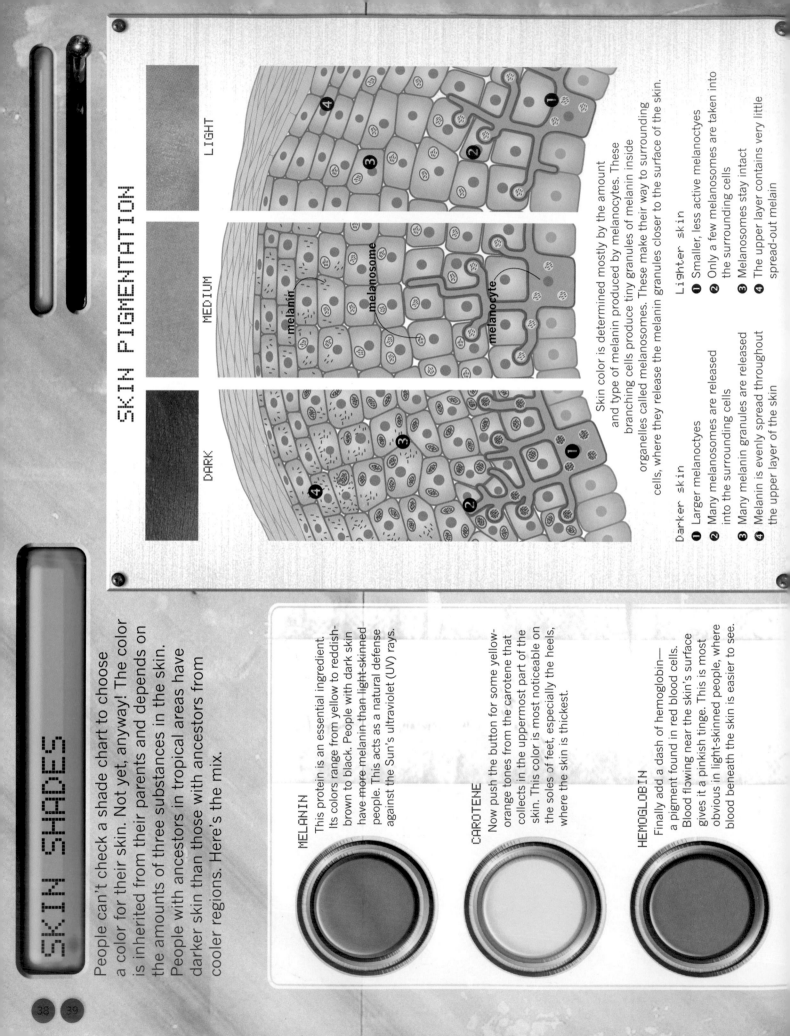

SPECTACULAR SPECTRUM

- ☐ 100% NATURAL INGREDIENTS
- ☐ COLOR TAILOR-MADE JUST FOR YOU
- ☐ AVAILABLE IN PINKISH-WHITE, EBONY BLACK, AND LOTS OF SHADES IN BETWEEN

FRECKLES

Concentrated clusters of melanin create freckles—sprinklings of tiny brown spots most obvious on people with light skin. Freckles may become more noticeable when the person spends time in the Sun and less obvious in the winter months.

WARNING!

Ultraviolet (UV) rays in sunlight increase the production of melanin in the skin, creating a tan. Invisible to human eyes, UV rays also penetrate and damage skin cells. This can cause permanent skin damage, even cancer. Sunscreen should be applied regularly to protect the skin.

SKIN COLOR

ORGAN EXHIBITION

Not for the squeamish, this new gallery opens to the public with an astonishing exhibition of the body's main organs. Some organs are displayed in specially constructed cases that give the viewer an all-around view of the inner workings. Peer inside the chambers of the heart or discover how the digestive system fits inside the body—or simply admire the detail in the painted lungs. Tickets include entry to further displays that include the skin, spleen, bladder, and reproductive organs.

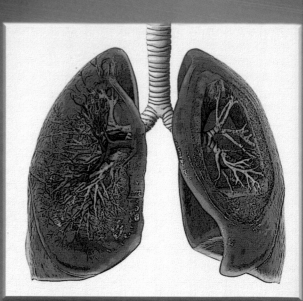

PAIR OF LUNGS
This detailed painting shows a pair of lungs. Soft and spongy, they sit inside the chest, expanding and shrinking with every breath to get air in and out of the body. It is through the lungs that life-giving oxygen gets into the bloodstream.

CUTAWAY HEART
In this display, part of the heart's muscular wall has been removed for a view inside. Get close up to see the chambers that fill and empty with blood every time the heart beats. Notice the thick walls, made from a special type of muscle that squeezes without ever tiring.

MAKE US SMILE
Stripping away the skin and fat reveals a different face. Muscles work by pulling, usually on bones, to make the body move. A few, however, tug the skin, like those that make a person smile or frown.

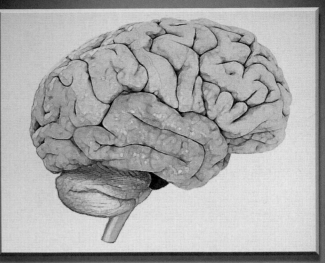

THE BRAIN

The body's most complex organ, the brain is shown here with its main areas color tinted. Under that wrinkly covering, millions of electrical signals are whizzing through a network of brain cells that make you think, feel, and be you.

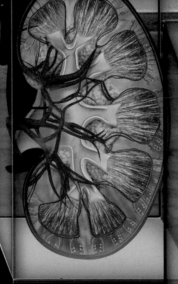

FOOD PROCESSOR

When organs work together for a common purpose, they form a system. The teeth, tongue, esophagus, stomach, intestines, liver, and other organs make up the digestive system, which processes food and extracts substances that the body can use.

INSIDE A KIDNEY

Beneath the kidney's protective surface lie around one million tightly packed filtration units known as nephrons.

OUTSIDE A KIDNEY

The main role of our two kidneys is to filter waste and water out of the blood in order to make a pale yellow liquid called urine.

SPARE PARTS

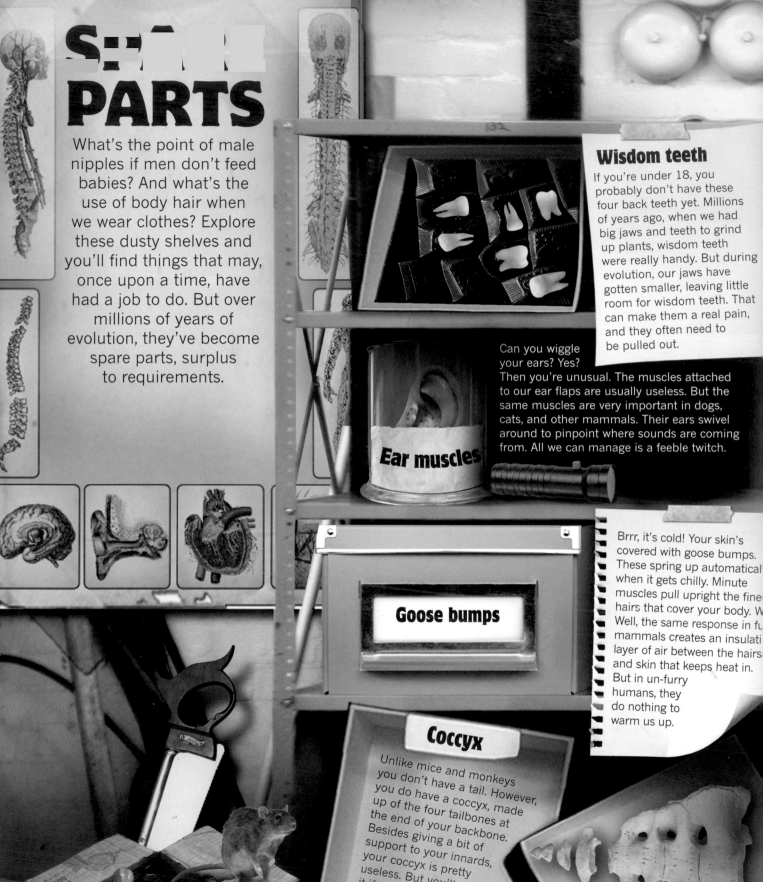

What's the point of male nipples if men don't feed babies? And what's the use of body hair when we wear clothes? Explore these dusty shelves and you'll find things that may, once upon a time, have had a job to do. But over millions of years of evolution, they've become spare parts, surplus to requirements.

Wisdom teeth

If you're under 18, you probably don't have these four back teeth yet. Millions of years ago, when we had big jaws and teeth to grind up plants, wisdom teeth were really handy. But during evolution, our jaws have gotten smaller, leaving little room for wisdom teeth. That can make them a real pain, and they often need to be pulled out.

Can you wiggle your ears? Yes? Then you're unusual. The muscles attached to our ear flaps are usually useless. But the same muscles are very important in dogs, cats, and other mammals. Their ears swivel around to pinpoint where sounds are coming from. All we can manage is a feeble twitch.

Ear muscles

Brrr, it's cold! Your skin's covered with goose bumps. These spring up automatical when it gets chilly. Minute muscles pull upright the fine hairs that cover your body. W Well, the same response in fu mammals creates an insulati layer of air between the hairs and skin that keeps heat in. But in un-furry humans, they do nothing to warm us up.

Goose bumps

Coccyx

Unlike mice and monkeys you don't have a tail. However, you do have a coccyx, made up of the four tailbones at the end of your backbone. Besides giving a bit of support to your innards, your coccyx is pretty useless. But you'll notice it if you fall heavily on your backside and it gets bruised or broken.

Male nipples

Believe it or not, in the first few weeks of life, girls and boys share the same basic body plan—including nipples. That's why boys have nipples even though they're not really useful.

Third eyelid

Look in a mirror and you'll see this half-moon-shaped fold curving around the inner corner of your eye. It's probably the remains of the nictitating membrane, or "third eyelid," that swishes across the eyes of other animals. What does it do? It gathers dust to produce that crusty "sleep" you find when you wake up.

Appendix

If you were a rabbit, your appendix would be long as well as important. Without it, you wouldn't be able to digest grass. But we don't graze on grass and our short appendix didn't seem to have much purpose—although it can get inflamed, causing appendicitis! Scientists now believe the appendix helps defend us from germs and provides a rest home for "good" bacteria.

Body hair

Men's beards and chest hairs are a reminder of our hairier past, when our ancestors' thick hair kept them warm. Now we have special clothing that does the job instead.

Plantaris muscle

Can you bend your feet to grip tree branches? Most unlikely. Yet monkeys and other close mammal relatives can. That's because the plantaris muscle running down the backs of their legs helps curl the feet downward. If you have them, and one in ten people don't, your plantaris muscles will be slender and weak.

plantaris muscle

BODY BUILDERS

Everybody's body is put together using 25 different raw ingredients called elements. These are chemicals that can't be broken down to anything simpler and consist of very tiny particles called atoms. Inside the body, atoms are usually bonded together to make molecules. Two hydrogen atoms and one oxygen atom, for example, produce a water molecule. The four elements being added here make up 96 percent of body weight. Now back to work!

OXYGEN

Inside the body, a generous amount of oxygen should be combined with hydrogen to make water. Freshly breathed-in oxygen goes directly to cells to release energy.

NITROGEN

This makes a small but important contribution to the body. Nitrogen is part of key molecules such as proteins and DNA.

HYDROGEN

Hydrogen atoms are needed inside every complex molecule, including carbohydrates, fats, and proteins.

If I fall in here, I'll really be in my element.

There should be seven trillion quadrillion atoms going in here, and I want every one of them accounted for. Any missing atoms will be deducted from your pay.

Don't seem to have the strength for scaling bodies today. I must be lacking in iron.

CARBON

Carbon atoms bond together in chains and form the "backbones" of just about all the molecules inside and outside the body's cells.

Don't forget to add a pinch of copper, chromium, tin, and zinc—the body won't work without them. And not too much or the body might start to rattle.

Must add calcium and phosphorus for strong teeth and bones. Every body has to meet the standard specifications.

Just a trace of magnesium should boost this body's immune system.

INGREDIENTS

Oxygen	65%
Carbon	18%
Hydrogen	10%
Nitrogen	3.0%
Calcium	1.5%
Phosphorus	1.0%
Potassium	0.35%
Sulfur	0.25%
Sodium	0.15%
Chlorine	0.15%
Magnesium	0.05%
Iron	0.008%
Iodine	0.00004%

Plus trace amounts of: chromium, cobalt, copper, fluorine, manganese, molybdenum, nickel, selenium, silicon, tin, vanadium, and zinc

SUPERCELLS

THEIR POWERS AND ABILITIES ARE LEGENDARY. THEIR SKILLS AND STRENGTHS FOR THEIR PARTICULAR JOBS ARE IMPRESSIVE. DAY IN, DAY OUT, THEY WORK TIRELESSLY AND WITHOUT REWARD. EVER WILLING TO SERVE AND ALWAYS DEDICATED TO THE TASK AT HAND, THESE ARE YOUR BODY'S SUPERCELLS. MEET THE TEAM . . .

NERVE CELL

HARD AT WORK IN THE BRAIN AND NERVOUS SYSTEM, THESE CELLS COLLECT AND SEND OUT INFORMATION THROUGH TINY ELECTRICAL IMPULSES. BRANCHES ON THE CELL BODY CALLED DENDRITES BRING DATA TO THE CELL, WHILE AXONS (THE MIDDLE PARTS) TAKE IT AWAY.

MANY CELLS COME AND GO, BUT WE'VE BEEN WORKING SINCE THE DAY YOU WERE BORN. NEVER SAY DIE!

ZAPPPPP!

MAKE NO BONES ABOUT IT, MY FRIEND, WE'LL KEEP YOUR SKELETON IN TIPTOP CONDITION.

PHOTORECEPTOR CELLS

THERE ARE TWO TYPES OF CELLS IN THE EYES. RODS ARE SENSITIVE TO LIGHT, DARK, SHAPES, AND MOVEMENT, WHILE CONES HELP YOU SEE COLOR. SPECIAL PIGMENTS IN THE CELLS CONVERT LIGHT INTO NERVE IMPULSES. WHEN THESE REACH THE BRAIN, IT TURNS THEM INTO PICTURES.

BONE CELL

YOUR BONES ARE A MIXTURE OF MATRIX—THE HARD STUFF THAT MAKES THEM STRONG—AND OTHER CELLS THAT HELP THEM GROW AND FIX THEMSELVES. BONE-BUILDING CELLS ARE CALLED OSTEOBLASTS, WHILE MAINTENANCE CELLS ARE CALLED OSTEOCYTES.

DAY OR NIGHT, WE CATCH THE RAYS TO GIVE YOU THE POWER OF SIGHT.

MUSCLE CELL
THESE HARD-WORKING HEROES CONVERT CHEMICAL ENERGY INTO MOVEMENT. THE SKELETAL MUSCLES, PACKED WITH THOUSANDS OF LONG MUSCLE-CELL FIBERS, CAN CONTRACT WHEN SET OFF BY A NERVE SIGNAL. AS THEY CONTRACT, THEY PULL OUR BONES TO MAKE US MOVE.

WE'RE HERE TO HELP YOU GET A MOVE ON. GO ON, PUT SOME MUSCLE INTO IT!

WE PROTECT YOUR ORGANS WITH A SHOCK-ABSORBING CUSHION AND A LAYER OF INSULATION TO KEEP YOU WARM.

FAT CELL
THESE ARE FOUND IN THE LAYER UNDER YOUR SKIN AND AROUND OTHER ORGANS. THE CELLS RESEMBLE PLASTIC BUBBLES FILLED WITH OIL. THE CELLS CAN GET BIGGER OR SMALLER DEPENDING ON HOW MUCH ENERGY-RICH FAT THEY STORE.

LIVER CELL
A KEY FUNCTION OF LIVER CELLS IS TO ADJUST THE COMPOSITION OF YOUR BLOOD, REMOVING TOXINS AND REGULATING LEVELS OF SUGARS, FATS, AND AMINO ACIDS.

EPITHELIAL CELL
YOUR OUTER SKIN—AS WELL AS INSIDE YOUR NOSE, MOUTH, LUNGS, AND DIGESTIVE TRACT—IS LINED WITH THESE CELLS. THEY STOP FLUIDS OR PATHOGENS FROM GETTING THROUGH TO THE TISSUE BELOW.

DOES YOUR BLOOD NEED CLEANING AND FINE-TUNING? WE GUARANTEE TO DE-LIVER!

KAPOOOW!

WANT TO KEEP OUT THE NASTY STUFF? WE'VE GOT YOU COVERED.

BODY CELLS

INSIDE A CELL

The human body is made from trillions of tiny cells, and each one is a hive of activity. They may be microscopic, but they contain many different structures called organelles, which are all hard at work. While we sleep, eat, work, or walk the dog, thousands of chemical reactions are taking place to keep our cells—and our bodies—alive.

Either I've shrunk or this is one seriously powerful magnifying glass! I'd give my wig to travel into the future and bring back one of those fancy new microscopes.

CELL STRUCTURE

Every cell has a membrane that surrounds a jellylike cytoplasm. This cytoplasm is dotted with a variety of organelles, which all have specific jobs to do, such as making proteins—the cell's key chemicals.

cell structure

nerve cell

1—MITOCHONDRIA
These sausage-shaped organelles provide the energy needed to power a cell's activities. They release energy from "fuels" in food, especially glucose.

2—LYSOSOMES
Powerful enzymes contained in membrane sacs break down worn-out organelles inside the cell. Any useful foreign matter that gets recycled, the pieces left behind are stored.

3—NUCLEUS
Instructions that build and run cells, are stored substances that build and run the cell's control centre.

4—CYTOPLASM
This thick fluid consists of water with lots of dissolved substances. Organelles float and move in the reactions occur.

5—ENDOPLASMIC RETICULUM
cytoplasm, where many chemical substances, where proteins (in the This system of linked cavities its surface.) and transports ribosome that stud the Golgi apparatus and other places, them to particles.

6—MICROTUBULES
Stiff but bendable, these hollow tubes form part of the "skeleton," that supports organelles shapes, like trains on tracks. They also move around, the cell. They are cell's the

7—PLASMA MEMBRANE
This flexible membrane surrounds the cell, separating its busy interior also controls surroundings. The membrane or exit the cell. which substances enter

8—GOLGI APPARATUS
The Golgi apparatus processes. Many are packages to build apparatus made the cell, but some used to build and run the plasma membrane are exported through for use elsewhere.

DISCOVERING DNA

In the early 1950s, biologists already knew that the nucleus of every cell contained DNA (deoxyribonucleic acid), a molecule that carries the instructions to operate cells and determine what the body looks like and what it does. But to understand more, they had to figure out the structure of a DNA molecule. It took four scientists—three men, and one woman—to knit the strands together.

JAMES WATSON

I was a young geneticist from the U.S., working in Cambridge, England, when I teamed up with Crick to try to crack the DNA puzzle. We both knew that if we didn't get there soon, someone else would. We made one model of the molecule, but it was a failure. We knew we had to get our hands on Rosalind's photograph.

ROSALIND FRANKLIN

Although generally modest, I must admit I was a brilliant physicist at a time when it was tough for women to get ahead. I produced an image of a DNA molecule using a technique called x-ray diffraction. A fuzzy "X" that was visible in the middle of the molecule would prove to be the key to DNA's structure. Somehow, Watson and Crick got ahold of a copy of the photograph.

FRANCIS CRICK
When Jim and I saw Rosalind's photograph, we realized that the DNA molecule was a double helix—imagine if you twist a ladder around and around, all the genetic instructions are carried on the rungs separating the outer supports. We built a model—and it worked! We had discovered the secret of life.

MAURICE WILKINS
I was working with Rosalind in London, England, although to tell the truth we didn't really get along. I knew that Crick and Watson were getting close to solving the DNA puzzle, and I arranged for them to see Rosalind's x-ray photograph. In 1962, I shared the Nobel Prize with them. By that time, though, Rosalind had died of cancer at age 37.

DISCOVERY OF THE DOUBLE HELIX

DNA

Every body cell holds the instructions needed to construct and maintain a human being. These instructions, called genes, are carried by chromosomes, each made of a long DNA molecule. Each gene is a coded message that is translated and used to make a particular substance called a protein. Proteins are vital for all cell activities. Follow these steps to see how it's done.

Step 1

BEFORE YOU START, CHECK THAT ALL THE PARTS ARE PRESENT—A LIVING CELL, ITS NUCLEUS, AND ALSO ONE CHROMOSOME.

CELL

CYTOPLASM

PORE

NUCLEUS

CHROMOSOME

INSIDE THE CELL'S NUCLEUS ARE 46 CHROMOSOMES, WHICH CARRY AROUND 20,000 GENES. LOOK AT ONE CHROMOSOME IN MORE DETAIL. IT'S A STRAND OF DNA, TIGHTLY COILED TO PACK ALL THE INFORMATION IT HAS TO STORE INSIDE THE NUCLEUS.

UNRAVEL THE DNA COILS TO REVEAL ITS STRUCTURE. YOU'LL SEE THAT DNA RESEMBLES A TWISTED LADDER, WITH ITS TWO STRANDS LINKED BY "RUNGS" CALLED BASES, OF WHICH THERE ARE FOUR TYPES (A, C, G, AND T).

PAIRED BASES LINK DNA STRANDS

FOUR TYPES OF BASES SHOWN HERE AS YELLOW (T), PURPLE (A), GREEN (G), AND BLUE (C)

Step 2

MRNA

MRNA BUILDING BLOCKS LINK TO COPY SEQUENCE OF BASES IN DNA

DNA STRANDS SEPARATE

SEPARATE THE STRAND IN THIS SHORT SECTIO OF DNA. IT'S A SINGLE GENE THAT HOLDS INSTRUCTIONS FOR MAKING A PROTEIN. TH BASES HOLD THE "LETTERS" THAT MAKE UP THE "WORDS" OF THOSE INSTRUCTIONS

"BACKBONE" C DNA STRAND I FORMED BY SUGAR AND PHOSPHATE MOLECULES

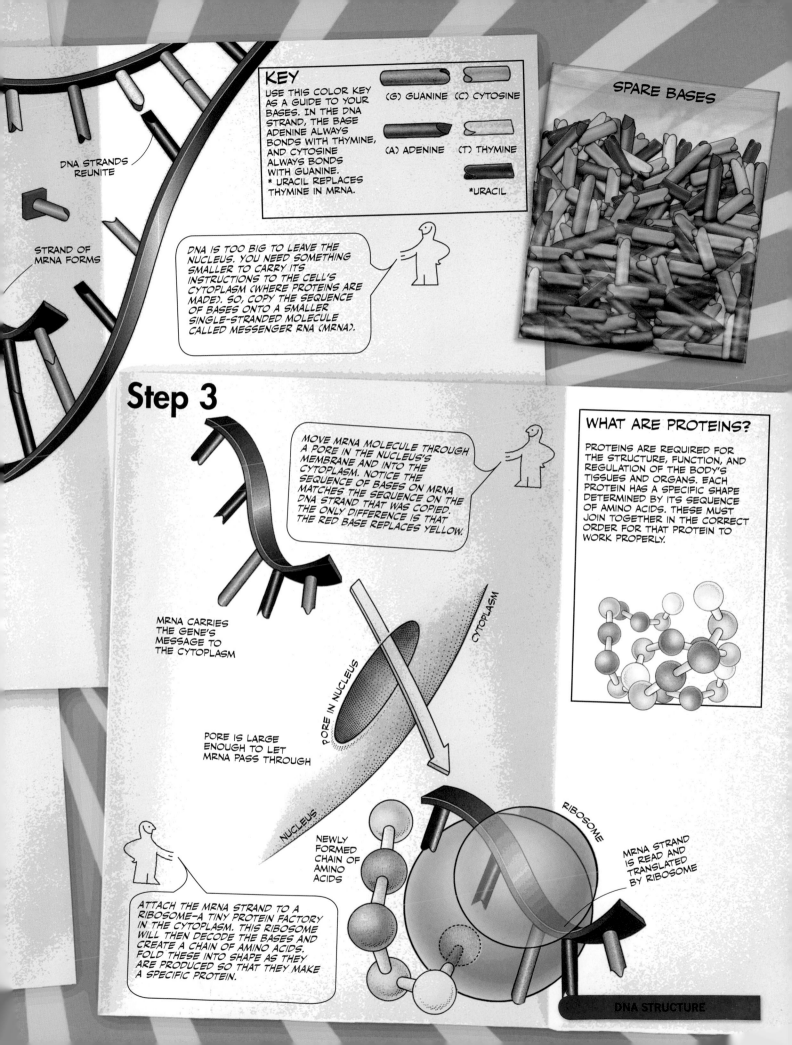

DNA STRANDS
REUNITE

STRAND OF
MRNA FORMS

KEY

USE THIS COLOR KEY
AS A GUIDE TO YOUR
BASES. IN THE DNA
STRAND, THE BASE
ADENINE ALWAYS
BONDS WITH THYMINE,
AND CYTOSINE
ALWAYS BONDS
WITH GUANINE.
* URACIL REPLACES
THYMINE IN MRNA.

(G) GUANINE   (C) CYTOSINE

(A) ADENINE   (T) THYMINE

*URACIL

SPARE BASES

DNA IS TOO BIG TO LEAVE THE
NUCLEUS. YOU NEED SOMETHING
SMALLER TO CARRY ITS
INSTRUCTIONS TO THE CELL'S
CYTOPLASM (WHERE PROTEINS ARE
MADE). SO, COPY THE SEQUENCE
OF BASES ONTO A SMALLER
SINGLE-STRANDED MOLECULE
CALLED MESSENGER RNA (MRNA).

Step 3

MOVE MRNA MOLECULE THROUGH
A PORE IN THE NUCLEUS'S
MEMBRANE AND INTO THE
CYTOPLASM. NOTICE THE
SEQUENCE OF BASES ON MRNA
MATCHES THE SEQUENCE ON THE
DNA STRAND THAT WAS COPIED.
THE ONLY DIFFERENCE IS THAT
THE RED BASE REPLACES YELLOW.

WHAT ARE PROTEINS?

PROTEINS ARE REQUIRED FOR
THE STRUCTURE, FUNCTION, AND
REGULATION OF THE BODY'S
TISSUES AND ORGANS. EACH
PROTEIN HAS A SPECIFIC SHAPE
DETERMINED BY ITS SEQUENCE
OF AMINO ACIDS. THESE MUST
JOIN TOGETHER IN THE CORRECT
ORDER FOR THAT PROTEIN TO
WORK PROPERLY.

MRNA CARRIES
THE GENE'S
MESSAGE TO
THE CYTOPLASM

CYTOPLASM

PORE IN NUCLEUS

PORE IS LARGE
ENOUGH TO LET
MRNA PASS THROUGH

NUCLEUS

NEWLY
FORMED
CHAIN OF
AMINO
ACIDS

RIBOSOME

MRNA STRAND
IS READ AND
TRANSLATED
BY RIBOSOME

ATTACH THE MRNA STRAND TO A
RIBOSOME—A TINY PROTEIN FACTORY
IN THE CYTOPLASM. THIS RIBOSOME
WILL THEN DECODE THE BASES AND
CREATE A CHAIN OF AMINO ACIDS.
FOLD THESE INTO SHAPE AS THEY
ARE PRODUCED SO THAT THEY MAKE
A SPECIFIC PROTEIN.

DNA STRUCTURE

CELL DIVISION

Hey, you! Yes, you eating the hot 'dog in the opposite stand. Check this out. We are celebrating our amazing body cells. Like you, we all started out as a single cell, but through a process called mitosis, that cell divided into two—each with identical DNA (genetic instructions)—and then those cells divided, and so on. Cell division enables us to grow and means our bodies can replace worn-out cells. Anyway, check out the other posters. We've gotta split.

1

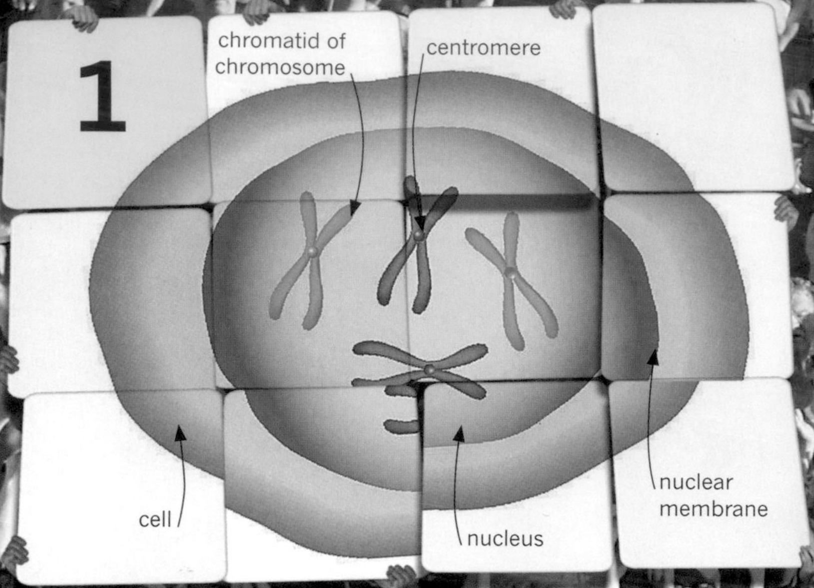

chromatid of chromosome

centromere

cell

nucleus

nuclear membrane

PREPARING FOR ACTION

All 46 chromosomes inside a cell's nucleus (four are shown here) consist of a single DNA molecule. The cell prepares for mitosis by duplicating those molecules. Each chromosome, now X shaped, has two identical strands, or chromatids, linked by a centromere.

5

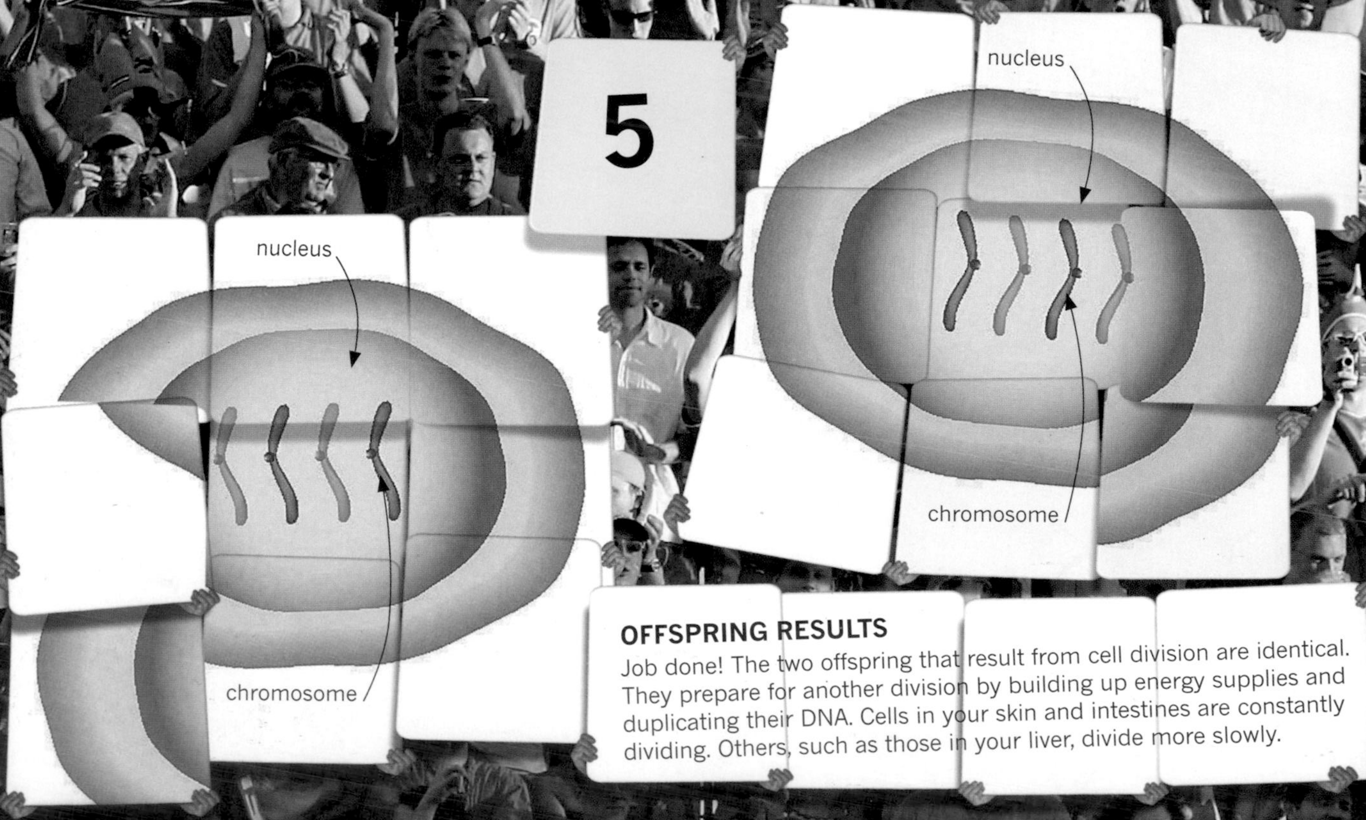

nucleus

nucleus

chromosome

chromosome

OFFSPRING RESULTS

Job done! The two offspring that result from cell division are identical. They prepare for another division by building up energy supplies and duplicating their DNA. Cells in your skin and intestines are constantly dividing. Others, such as those in your liver, divide more slowly.

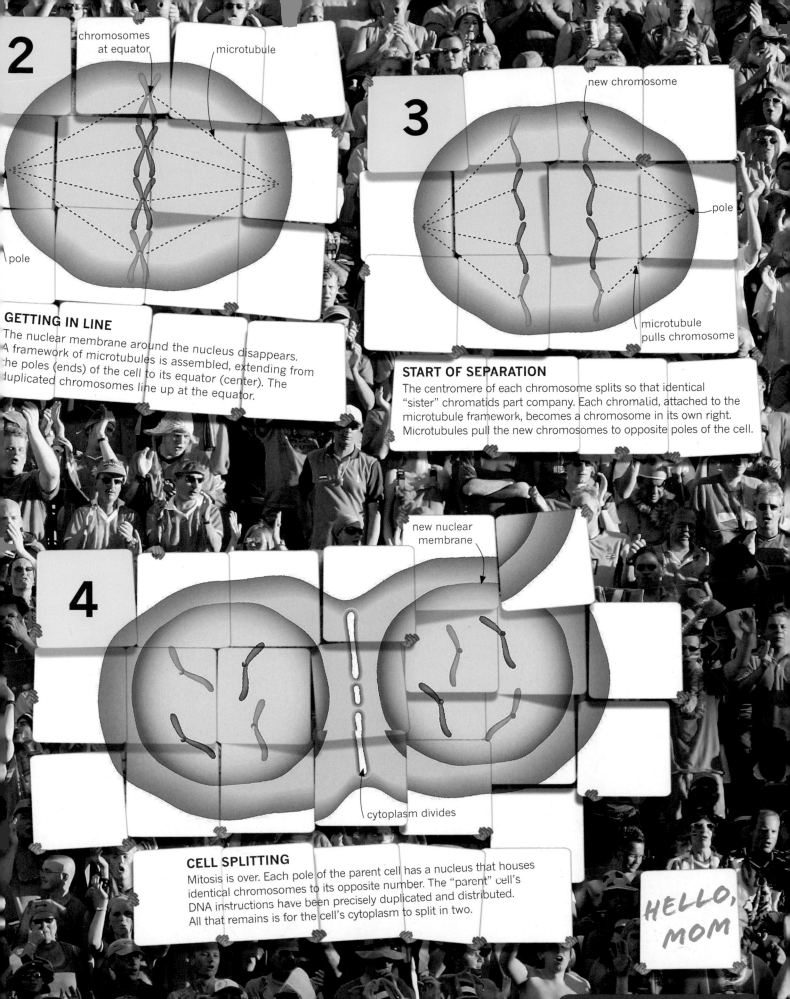

2

chromosomes at equator

microtubule

pole

GETTING IN LINE

The nuclear membrane around the nucleus disappears.
A framework of microtubules is assembled, extending from
the poles (ends) of the cell to its equator (center). The
duplicated chromosomes line up at the equator.

3

new chromosome

pole

microtubule
pulls chromosome

START OF SEPARATION

The centromere of each chromosome splits so that identical
"sister" chromatids part company. Each chromatid, attached to the
microtubule framework, becomes a chromosome in its own right.
Microtubules pull the new chromosomes to opposite poles of the cell.

4

new nuclear
membrane

cytoplasm divides

CELL SPLITTING

Mitosis is over. Each pole of the parent cell has a nucleus that houses
identical chromosomes to its opposite number. The "parent" cell's
DNA instructions have been precisely duplicated and distributed.
All that remains is for the cell's cytoplasm to split in two.

HELLO, MOM

GENETIC ID

What we are depends a lot on the genetic material contained in our cells. This consists of long molecules of DNA, sections of which form genes. Most of these genes are identical in all of us, ensuring we are all recognizably human. But some vary, giving each of us our own individuality. At the end of the 20th century, the Human Genome Project set about unraveling, analysing, and identifying our genetic identity.

WHAT IS A GENOME?
The nucleus of each human cell contains 22 pairs of "ordinary" chromosomes and two sex chromosomes, either XX (female) or XY (male). A genome is all of the DNA in one complete set of chromosomes, including both X and Y chromosomes.

HOW LONG IS THE HUMAN GENOME?
The genome of just one cell is 3.3 ft (1 m) long. The DNA molecules in a genome contain billions of pairs of bases—adenine (A) with thymine (T) and cytosine (C) with guanine (G). These bases form the "letters" of genes, the coded instructions that control how we work.

WHAT WAS THE HUMAN GENOME PROJECT?
The Human Genome Project (HGP) started in 1990 and was completed in 2003. It had two main goals. First, to figure out the sequence of base pairs that make up all the DNA in a genome. And second, to identify all the genes in a genome and to show which genes are found where.

WHO WAS INVOLVED?
The HGP involved thousands of scientists in 16 different research institutes in six countries. Their first task was to sequence the bases in gene "landmarks" on chromosomes that would guide them when they later sequenced complete DNA molecules (each being one chromosome).

THIS IMAGE SHOWS 22 PAIRS OF HUMAN CHROMOSOMES ARRANGED IN ORDER OF SIZE. THE OTHER TWO ARE THE SEX CHROMOSOMES, X AND Y. ONE MEMBER OF EACH PAIR COMES FROM A PERSON'S MOTHER, THE OTHER FROM THE FATHER.

WHERE DID THE DNA COME FROM?

DNA was provided by volunteers whose identity has been kept intentionally secret, although one well-known scientist also supplied DNA.

HOW WAS THE DNA SEQUENCED?

To determine the sequence of bases, the long strands of DNA were cut into short pieces. An instrument called a sequencer then worked out the order in overlapping fragments, before rejoining the pieces to construct a complete DNA molecule.

WHAT WAS DISCOVERED?

The human genome consists of 3.2 billion base pairs. There are around 20,000 genes in the genome, far fewer than the 100,000 thought originally. Only three percent of the genome is DNA that makes up genes. The rest is junk (noncoding) DNA that does not instruct a cell to make proteins.

WHAT'S NEXT?

Although the HGP is finished, analysis of its findings will continue for years. In particular, scientists are looking at why certain gene variations cause diseases. This should help doctors to understand each patient's health needs based on their genetic makeup, and precisely target problems using special drugs.

A RESEARCHER PREPARES SAMPLES FOR A SEQUENCER, WHICH WORKS OUT THE ORDER OF BASES.

A COMPUTER SCREEN DISPLAY SHOWS THE DNA SEQUENCE AS A SERIES OF COLORED BANDS.

64–65 THE "X" MAN
The discovery of x-rays, and the impact it had on medicine

60–61 SKELETON GALLERY
The bones that make up the human skeleton

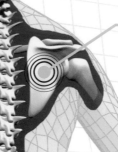

70–71 SPACED OUT
The effects of space travel on the human body

68–69 MUSCLE GYM
The body's skeletal muscles, their structure, and how they work to make you move

62–63 BREAK A LEG
What happens when you fracture a bone and how your body fixes it

72–73 CAN YOUR FACE SPEAK WITHOUT WORDS?
How small facial muscles work to produce many different expressions

76–77 IN HAND
Forearm muscles and their long tendons produce a wide range of hand movements

How the skeletal framework supports the body and how the muscles work with it to make you move.

80–81 REPLACEMENT PARTS
A look at prosthetic limbs through the ages and how they work

78–79 ON THE MOVE
How a great deal about the way humans move was revealed by two early photographers

74–75 FITNESS FIRST!
The benefits of doing regular exercise

66–67 JOINTS
How different types of joints allow the body to make many different movements

MOVING FRAMEWORK

SKELETON GALLERY

The skeleton **supports the body.** Without it, humans would be soggy heaps of muscles, guts, and organs.

♫ . . . With the hipbone connected to the backbone, And the backbone connected to the neck bone, And the neck bone connected to the head bone . . . ♫

You should audition for Bone Idol!

Humans have lots of bones in their **hands**—27 in each! I guess this is why they are so good at using tools. The bones in the wrist are called carpals, palm bones are metacarpals, and the finger bones are **phalanges.** It's a similar story with the **feet.** Tarsals are the anklebones, metatarsals link the ankle and toes, and phalanges are the toe bones.

The **rib cage** surrounds and protects the heart and lungs. The ribs are connected to the **spine.**

Check out its noggin! The **skull** is made up of 22 separate bones. Some parts protect its superpowerful brain, others make up the face, and the **mandible** is the jawbone. I find a longer snout much more attractive.

What are you staring at?

What an extraordinary creature the human is—**206 bones** connected together to make a **strong, flexible skeleton** framework. Truly awesome!

Homo sapiens skeleton

Homo sapiens, or human beings, first appeared 150,000 years ago. They are vertebrates. This means they have an internal skeleton with a backbone (spine) and braincase (cranium). Humans have four limbs but walk upright on their two legs. Human hands have opposable thumbs, which means that each thumb can touch the tips of the other four fingers. This enables humans to grip tools and objects.

The bones are made of **hard tissue,** with a **honeycomb** structure on the inside. This makes them strong but light, so humans can move around easily. Some bones are filled with jellylike red **marrow,** and this is where the human's **red blood cells** are made.

And the **spine** runs from the head to the hips. It is a tower of bones called **vertebrae.** Discs of **cartilage** between the vertebrae allow movement. Add some muscles and this fellow could bend over and touch his toes.

BREAK A LEG

The hundreds of bones in your skeleton are lightweight but strong and can bend slightly under pressure. However, a sharp blow or repeated stress can lead a bone to break, or fracture. There are different types of fracture from tiny hairline cracks to complete fractures, which break the bone into two pieces, and compound fractures, where the broken bone pierces the skin. Ouch!

ACCIDENTS HAPPEN

Fractures can result from all sorts of accidents. Strain from a repeated activity like a sport can cause stress fractures. Or an awkward tumble or collision with a hard object can cause impact fractures. Falling out of a tree might do the trick!

FIRST AID

To treat a fracture, you should first elevate it to reduce the swelling and apply a cold compress to numb the pain. Sometimes it is not obvious whether an injury is a break or just a bad sprain—to know for sure you'll have to go to the hospital.

SWELL TIME!

The shock of the accident causes a rush of endorphins (body chemicals) that act as natural painkillers. After the initial shock wears off, though, the pain kicks in. The area swells up as the body's defense mechanisms swing into action, sending extra oxygen and nutrients to start the healing process. Bruises start to develop.

AT THE HOSPITAL

At the hospital's emergency room, a nurse assesses the damage and can give out painkillers. An orderly wheels you to the x-ray room, where a picture can be taken of the fracture for a doctor to examine.

SEEING THE DOC

A specialist called an orthopedist examines your leg and the x-rays to see exactly where and how bad the break is. If it is a really nasty fracture, the doctor might need to realign the bone, or insert metal pins to hold it in place. Most people just need a splint or a cast, and their bodies do all the hard work of healing.

X-RAY

With a special plate behind your leg, a blast of x-rays is sent through the machine. The plate absorbs the x-rays, except where your bones block their path. This creates a negative image on the plate. The radiologist takes x-ray pictures from more than one angle, so your doctor has a full picture of the fracture.

IN A CAST

With your limb in the right position, a doctor or nurse applies a dressing that will set solid to keep your bone aligned correctly, making it easier for the bone to heal itself. Over the next few months, it does just that. Bone cells called osteoclasts eat away the dead tissue, and cells named osteoblasts build up new bone, fusing the fracture back together again. Phew—back to climbing trees!

THE "X" MAN

IT STARTED AS AN INNOCENT LABORATORY EXPERIMENT . . .

GASP! AS HE MAKES ONE OF THE MOST IMPORTANT CENTURY . . . DISCOVERY THE 19TH **BY ACCIDENT!**

STARRING NOBEL-PRIZE WINNING **PROFESSOR WILHELM KONRAD ROENTGEN** THE MAN WHO DISCOVERED X-RAYS!

SWITCHED-ON SCIENTIST One night in 1895, Wilhelm Roentgen was experimenting with a Crookes tube (a glass bulb emptied of air). He knew that when an electric current passed between two electrodes in the tube, a cathode ray (stream of electrons) was released, making the tube glow. What would happen if he covered the tube with thick black cardboard?

DISTANT GLOW A screen painted with luminescent paint was standing on a chair a few feet away. As soon as the current was turned on, it began to shimmer with a greenish-yellow glow, even though the black cardboard had made the tube light-tight

THE X FACTOR

Roentgen realized this distant glow must be an unknown type of radiation. Uncertain what he was dealing with, he'd discovered the new rays he'd decided to call the new rays has stuck, but we now know them to be invisible high-frequency electromagnetic waves. The name

PENETRATING RAYS

Roentgen placed various objects between the tube and screen. He found that the x-rays passed straight through soft materials such as paper, but that metal objects blocked (absorbed) the rays.

SKELETON HAND

Finally, Roentgen aimed the x-rays at his wife's hand as it rested on a photographic plate. Not only did the ring on her finger show up sharply, but all the bones of her hand were also visible. He'd stumbled on an amazing technique for looking inside the living body without cutting it open! Roentgen's discovery would revolutionize medicine.

MEDICAL BOMBSHELL

At first doctors used x-rays to examine broken bones and locate swallowed metal objects. As the technology improved, they used them to diagnose cancers and other diseases. But exposure to x-rays (radiation) carries hidden dangers. Many doctors and radiologists (x-ray technicians) got sick and died before the introduction of protective lead clothing in the 1920s.

WORRIED ABOUT PRYING RAYS?

FEAR NOT WITH LEAD-LINED UNDERWEAR

Worried that people with x-ray vision are seeing more than they ought to. That's why we've invented lead-lined undies to block the rays in their tracks. Customers tell us they're worried

WEDDING RINGS ON YOUR FINGERS

THE LATEST MUST HAVE FOR YOUNG COUPLES

Create a permanent memento of your wedding day with his-and-her hand x-rays.

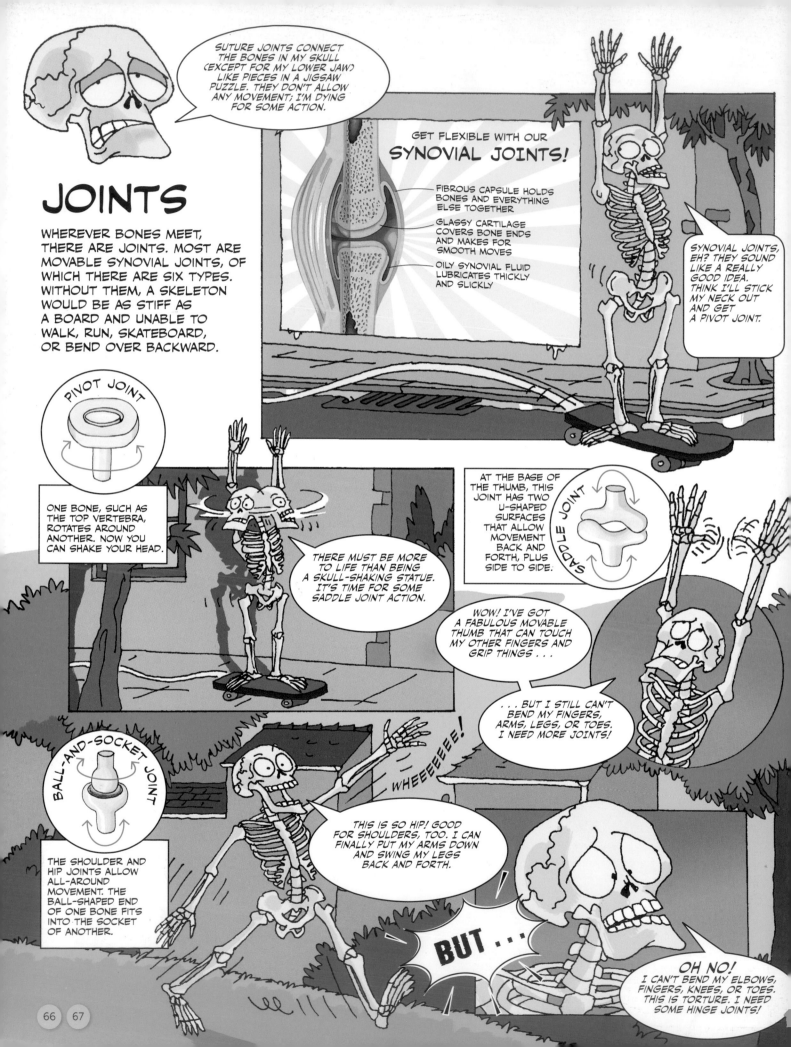

JOINTS

WHEREVER BONES MEET, THERE ARE JOINTS. MOST ARE MOVABLE SYNOVIAL JOINTS, OF WHICH THERE ARE SIX TYPES. WITHOUT THEM, A SKELETON WOULD BE AS STIFF AS A BOARD AND UNABLE TO WALK, RUN, SKATEBOARD, OR BEND OVER BACKWARD.

SUTURE JOINTS CONNECT THE BONES IN MY SKULL (EXCEPT FOR MY LOWER JAW) LIKE PIECES IN A JIGSAW PUZZLE. THEY DON'T ALLOW ANY MOVEMENT; I'M DYING FOR SOME ACTION.

GET FLEXIBLE WITH OUR SYNOVIAL JOINTS!

FIBROUS CAPSULE HOLDS BONES AND EVERYTHING ELSE TOGETHER

GLASSY CARTILAGE COVERS BONE ENDS AND MAKES FOR SMOOTH MOVES

OILY SYNOVIAL FLUID LUBRICATES THICKLY AND SLICKLY

SYNOVIAL JOINTS, EH? THEY SOUND LIKE A REALLY GOOD IDEA. THINK I'LL STICK MY NECK OUT AND GET A PIVOT JOINT.

PIVOT JOINT

ONE BONE, SUCH AS THE TOP VERTEBRA, ROTATES AROUND ANOTHER. NOW YOU CAN SHAKE YOUR HEAD.

THERE MUST BE MORE TO LIFE THAN BEING A SKULL-SHAKING STATUE. IT'S TIME FOR SOME SADDLE JOINT ACTION.

AT THE BASE OF THE THUMB, THIS JOINT HAS TWO U-SHAPED SURFACES THAT ALLOW MOVEMENT BACK AND FORTH, PLUS SIDE TO SIDE.

SADDLE JOINT

WOW! I'VE GOT A FABULOUS MOVABLE THUMB THAT CAN TOUCH MY OTHER FINGERS AND GRIP THINGS . . .

. . . BUT I STILL CAN'T BEND MY FINGERS, ARMS, LEGS, OR TOES. I NEED MORE JOINTS!

BALL-AND-SOCKET JOINT

THE SHOULDER AND HIP JOINTS ALLOW ALL-AROUND MOVEMENT. THE BALL-SHAPED END OF ONE BONE FITS INTO THE SOCKET OF ANOTHER.

THIS IS SO HIP! GOOD FOR SHOULDERS, TOO. I CAN FINALLY PUT MY ARMS DOWN AND SWING MY LEGS BACK AND FORTH.

WHEEEEEEE!

BUT . . .

OH NO! I CAN'T BEND MY ELBOWS, FINGERS, KNEES, OR TOES. THIS IS TORTURE. I NEED SOME HINGE JOINTS!

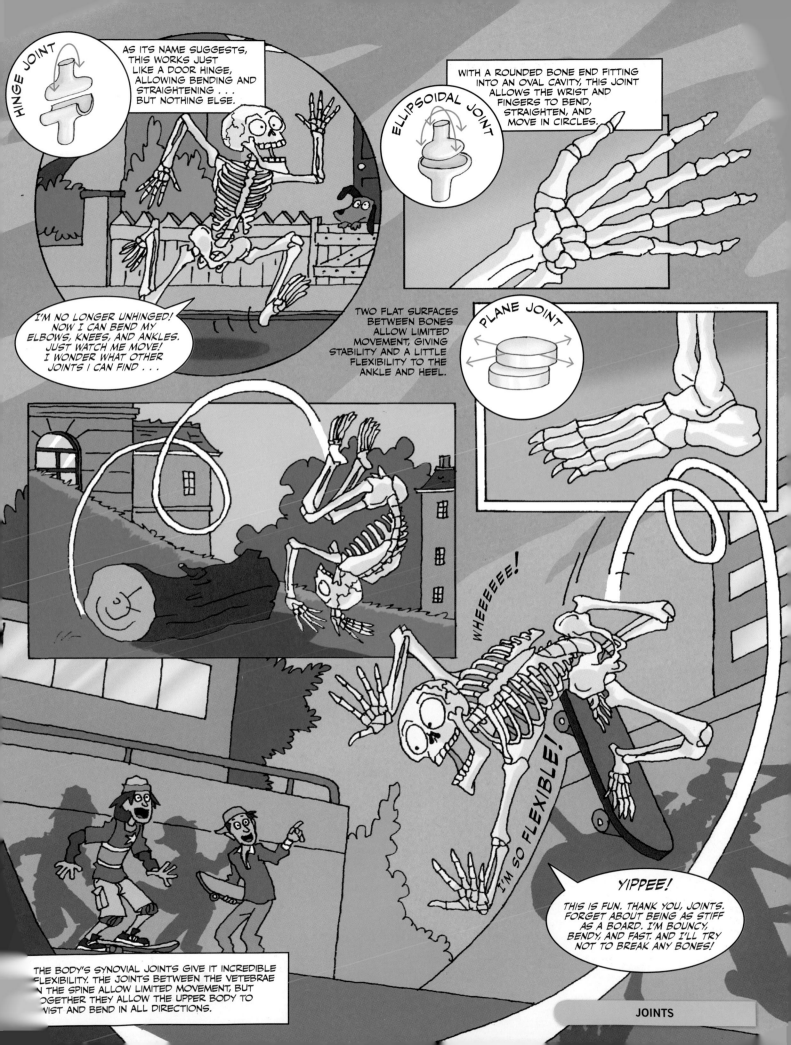

Flexing his pecs and clenching his glutes, our star graduate shows off his muscular body. Rippling restlessly beneath his skin, the shapes and outlines of the most prominent of his 640 skeletal muscles are clearly defined. Remove his skin and you would expose the red, glistening muscles that are attached at each

1. FRONTALIS wrinkles the forehead.
2. ORBICULARIS OCULI closes the eye, causing blinking.
3. STERNOCLEIDOMASTOID bends the head forward and tilts it sideways.
4. PECTORALIS MAJOR pulls the arm forward and toward the body and twists it.
5. BICEPS BRACHII bends the arm at the elbow.
6. DELTOID raises the arm to the side, front, and rear.

7. EXTERNAL OBLIQUE rotates the trunk and bends it sideways.
8. RECTUS ABDOMINIS bends the trunk forward and pulls in the abdomen.
9. QUADRICEPS FEMORIS straightens the leg at the knee and bends the thigh at the hip.
10. SARTORIUS rotates the thigh outward and bends it at the hip.
11. ADDUCTOR LONGUS pulls the thigh in toward the body.
12. TIBIALIS ANTERIOR bends the foot upwards.

Blood capillary carries oxygen and food to the muscle fibers

Muscle fiber has a striped appearance

Bundle of muscles fibers

Myofibrils are packed inside fiber

Skeletal muscle

STRUCTURED WORKOUT

Muscles have a very organized structure. Each muscle is a bundle of long, cylindrical muscle cells called fibers. Each fiber is packed with long, parallel myofibrils, inside which, again in parallel, are overlapping myosin and actin filaments.

...end to bones by cablelike tendons. By contracting and pulling, the muscles allow him to lift dumbbells, wrestle bears, pick flowers, and perform a multitude of other movements. They also, fortunately, release heat to keep him warm. And whether deltoids or hamstrings, all his muscles contract in the same way.

Thick myosin filament

Head of myosin interacts with actin to form a bridge

Thin actin filament

13. TRAPEZIUS pulls the head and shoulder backward.
14. LATISSIMUS DORSI pulls and rotates the arm and pulls it downward and backward.
15. TRICEPS BRACHII straightens the arm at the elbow.
16. GLUTEUS MAXIMUS straightens the thigh at the hip when running or jumping.

17. "HAMSTRINGS," INCLUDING BICEPS FEMORIS, bend the leg at the knee and straightens the thigh at the hip.
18. GASTROCNEMIUS pulls on the heel to bend the foot downward.

Relaxation (filaments are not interacting)

Contraction (filaments are interacting)

IMPULSIVE CONTRACTION

When a nerve signals a muscle to contract, myosin and actin form bridges that pull actin filaments inward, shortening the muscle fiber—and thus the muscle.

SKELETAL MUSCLES

SPACED OUT

Space travel may be the ultimate adventure, but a weightless environment can take its toll on even the healthiest astronauts. Without the effects of gravity to keep their feet on the ground (or deck), the floating astronauts have to work a lot harder to maintain their fitness.

Talk about a growth spurt! Astronauts grow 2–3 in (5–8 cm) taller in space. With no gravity pressing down on the spine, the back lengthens in space but soon returns to its original size back on Earth.

No danger of bird flu in space, but watch out for bird legs! With no gravity to push blood to the lower limbs, astronauts' legs get increasingly thinner in space.

Bumpy ride? Feeling queasy? Astronauts often experience space adaptation syndrome in their first few days in space. Unlike Earth—where gravity keeps most body fluids below the heart—in space some of these fluids move to the head. This can lead to dizziness and vomiting as the astronauts adapt to a new environment.

A SIX-MONTH TRIP TO MARS WOULD LEAVE ASTRONAUTS WITH WEAKER BONES OWING TO THE LACK OF GRAVITY. ONCE THERE, THINGS WOULD BECOME EVEN TOUGHER, AS THE PULL OF MARS'S GRAVITY—AROUND ONE-THIRD THAT OF EARTH'S GRAVITY—WOULD PRESS DOWN ON THEIR FRAGILE BONES.

There is nothing out of this world about getting sick. As bodily fluids rise to the head, astronauts get a stuffy nose and a puffy face. Their eyes may also swell up, and veins can bulge out from the neck.

Dust in space does not settle. It goes up astronauts' noses and makes them sneeze more than 100 times a day!

Astronauts on the International Space Station can see a sunrise every 90 minutes. This makes sleeping difficult, so they need to cover up the windows and put on sleeping masks just to get some rest.

Bones become weaker in space, and this reduces bone mass by up to ten percent. Back on Earth, it can take six months for astronauts to recover their bone mass.

ASTRONAUTS' MOVEMENTS ARE NOT THE ONLY THINGS TO SLOW DOWN IN SPACE— THE HEART DOES MUCH LESS PUMPING OWING TO THE ABSENCE OF GRAVITY, CAUSING HEART TISSUE TO SHRINK.

WITHOUT THE FORCE OF GRAVITY TO WORK AGAINST, MUSCLE TONE DIMINISHES IN SPACE. TO COUNTERACT THIS, ASTRONAUTS SPEND AT LEAST TWO HOURS A DAY IN THEIR SPACE GYM . . . ALTHOUGH THEY NEED TO BE STRAPPED TO THEIR EXERCISE EQUIPMENT SO THAT THEY DON'T FLOAT AWAY!

The body is not the only thing that change shape in space. Red blood cells, normally concave disks, become more spherical.

CAN YOUR FACE SPEAK WITHOUT WORDS?

ACTORS WANTED NOW

SILENT MOVIE AUDITIONS

BRING YOUR FACE WITH YOU. LEAVE YOUR VOICE AT HOME!

FRONTALIS raises the eyebrows and wrinkles the forehead

PROCERUS pulls the eyebrows together and downward

ORBICULARIS OCULI closes the eyelids and blinks and winks

LEVATOR LABII SUPERIORIS raises and curls the upper lip

ORBICULARIS ORIS closes and purses the lips

CORRUGATOR SUPERCILII draws the eyebrows together and wrinkles the forehead in a frown

ZYGOMATICUS MINOR (TOP MUSCLE) AND MAJOR (BOTTOM) pull the corners of the mouth upward and outward

RISORIUS pulls the corners of the mouth to the side

PLATYSMA pulls the lower lip back and down

DEPRESSOR ANGULI ORIS pulls the corners of the mouth to the side and downward

DEPRESSOR LABII INFERIORIS pulls the lower lip downward

MENTALIS wrinkles the chin and sticks out the lower lip

Your face says it all. So don't imagine smooth talking will convince us that you're right for the part. Understand this. More than 20 small muscles, fixed at one end to your skull, tug at the skin to create an array of facial expressions, from a surly sneer to a giant grin. They do it without you realizing, so you can't conceal your feelings. There's no language barrier either. Worldwide, people recognize six basic expressions—happiness, sadness, fear, surprise, anger, and disgust. And don't bother trying to win us over with that fake smile. We can see right through it.

THE HAPPY MAN

Simon Glee won the lottery…
No wonder he's so happy!

You'll cry like a baby and love every minute. Bring your tissues.

SURPRISED

Winona Wonder looks very shocked—and so will you when you discover why!

If her looks could kill, Maddy Cross would be jailed for life.

When Maddy gets mad, take cover— she's very, very, very

!ANGRY!

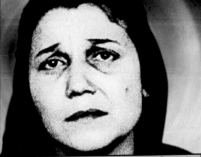

The saddest, soggiest saga since Sob Story. See it and weep BUCKETS!

SAD

THE MAN WITH TWO SMILES

One is false, one is real, but even he doesn't know which is which!

FAKE SMILE

* Only uses muscles around the mouth
* No wrinkles around, or bags under, eyes
* Pupils are small
* Smile is asymmetrical
* Not infectious

REAL SMILE

* Uses muscles around the mouth and eyes
* Wrinkles appear around, and bags under, the eyes
* Pupils widen
* Smile is symmetrical
* Highly infectious

DISGUSTED

SIX REELS OF UTTER REVULSION

Dinah Devine is disgusted with EVERYTHING!

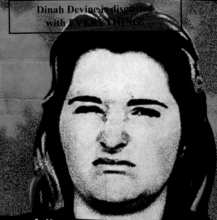

A lip-curling legend of distasteful detestation

COMPETITION

See the movie and count the number of real smiles you see.

Hand in your answer at the box office and, if you are right, win two tickets to the movie of your choice.

Watch in horror as your face becomes contorted by fear.

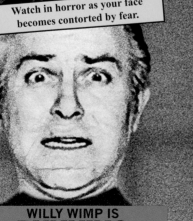

WILLY WIMP IS
RUNNING
SCARED

FACIAL MUSCLES

THE HEART ❶

The rapid, repeated movements of aerobic exercise help keep your heart healthy. As you exercise, your heart rate speeds up and your capillaries increase in number to get more oxygen to the muscles quicker. The more you work out, the more efficient your heart gets at delivering oxygen-rich blood to the rest of your body.

THE LUNGS ❷

Regular aerobic activity can also help your lungs get stronger. When you work out, your breathing rate more than doubles and you breathe deeper to get more oxygen into the body. This increases your lung capacity, making them work more efficiently and providing you with plenty of puff to keep going.

Pushups are a type of anaerobic exercise, using a high-intensity burst of activity over a short time to build muscle strength.

Long-distance cycling and similar activities, such as marathon running, build up stamina

FLEXIBILITY

Exercising stretches out your muscles and joints and helps make your body more flexible. Being able to bend and stretch with ease prevents muscle strain or injury, improves coordination, and generally makes you a smoother mover. Yoga, martial arts, gymnastics, and dance all help your joints move as they should and build flexibility.

STRENGTH

Building strong muscles enables you to stay on the move for longer and helps support your moving joints so that it is less likely you will injure them. Strength training also helps maintain a healthy weight, as muscles burn many more calories—even when you're resting—than an equal amount of body fat does.

Keeping joints flexible enables them to move smoothly through their full range of motion.

FITNESS FIRST!

Regular exercise helps build a strong, flexible, energetic body, benefiting just about every part of it. Staying in shape can help you live longer by lowering the risk of developing certain diseases and helping you maintain a healthy body weight. And here's another heads-up: when you work out, your body produces chemicals called endorphins—a natural pick-me-up that helps you feel relaxed and happy.

A strong upper body and a good sense of balance and coordination can enable tricky physical feats like this one-handed handstand.

STAMINA

Working out is hard work (it's not called working out for nothing), and your body can get tired while you exercise. But the more you exercise, the more your stamina increases. Building up your stamina means you are able to stay active for longer periods of time, making it easier for you to find that extra bit of energy to keep going when fatigue sets in.

In Hand

FROM WRITING A LETTER TO WIELDING AN AXE, HANDS ARE CAPABLE OF A MULTITUDE OF MOVEMENTS, BOTH PRECISE AND POWERFUL. THEY OWE THIS VERSATILITY TO THE FOREARM AND HAND MUSCLES THAT MOVE THEIR FLEXIBLE BONY FRAMEWORK.

Flexor carpi radialis bends the wrist and turns the hand outward

Flexor digitorum superficialis bends all the fingers (excluding the thumb)

Flexor retinaculum is a ligament band that holds the flexor tendons in place

Finger bends when its middle-finger bone is pulled by a flexor tendon

The benders (front of arm)

Most of the muscles in the front of the forearm are flexors that bend either the wrist, by pulling on the wrist and palm bones, or the fingers and thumb. These forearm muscles have long tendons that extend into the hand and fingers and anchor them firmly to each bone.

Tendon of flexor digitorum superficialis runs from the forearm to one of the fingers

Small muscles in the ball of the thumb move it toward the fingers to produce a precision grip like this

The straighteners (back of arm)

At the back of the forearm are the extensor muscles that, like their flexor equivalents, give the forearm its fleshiness. They, too, have long, cablelike tendons, kept in order by a wristband retinaculum. These extensor muscles straighten either the wrist or the fingers and thumb.

Index finger straightens when its middle-finger bone is pulled by an extensor tendon

Extensor retinaculum is a ligament band that holds the extensor tendons in place

Extensor digitorum straightens all the fingers (excluding the thumb)

Tendon of extensor digitorum runs from the forearm across the back of the hand and into a finger

Extensor carpi ulnaris straightens the wrist and pulls the hand out to the side

Extensor digiti minimi straightens the pinkie

Get a grip: precision vs. power

While forearm muscles create a power grip, smaller muscles inside the hand itself create precision movements such as holding a paintbrush. Humans' unique ability to move the thumb across the palm so that it can touch the tips of the other fingers enables us to perform such delicate actions.

On the move

Not even the most learned of anatomists could describe precisely how the human body behaves when it moves. The separate movements of the muscles, joints, and limbs are simply too rapid for the human eye to see.

Until, that is, the invention of photography in the mid-1800s. This new technology meant that body movement could be captured in a still image, and it inspired the work of the two pioneering photographers exhibited here.

Great leap forward

English-born Eadweard Muybridge was an artist rather than a scientist. He leaped into the public eye in 1877 when he published the first photographs ever taken of a moving horse. After that, Muybridge went on to produce thousands of images of men and women walking, running, leaping, and jumping. His technique involved setting up a row of up to 24 cameras with shutter releases electrically timed to go off in sequence. The dynamic images shown here reveal the subtle movements of walking and the more pronounced body positions of jumping and running. His work allowed people to see themselves on the move, and proved to be a huge success with the public.

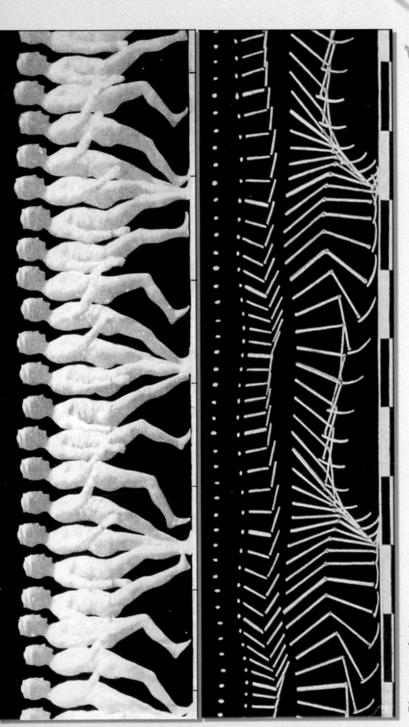

Picture perfect

A French professor of physiology, Étienne-Jules Marey had already experimented with various ways of recording and measuring movement before turning to photography, inspired by Muybridge's horse studies. To create his famous sequences of moving people, he used a single camera and placed a revolving disk, with slots cut into it at intervals, behind the lens. This produced a succession of images on a single plate of film, giving a more fluid "picture" of movement. He then broke the images down into skeletal outlines to analyse the separate movements made by the running figure.

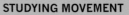

REPLACEMENT PARTS

1. BRONZE LEG
Prostheses are artificial substitutes for missing body parts. One of the oldest existing examples—which dates from around 300 B.C.—is this artificial leg. Unearthed from a grave in Capua, Italy, in 1858, it is made of bronze and iron plates hammered over a wooden core. Its owner may have been injured in battle.

2. PARÉ'S PROSTHETICS
In the 1500s, French military surgeon Ambroise Paré used amputation as a lifesaving method on the battlefield, removing many a soldier's shattered arm or leg. He then began to design and build artificial limbs for his amputation patients. Paré's devices introduced features still in use today, from locking knees to leather harnesses for attaching a leg.

3. PEG LEGS
These simple, foot-free devices with no moving parts were made of wood, plastic, or metal. They did the job, but the world wars and conflicts that followed led to a rise in amputees and a greater demand for more functional and realistic limbs.

4. COMPUTERIZED LEGS
Medical and technological developments have led to lighter, more lifelike legs made of plastic and foam. The Otto Bock C-Leg is equipped with microprocessors that adapt to each move the wearer makes, so walking feels natural.

5. LEGS FOR ATHLETES
In 1984, American athlete and amputee Van Phillips introduced the Cheetah. This C-shaped carbon graphite foot acts like a giant spring, enabling its wearer to jump, land, and run. Sprinters wearing Cheetahs can give able-bodied athletes a run for their money.

1. HELPING HANDS
In 1504, German knight Gotz von Berlichingen lost his forearm on the battlefield. A glovelike replacement was created for him, known as the Iron Hand. The fingers could be moved with small gears and fixed into position, so Gotz could grip a sword and continue battling.

2. LEFT HOOK
The most common type of prosthetic arm for hundreds of years was tipped with a metal hook. Today's models use straps that connect the hook to an anchor on the opposite shoulder. When the opposite elbow moves, the hook opens or closes to grip objects.

3. REPLACEMENT ARM
The medical and technological advances that improved prosthetic legs over the last hundred years have also led to artificial arms that increasingly resemble real ones. Motor-operated devices let the wearer move the fingers on a prosthetic arm by pushing a button or toggling a switch to perform a specific task.

4. BIONIC ARM
On the cutting edge of prosthetics is bionics—the combination of biology and technology to replicate human body parts. Bionic arms are not manually operated; instead, the nerves in the amputated stump are rewired to the chest muscles. When the wearer thinks about moving his or her hand, messages travel along the rewired nerves to the chest. The chest muscles then send out tiny electrical signals that alert microprocessors in the arm to move the hand.

ARTIFICIAL LIMBS

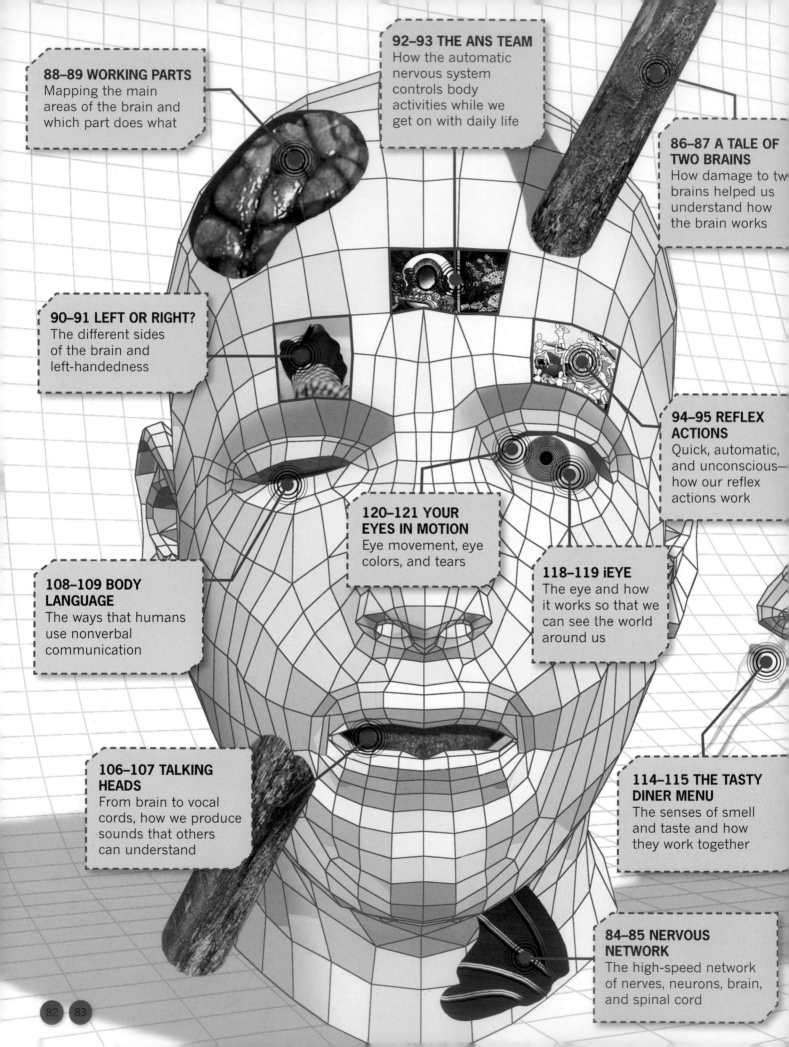

88–89 WORKING PARTS
Mapping the main areas of the brain and which part does what

92–93 THE ANS TEAM
How the automatic nervous system controls body activities while we get on with daily life

86–87 A TALE OF TWO BRAINS
How damage to two brains helped us understand how the brain works

90–91 LEFT OR RIGHT?
The different sides of the brain and left-handedness

94–95 REFLEX ACTIONS
Quick, automatic, and unconscious—how our reflex actions work

120–121 YOUR EYES IN MOTION
Eye movement, eye colors, and tears

118–119 iEYE
The eye and how it works so that we can see the world around us

108–109 BODY LANGUAGE
The ways that humans use nonverbal communication

106–107 TALKING HEADS
From brain to vocal cords, how we produce sounds that others can understand

114–115 THE TASTY DINER MENU
The senses of smell and taste and how they work together

84–85 NERVOUS NETWORK
The high-speed network of nerves, neurons, brain, and spinal cord

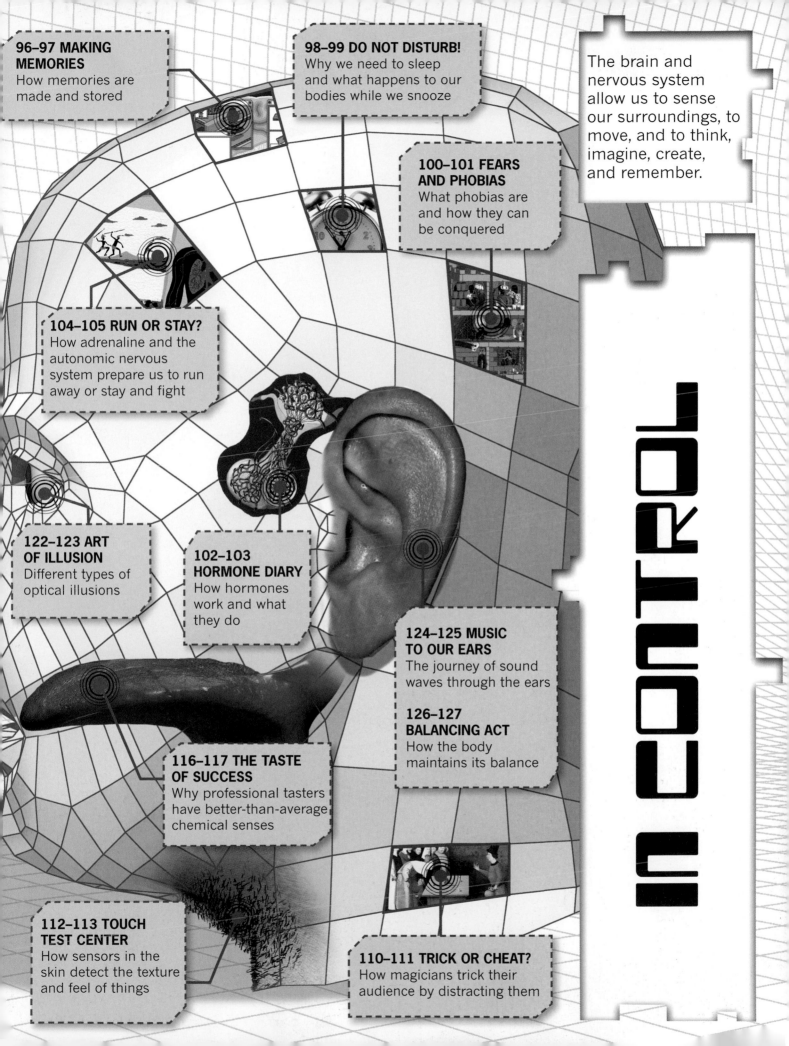

96–97 MAKING MEMORIES
How memories are made and stored

98–99 DO NOT DISTURB!
Why we need to sleep and what happens to our bodies while we snooze

100–101 FEARS AND PHOBIAS
What phobias are and how they can be conquered

The brain and nervous system allow us to sense our surroundings, to move, and to think, imagine, create, and remember.

104–105 RUN OR STAY?
How adrenaline and the autonomic nervous system prepare us to run away or stay and fight

122–123 ART OF ILLUSION
Different types of optical illusions

102–103 HORMONE DIARY
How hormones work and what they do

124–125 MUSIC TO OUR EARS
The journey of sound waves through the ears

126–127 BALANCING ACT
How the body maintains its balance

116–117 THE TASTE OF SUCCESS
Why professional tasters have better-than-average chemical senses

112–113 TOUCH TEST CENTER
How sensors in the skin detect the texture and feel of things

110–111 TRICK OR CHEAT?
How magicians trick their audience by distracting them

IN CONTROL

Nervous network

Controlling everything the body does is a complex communication network called the nervous system. Working 24/7, it gathers information about the body and issues instructions that make it react. Electrical signals are flashed to and from the network's headquarters in the brain at speeds of up to 328 ft (100 m) a second via a circuit of nerves packed with specialized cells called neurons.

CONTROL CENTER

The brain is a living computer. Its 100 billion neurons work together to analyse information being transmitted continuously from the body's network of nerves. The brain makes instant decisions about what instructions to send out, such as stimulating an arm muscle to contract and move.

INFORMATION SUPERHIGHWAY

Composed of the brain and the spinal cord, the central nervous system (CNS) coordinates the activities of the entire body. The spinal cord relays information to spinal nerves, branches of which control most of the body's skeletal muscles. It can also work independently of the brain, controlling reflex actions such as pulling the hand away from something hot.

FUNNY BONE

Most nerves are buried deep in the body, but the ulnar nerve at the elbow sits close to the surface. A sudden knock against the humerus, or funny bone, sends a tingling sensation shooting down the arm.

Pressure receptors in the hand tell the brain that the hand has contact with the ball

Optic nerve from the eye sends a stream of signals to the brain to track the ball's position

Intercostal nerves control the muscles that move the ribs to control breathing

TWO-WAY TRAFFIC

The network of nerves spanning out from the brain and spinal cord to the rest of the body is known as the peripheral nervous system (PNS). These nerves contain sensory neurons, which gather information from organs, blood vessels, muscles, and other body parts to update the CNS, and motor neurons, which deliver instructions from the CNS to skeletal muscles.

NERVE STRUCTURE

Each neuron (nerve cell) has a long filament, or axon, that carries nerve impulses to the next neuron. Cablelike nerves are made up of individual axons grouped into fascicles and wrapped in tough, elastic perineurium tissue. Fascicles are bundled together, protected by an outer layer called the epineurium and cushioned by blood vessels and fat-containing cells.

Tiny electrical signals speed along length of axon

Perineurium

Fascicle is a collection of axons surrounded by perineurium tissue

Fat protects fascicles and allows nerve to bend

Epineurium surrounds the entire nerve

MAJOR NERVES

Arising from the brain, 12 pairs of cranial nerves service the head and neck. Branches of the 31 pairs of spinal nerves, which originate from the spinal cord, form an extensive network that supplies the rest of the body, right down to the tips of the toes.

Nerve impulses from the brain carried by motor neurons instruct muscles to contract to straighten the thigh at the hip

Sciatic nerve is the thickest and longest in the body and controls thigh muscles that bend the leg at the knee

Calf is served by the internal popliteal nerve, which is a branch of the sciatic nerve

A Tale of Two Brains
Curious cases that helped explain the brain

*I*t was the best of times; it was the worst of times . . . at least it was for those delving into the mysteries of the human brain. By the middle of the 1800s, scientists had developed many theories about how this spongy gray matter worked, yet the limits of technology meant their ideas could not be tested. Had this chapter in medical research come to a dead end? Dear reader, no. Scientific proof that each region of the brain had a different function was confirmed by the strange behavior of two patients suffering from brain damage. What the dickens was going on? Read their two tales here.

Phineas Gage and the Rod of Doom
1848: Vermont

The young foreman of a gang of railroad construction workers, Phineas Gage must have found his job a blast . . . literally. Gage and his men were employed to clear the way for a railroad line to run through the mountains, and Gage's task was to fill holes drilled in the mountainside with enough explosives to shatter the rock. After filling the holes with gunpowder, Gage used the pointed end of his metal tamping iron to push a fuse into the gunpowder, before the hole was filled up with sand. Gage then tamped down the sand to plug the hole so that the blast went in, not out. True, it was a tricky job, but Gage had done this countless times without incident . . . until that fateful afternoon of September 13.

As Gage stood over a hole filled with explosives and a fuse, he lost his grip—or maybe he was just distracted. No one knows what was running through his head when he dropped the iron rod. It struck granite, created a spark, and set off an explosion. The blast drove the rod straight through his head, entering under his cheekbone, then traveling through his brain and out of his forehead. The tamping rod fell with a clang, covered in blood and brains.

Gage's gang raced through the smoke to find him knocked flat on his back, but conscious. Within moments he was sitting up and talking. Nonetheless, they rushed him to his hotel as another worker raced to find the town doctor. As he examined the wound, Dr. John Harlow could hardly

Fig. 1
How the tamping iron entered Gage's head

believe Gage had survived. His skull had shattered, his brain was exposed, yet Gage suffered no loss of speech or movement. Harlow cleaned the bloody wound, pressed the skull bones back in place, and wrapped a bandage around Gage's head. He assumed that Gage had gotten off so lightly because the front of the brain was not vital.

The following spring, Dr. Harlow examined Gage. Although he looked the same (bar the scar), Gage's personality had changed beyond recognition. He swore, insulted friends, and was very selfish. When Dr. Harlow wrote a paper about the case, it sparked a worldwide wave of interest. Gage's accident had proved that the front of the brain controls personality and that damage to this region, despite its consequences, need not be fatal.

Dr. Broca and the Tan Man
1861: Paris, France

Some years later, a strange patient checked into the Bicêtre Hospital in Paris. He was intelligent and able-bodied, yet he had lost the power of speech, replying to any question with a single word: tan. This became his nickname. While living in the French hospital, Tan also lost movement in his right arm and leg. By complete coincidence, in April 1861, Tan encountered influential French doctor and medical investigator Paul Broca when his paralysed leg became swollen. Broca had been tinkering with the idea that the frontal lobes of the cerebrum control speech. He noted with great interest Tan's speech problems as well as the paralysis on the right side of his body.

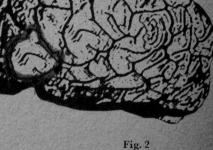

Fig. 2
Part of the brain now known as Broca's area

A short time later, Tan died. During the autopsy, Broca could see a dark lesion in the left frontal lobe of Tan's brain. He presented his findings to a leading French medical research group, and for the first time, it became clear that there was a link between a defect in a specific part of the brain and a loss of body function. The region of the brain that controls speech was later named Broca's area.

The tales of these two men must now end. It was a far, far better thing that they did than I have ever done for the study of how the brain works.

I remain, your humble servant,
Dr. Ed Case

Paul Broca (1824–1880)

When we plan to move our bodies in a pattern that we've learned before—such as doing a particular skateboard trick or playing tennis—we rely on this area of the brain. It decides which muscles we are going to need and sends signals to them.

This area activates muscles or groups of muscles to contract and pull on the skeleton to get us on the move. Most of the movements we make are controlled right here.

PREMOTOR CORTEX

Found at the front of the brain, the prefrontal cortex is key to our personality and intelligence. This is where we make plans and decisions, sort out our thoughts, and learn complex ideas.

PREFRONTAL CORTEX

BROCA'S AREA

This part of the brain helps us speak and understand what other people say to us. Broca's area allows us to figure out what we are going to say, and then it instructs the muscles used in speaking (in the throat, tongue, and mouth) to move.

WORKING PARTS

It's not very large, but the brain is certainly in charge. Within its folds and grooves, it contains our intelligence, memory, emotions, and the ability to move, feel, and speak. All the information collected via the senses is processed in the cerebral cortex, which has distinct parts to perform different jobs. Motor areas tell muscles to move, sensory areas gather information from the senses, and association areas help us interpret data so what we understand and learn.

Signals from the primary auditory cortex undergo further analysis here so that we can identify and "hear" them. In the association cortex, we identify a sound, locate the source, and figure out what made the sound.

PRIMARY MOTOR CORTEX

PRIMARY SENSORY CORTEX

SENSORY ASSOCIATION CORTEX

WERNICKE'S AREA

PRIMARY AUDITORY CORTEX

AUDITORY ASSOCIATION CORTEX

VISUAL ASSOCIATION CORTEX

PRIMARY VISUAL CORTEX

When we touch something, messages about pressure, heat, pain, and vibration rush from receptors in the skin to this area of the brain. Fingertips and lips are especially packed with sensitive nerve endings.

Messages received via the primary sensory cortex go to this part of the brain for processing. The sensory association cortex is like a database of items you've touched before. Here, messages are analysed and compared so that you can identify what you've just touched.

The primary visual cortex sends basic information about what we see to this association area of the brain. Complex analysis then sorts through our visual memory to identify what we are looking at and where it is in relation to us.

When light hits the neurons in the retina at the back of the eye, they fire off messages to the primary visual cortex. Here, the brain begins to process the visual information in a very simple way: outlines, shapes, colors, and motion.

Figuring out what we are hearing starts in this area of the brain. The ears detect sounds and signal the primary auditory cortex. The signals are then analysed for volume (loud or quiet) and pitch (high or low).

German neurologist (brain doctor) Karl Wernicke gave his name to this area of the brain, involved in giving meaning to written or spoken language. In 1871, he noticed that people who had damage here could speak, but in gobbledygook. It is connected to Broca's area by a large bundle of nerve fibers.

BRAIN ACTIVITIES

LEFT OR RIGHT?

The report cards are in and the two halves of the cerebrum (the largest part of the brain) have excelled in very different subjects. Frankly, if it wasn't for the band of nerve fibers linking the pair, it would be difficult to believe they are even related!

REPORT CARD

Name **LEFT BRAIN**   Class **6A**

SUBJECT	GRADE	TEACHER'S REMARKS
MATH Miss Take	A	Left Brain is a natural mathematician. He readily applies newly learned skills to a variety of complex problems and processes information accurately and with attention to detail. He presents his work in a logical order, but it is sometimes difficult to read his rushed and messy writing. Left Brain needs to slow down and let his hand catch up with his speedy mind.
SCIENCE Dr. Fizz	A+	*Left Brain is a proven science whiz. He enjoys doing experiments and is able to provide a thorough account of his observations in a clear step-by-step fashion.*
HISTORY Mr. Oldman	A	With his analytical approach to learning, Left Brain has a sound grasp of historical events. The timeline he constructed was both accurate and exhaustive—most of the facts he chose to explain were not even taught in any of the lessons. This demonstrates his excellent individual research skills.
LANGUAGES Frau Deutsch	B+	Left Brain continues to excel in German, and he copes well with the growing vocabulary and complex grammatical rules. Wunderbar!
ART Miss Color	C-	Left Brain has a love-hate relationship with art. While he is able to talk at length about Pablo Picasso's life and work, he is reluctant to pick up a paintbrush.
SPORT	B	*A strategic athlete, Left Brain is always willing to take the captain role and appoint positions on the field. He plays by the rules.*

BEING LEFT-HANDED:

What do Barack Obama, Leonardo da Vinci, and Isaac Newton have in common? They are all left-handed. For most people, the left half of the brain—which controls the right side of the body—is the dominant side, and that is why most people are right-handed. But in ten per cent of the population, the creative right side of the brain dominates and, because it controls the left side of the body, right-brain people are left-handers.

REPORT CARD

Name **RIGHT BRAIN**

Class 6A

SUBJECT	GRADE	TEACHER'S REMARKS
MATH Miss Take	B̶ C	Right Brain is making slow progress. He becomes confused by long division and subtraction problems. On the bright side, all the mathematical symbols are presented like works of art.
SCIENCE Dr. Fizz	B	Right Brain is a risk taker and continues to impress me with his "outside-the-box" thinking, but it would be good to see him apply more logic when solving problems.
HISTORY Mr. Oldman	B+	Not one for getting bogged down in facts and dates, Right Brain is more interested in understanding the dominant philosophies of a historical period and empathizing with the experiences of historical figures.
LANGUAGES Frau Deutsch	C+	Right Brain enjoys the vibrant atmosphere in German class, yet I cannot help but feel that he takes undue advantage of the discussion-based learning that is so important when discovering a new language. More to the point, I am a little concerned with some of his rather colorful vocabulary. He seems to have learned some new words that have no place in the classroom.
ART Miss Color	A+	Adventurous. Dazzling. Strange. These three words probably sum up Right Brain's original works best. He is exceptionally creative and lets his imagination run wild.
P.E. Mr. Ball	B-	Right Brain is clearly a passionate athlete, and will often steam in impulsively rather than coolly strategizing the best way to play.

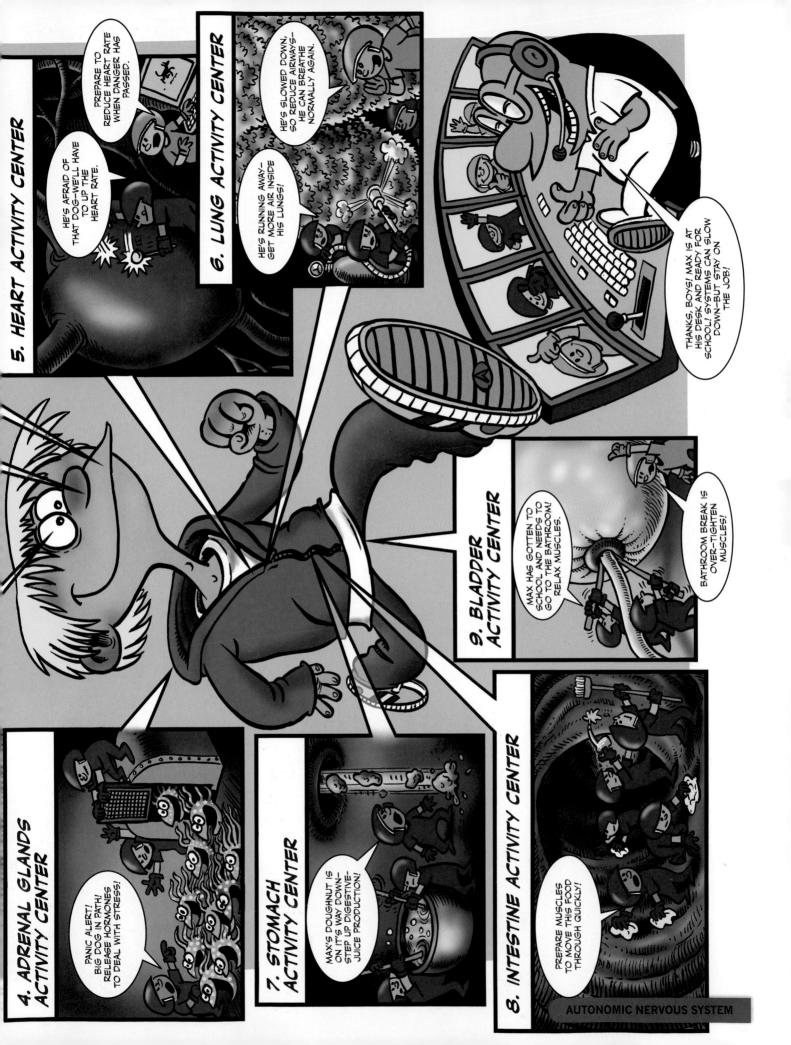

REFLEX ACTIONS

Touch something that's hotter than you thought and your hand will jerk back without your having to think about it. That's a typical reflex action. Reflexes are rapid automatic responses that always work in the same way—often to protect you from harm. Many responses involve the spinal cord alone, while others go via the brain.

1 Something irritating your nose? Hay fever? A winter cold? The sneeze reflex will send a blast of air from your lungs through your nasal cavity to clear the irritation.

2 The artist has swung the paintbrush around without looking. Fortunately this guy saw it coming, and ducked automatically to avoid being hit.

3 It's important to pull your hand away from something hot to stop it from getting burned. That's what the split-second withdrawal reflex does.

4 If you're unlucky enough to slip and stumble, a reflex action can break your fall. Automatically putting your arm out might prevent you from falling.

5 The figure carrrying the thumbtacks has spotted the stumbling man. Without thinking, he jumps out of the way.

6 Step on a pin and messages whiz to your spinal cord and then straight back to the leg muscles to lift your foot. It is only when the messsages travel on from the spinal cord to your brain that you feel the pain.

7 Tap gently just below the kneecap and the lower leg kicks forward. Doctors check this reflex to make sure the spinal cord is working properly.

8 The soft touch of a feather on the skin produces a tickle. This results in involuntary twitching and, possibly, laughter. However, it's interesting that you can't tickle yourself.

9 Babies are born with several reflexes, including grasping at objects, sucking, and "walking" if held upright. These early reflexes all disappear within a few months.

SPINAL CORD

This column of nervous tissue extends down your back from your brain, surrounded and protected by the backbone. It's in charge of lmany automatic responses, including the withdrawal and knee-jerk reflexes. It communicates with the body through spinal nerves, which emerge from spaces between vertebrae in the spine.

This branch of the spinal nerve carries signals to muscles, instructing them to contract and move the body.

— Vertebra

The spinal cord enables reflexes to happen by processing signals from receptors and sending out signals to muscles.

This branch of the spinal nerve carries signals from heat, pain, and other receptors into the spinal cord.

MAKING MEMORIES

Imagine if you couldn't remember your best friend's name and had to be reintroduced each time you met. It doesn't happen, of course, because your memory effortlessly stores and recalls not just names but also events, facts, and skills, enabling you to think, learn, and be creative. How memory works is still not fully understood, but what is known is that it has three basic levels—sensory, short-term, and long-term.

MEMORY CAM

SENSORY MEMORY

When you're on the move, you're constantly aware of your surroundings. That's due to your sensory memory. For a split second, it stores a fleeting impression, or sense, of the sights and sounds around you before being updated and, usually, lost. However, something that grabs your attention may pass into your short-term memory.

SHORT-TERM MEMORY

Most sensory information that enters the brain is lost. If we remembered everything that happened, our brains would be overwhelmed.However, significant sights, sounds, and sensations are kept for a few seconds or minutes in short-term memory. This temporary storehouse gives the brain time to process and act on incoming information, such as reading, counting, or dialing a phone number.

WORD SEQUENCE
When you read a sentence, your short-term memory stores the words in order. Without it, you would register only one word at a time and the sentence would be meaningless.

PHONE NUMBERS
You've just looked up the number of a person you want to call. Short-term memory holds onto the digits of that number long enough for you to dial it. Some people can remember numbers for much longer.

COIN COUNTING
Seen something tasty to eat? You can briefly store its cost in your short-term memory while counting your money in order to calculate if you've got enough cash to buy a snack.

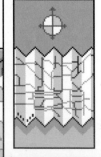

MAP READING
Being able to read a map depends on short-term memory. This momentarily stores the map markings so that the you can bring the details together and interpret them, allowing you to get where you want to go.

LONG-TERM MEMORY

Most short-term memories last for seconds and then vanish. But some persist and are moved to long-term memory. This permanent storehouse has a limitless capacity, and its memories can last for a lifetime. More importantly, memories stored here can be retrieved and reused. The three types of long-term memory are procedural, semantic, and episodic.

PROCEDURAL

This is where movement skills, such as playing a musical instrument or riding a bike, are stored. These are skills achieved through practice, and once learned, they are rarely lost.

SEMANTIC

Whenever you read something, you use your semantic memory to understand what's in front of you. It stores learned words, languages, and facts and their meanings.

EPISODIC

Specific occasions, such as a music festival or a vacation, are recorded in your episodic memory. Anything that later "jogs" your memory lets you recall the main events of that occasion.

LONG-TERM MEMORY

SHORT-TERM MEMORY

SENSORY MEMORY

MEMORY DOWNLOADS

MAKING CONNECTIONS

If your brain rates incoming information—such as a superscary moment in a movie—as being important, it is relayed back and forth between the hippocampus and the cerebral cortex (the "thinking" part of the brain). This process makes neurons (brain cells) create new connections that store the experiences in long-term memory, ready for retrieval.

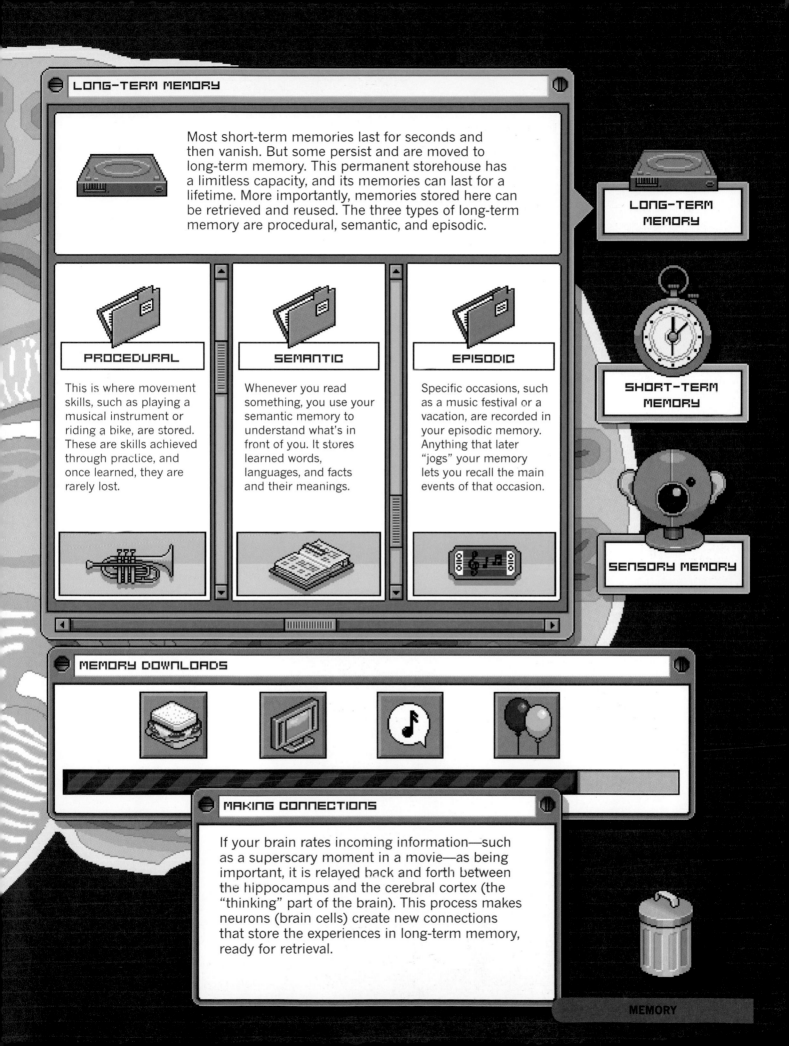

DO NOT DISTURB!

Your body needs a break at the end of the day, and a good night's sleep lets you rest and recover. Snoozing also allows your brain to sort and store information, release important chemicals, and work on tricky problems. If you don't get enough sleep, it's difficult to think clearly and you may become cranky.

STAGE 1 (NREM)

As you close your eyes and drift into the first stage of sleep, your brain tells your muscles to relax, although they may jerk suddenly in movements known as sleep starts. Brain activity when you are awake (beta waves) changes to alpha waves. Although drowsy, even a slight noise may wake you, so let the cat out.

STAGE 2 (NREM)

After awhile, you enter the next stage, when your body temperature drops slightly and your breathing rate slows down. The only moving you might do is a bit of tossing and turning, so your heart rate slows down to compensate. Sudden loud noises like a siren outside can rouse you, but you might sleep right through other sounds.

SLEEP PATTERNS

After your head hits the pillow, the brain signals your body to fall sleep. During the stages of nonrapid eye movement (NREM), you gradually sleep deeper and deeper, but you can still move around. In rapid eye movement (REM) sleep, your eyes dart back and forth under your eyelids, your heartbeat speeds up, and your skeletal muscles freeze. This is the stage when people dream.

▮	NON-REM SLEEP
▮	REM SLEEP

Every night, you repeat the NREM and REM stages around every 90 minutes until you wake up. The REM periods become a little longer as the night passes, which is why your longest dreams happen in the morning.

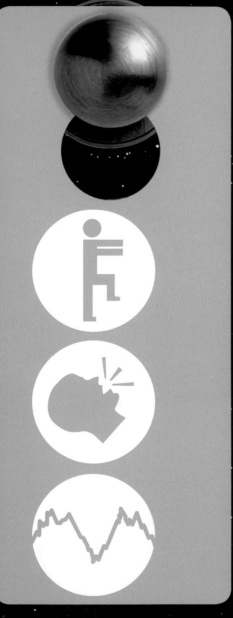

STAGE 3 (NREM)

This deeper sleep is called slow-wave sleep, when alpha waves slow into delta waves. Your blood pressure drops, and your body is less sensitive to changes in temperature. It's much harder to wake up, and if you did, you'd be confused and out of it. In this stage, some people sleepwalk, talk in their sleep, and snore.

STAGE 4 (REM)

Alpha waves appear in the brain as it becomes active—sometimes even more so than when you are awake. Your eyes move back and forth, perhaps in response to the images in your dreams or nightmares. Breathing rate and blood pressure both rise, but many of your muscles are paralysed, so you cannot act out your dreams.

FEARS AND PHOBIAS

Take a ride on the ghost train and see what scares you most. Everyone has some level of fear that protects them from danger. These rational fears are "built in" to our brains and were passed down from our ancestors, who had good reasons to be wary of anything that posed a threat to life. A fear of clowns or paper is not rational and may be linked to an early experience or being raised by someone with similar fear. When fears seem out of proportion to the potential dangers, they are known as phobias. All fears are stored in the memory section of the brain.

Dentophobia
Fear of dentists

Open wide!

Acrophobia
Fear of heights

Astraphobia
Fear of thunderstorms

Chiroptophobia
Fear of bats

Amathophobia Fear of dust

Achooo!

Arachnophobia Fear of spiders

Alektorophobia Fear of chickens

Lachanophobia Fear of vegetables

But vegetables are good for you!

FAMILIAR FEARS

Some phobias are so weird that they are difficult to understand, while others are quite common. One is claustrophobia—when a person feels terrified of being trapped in an enclosed space such as an elevator or a tunnel. Another is agoraphobia—a fear of being in an open place where the person does not feel safe and is desperate to escape—in most cases, to their home (unless it needs to be cleaned of course).

FIGHTING THE FEAR

Fears and phobias can trigger physical reactions such as shaking, rapid heartbeat, and nausea. Most people can live with their phobias by avoiding what scares them. If you suffer from lutraphobia, steer clear of otters. Severe phobics may need help from a psychologist.

Humans scare the whiskers off me!

FAMOUS PHOBICS

Even the famous have their fears . . . Napoleon Bonaparte, the emperor of France, suffered from a fear of cats (ailurophobia). Movie director Alfred Hitchcock was afraid of eggs (ovophobia), and psychiatrist Sigmund Freud was scared of traveling by train (siderodromophobia). He certainly wouldn't have taken a ride on this ghost train!

HORMONE DIARY

Mom's always saying I've got hormones zooming around inside me. I decided to find out what she was talking about, and guess what? Hormones are chemicals that make other things happen. They're oozed out from glands in the endocrine system straight into the blood. Like tiny messengers, they zip all over the place to control and regulate lots of body functions. I'm a living science experiment . . . How cool is that?

My ex little brother

Leaky tent!

Leaky me, almost!

July 28

Grrrr. My worst nightmare: my brother is officially taller than me. He's done nothing but talk about it this week, and it's GETTING ON MY NERVES. He says his pituitary gland is working overtime. That's the gland that tells bones and other body tissues to hurry up and grow, among other tasks. It's a big deal in the body, even though it's no bigger than a pea. Same size as said brother's BRAIN.

July 31

Just got back from my first-ever music festival! Cool! I went with Suzie and Mouse, plus Suzie's mom as chaperone. We saw so many great bands, and camping was a blast, despite the mud and rain. The lines for the restroom were pretty awful, though. I need to figure out how to up my levels of antidiuretic hormones, which target the kidneys, in order to reduce urine production, or I'll be forever in a line for the bathroom.

August 5

Give this girl a gold star! I finished my nutrition project on time (phew) and actually learned a lot. Did you know that hormones called insulin and glucagon work together to keep a steady supply of glucose (that's body sugar, your main fuel and energy source) in your bloodstream, no matter how often or not you eat? Now I feel better about the burger I gobbled to celebrate the end of the project . . .

Yummy!

GERMS!

August 7

Ewwww! This disgusting guy sat next to me on the subway, sneezing and spewing out all kinds of nasty germs . . . . He didn't even cover his mouth. Honestly, I felt like putting up my umbrella. Instead, I thought of my thymus gland pumping out T lymphocyte cells to boost my immune system. All those helpful chemicals diving right into my bloodstream, and I didn't have to do a thing. Thanks, thymus.

YUCK! Germ factory!

August 8

Time for period cramps. So annoying. Yep, it's those hormones at work again. Estrogen and progesterone made in the ovaries are in charge of my menstrual cycle. All the changes I've been through in puberty (and that includes changing my mood about every ten seconds . . . Mom was right) are down to hormones.

GRRRRR!

August 12

OMG, big, big news—Auntie Alice is having a baby! She's wanted one for ages. I'm so happy for her (plus there's all that money I'll earn as her babysitter). We were giggling about how much her body will change, and yes, hormones are definitely involved. A chemical called oxytocin is going to get her contractions started when it's time to have the baby, and prolactin will help her make milk.

August 13

Went to Suzie's for a sleepover. After a movie and pizza, we fixed each other's hair in different styles. I started to doze off, even though part of my hair was still rolled around a hairbrush . . . Is that dumb, or what? Later on I looked it up and you guessed it, a hormone called melatonin peaks at night to make you drowsy. During the day, there's less of it around.

RUN OR STAY?

There are some situations where we react in the same way as our ancient ancestors. This is most obvious in the body's response to stress, with modern man (or woman) experiencing identical reactions to those that took place when cavemen faced danger. Now, as then, the nervous system comes to our aid and sets off a series of changes that prepare us to either run from the situation or stay to confront it.

RIDING THROUGH THE BUSY CITY STREETS, MODERN MAN HAS TO NEGOTIATE ALL KINDS OF POTENTIAL THREATS, SUCH AS CARS AND PEDESTRIANS. STRESS RESULTS IN A RAPID HEART RATE, FASTER BREATHING, "BUTTERFLIES" IN THE STOMACH, AND SOMETIMES A REALLY SHORT TEMPER!

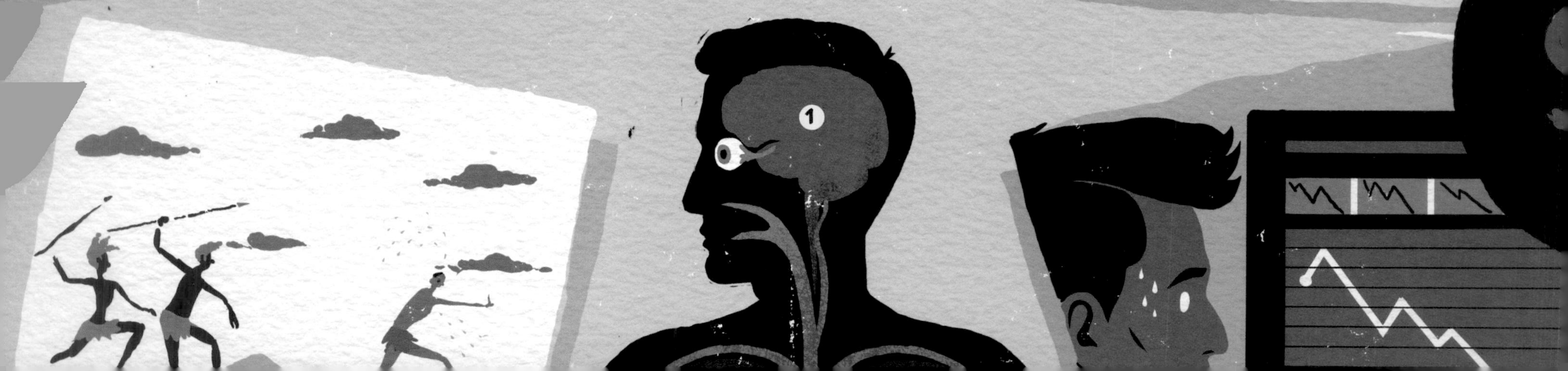

MODERN MAN

PREHISTORIC MAN

CORNERED BY A DANGEROUS ANIMAL—SUCH AS THIS FEARSOME FANGED SERPENT—OUR CAVEMAN'S BREATHING IS STIMULATED TO TAKE DEEPER BREATHS. THIS ALLOWS MORE OXYGEN TO ENTER THE BLOODSTREAM FOR DELIVERY TO THE BRAIN AND MUSCLES.

STOP

CHECKING STOCKS AND SHARES IS A STRESSFUL SCENARIO FOR MODERN MAN—IN A SECOND, HE COULD SEE HIS SAVINGS WIPED OUT. ONE REACTION IS A DRY MOUTH, CAUSED BY THE DIGESTIVE SYSTEM SLOWING DOWN AND MINIMAL SALIVA BEING PRODUCED.

RIDING A ROLLER COASTER MAY BE FUN, BUT IT ALSO TRIGGERS THE BODY'S EMERGENCY-RESPONSE SYSTEM. THE PALE COMPLEXION IS THE RESULT OF BLOOD DRAINING FROM THE FACE AS IT IS DIVERTED TO OTHER AREAS OF THE BODY THAT NEED IT MORE.

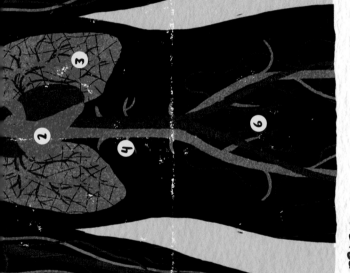

1 BRAIN
When a stressful situation occurs, part of the brain sends high-speed signals through the autonomic nervous system (ANS) to the rest of the body to prepare itself for action.

2 HEART
A rise in the rate at which the heart beats ensures that an increased blood flow carries extra supplies of oxygen and energy-rich glucose to the muscles and brain.

3 LUNGS
The airways inside the two lungs get wider in order to get more air inside the lungs and more oxygen—essential for energy release—into the blood.

4 ADRENAL GLANDS
These two glands release the hormone adrenaline, which reinforces the efforts of the ANS by, for example, making the liver release extra glucose from its store.

5 MUSCLES
Small arteries, called arterioles, inside arm and other muscles widen to boost blood flow to muscle cells so that they are powered up and ready to work.

6 DIGESTIVE SYSTEM
In readiness for an emergency situation, blood vessels in the stomach and digestive system contract as blood is diverted to other areas of the body.

BEING CHASED BY WEAPON-WIELDING ENEMIES SEES OUR CAVEMAN'S HEART BEAT FASTER. THIS ENABLES BLOOD TO BE PUMPED MORE QUICKLY TO ORGANS SUCH AS THE LUNGS TO PICK UP OXYGEN AND TO MUSCLES IN HIS (FAST-RUNNING!) LEGS.

AS OUR CAVEMAN SENSES THAT HE RUNS A REAL RISK OF BEING INJURED OR KILLED BY A FALLING ROCK, THE PUPILS IN HIS EYES DILATE (WIDEN). THIS ALLOWS MORE LIGHT INTO THE EYES AND IMPROVES HIS VISION SO THAT HE CAN JUDGE THE SITUATION MORE CLEARLY.

TALKING HEADS

HOW LORD SNOBBERY RECEIVED A SPOKEN MESSAGE FROM HIS GRANDSON VIA HIS EARS AND RESPONDED WITH APPROPRIATE SOUNDS GENERATED BY HIS VOCAL CORDS

It is a fine if blustery spring day in Lower Mawkishberry, near Maidstone in the county of Kent. In the drawing room of Moldering Masonry Mansions, young Master Cuthbert de Snobbery Witless, Esquire, addresses his ancient grandfather Lord Snobbery de Witless, the 12th Earl of Mawkishberry twice removed (and once merely misplaced). He leans in to hear his young charge, ear trumpet at the ready . . .

"Good afternoon, Gramps. You look dapper today. I bring a message from Mama: luncheon is being served in the garden. Nanny's made toad in the hole as a special treat! Shall we go down?"

"Squeak up, my boy. I can't hear you. I say, using a truncheon to dispose of a toad is rather heavy handed. In my day, we'd tell it to hop off."

"As a consequence of age (the master turned 90 on his last birthday), his auditory system is not functioning so well . . . Either that, or he's crazy. Woof!"

What the devil's going on here? The ear trumpet collects the sound of Cuthbert's voice and directs it to Lord Snobbery's ears. Inside the ear, sound waves from Cuthbert's words are turned into nerve impulses that are sent to the brain. Extraordinary!

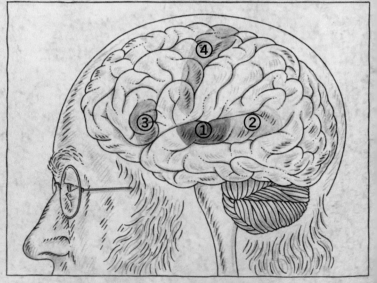

Inside the brain, the primary auditory cortex (1) identifies the signals as speech. Signals travel to Wernicke's area (2), where meaning is attached to the words. In Broca's area (3), the brain figures out a response, and in the primary motor cortex (4), instructions are sent to the muscles that will make him talk. Eventually.

Speech is produced in the larynx (1), at the top of the trachea (2). The vocal cords stretch across the larynx. When breathing, the cords are open, but to speak, the larynx muscles pull the cords together (3). Breath passes over them, so they vibrate, making sounds. The cavities of the head and neck help make the sounds louder.

"Did you say it's time for my lunch?"

After what seems an eternity, Snobbery's brain instructs muscles in the lips, tongue, and lower jaw to move so that he can form the words and reply to young Cuthbert.

"Yes, Gramps, do let's go. I'll help you into your wheelchair. Get down, Raffles, you soppy dog!"

"Make it snappy, won't you, Cuthbert? I'm not getting any younger here. And you do want to stay in my will, don't you?"

Cuthbert's brain interprets his beloved relation's question following the same process, but due to his relative youth, his response is a bit quicker.

HOW SPEECH IS PRODUCED

BODY LANGUAGE

Mission objectives:

» Observe behavior of earthling humans
» Locate and identify hand gestures and other forms of nonverbal communication
» Search intergalatic translation directory to interpret and classify human body language
» Return to home planet and report to invasion task force's Understanding Earthlings Subcommittee

BODY LANGUAGE:
Alien tourist seems to be biting her nails
TRANSLATION:
Nervous female who has lost her way

BODY LANGUAGE:
Devoted mother tilts her head
TRANSLATION:
Showing genuine interest in her earthling brat

BODY LANGUAGE:
Earthling walks briskly with upright stance
TRANSLATION:
Confident he knows where he's going

BODY LANGUAGE:
Alien tourist has arms crossed on his chest and looks glum
TRANSLATION:
Defensive because he knows he will be blamed for not checking the map

BODY LANGUAGE:
Hairy male sits with legs apart. Strange footwear!
TRANSLATION:
Relaxed and "ready to chill out," as earthlings say

BODY LANGUAGE:
Woman has legs crossed and kicks her shoe off. Eyes seem to be glazed
TRANSLATION:
Bored as geeky male explains theory of relativity, again

BODY LANGUAGE:
Male leans back with hands behind head. Smiling face

TRANSLATION:
Confident character in a relaxed mood

BODY LANGUAGE:
Large male rubs hands and licks lips

TRANSLATION:
Eager anticipation at thought of approaching tower of food

BODY LANGUAGE:
Sneaky male covers mouth with hand

TRANSLATION:
Dishonest earthling is about to steal French tries

BODY LANGUAGE:
Female with hands placed on hips and a tight mouth

TRANSLATION:
Angry that her date is late or posssibly a no-show

BODY LANGUAGE:
Male walks with hands in pockets and shoulders hunched forward

TRANSLATION:
Dejected because no money to buy cup of strange brown earthling drink

BODY LANGUAGE:
Skinny woman fiddles with hair and looks at earthling watch—a strange device for measuring time

TRANSLATION:
Feeling nervous about job interview. Lack of confidence very obvious

BODY LANGUAGE

TRICK OR CHEAT?

Magicians perform tricks that seem impossible. But in reality, they're an illusion. Magicians cheat by distracting their audience's attention from what is really happening. This image, by Dutch painter Hieronymus Bosch, shows a conjurer in action. Keep your eyes on the ball!

1 I'm performing tricks using cups and balls. I can make the ball pass through the solid bottoms of the cups, jump from cup to cup, or even disappear altogether.

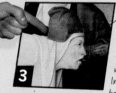

2 By distracting the audience's attention away from my hands, I can move the balls without anyone noticing, or lift a cup to make it seems as though the ball on top has passed through.

3 This audience member is looking a little too closely! I will distract him to make him look where I want him to. In this way, he won't be aware of my sleight of hand. His gazing also distracts the rest of the audience.

4 Oh dear! While the observer is watching the cup-and-ball trick, a thief standing behind him picks his pocket. The thief knows that his victim's attention is directed toward my trick.

5 Notice how the pickpocket gazes at the sky to direct the audience's attention away from his theft. It's a tactic a lot of magicians use. Seems I have some competition!

Audiences have been fooled by cup-and-ball tricks for more than 2,000 years.

TOUCH TEST CENTER

You have to touch—or be touched—by something to find out whether it feels hard or soft, warm or cold, tickly or scratchy—or if it just plain hurts! Here at our special center, a volunteer is putting a range of sensations to the test. She will demonstrate the versatility of the millions of skin receptors that send signals to the brain, which lets her know what she's feeling.

5 GOOD VIBRATIONS
Perched on a pulsating chair, our volunteer can feel the vibrations through receptors deep in her skin, the same ones that pick up heavy pressure. Vibrations move those receptors back and forth. That's why they fire off signals to her brain.

1 HAIR TUG
Most receptors in the skin are activated when they are bent, squashed, or tweaked. The receptors wrapped around hair roots are no exception. Anything that tugs on those hairs will pull at the receptors, which signal the brain to feel pain. Ouch!

2 GENTLE PROD
A finger, gently pressing the volunteer's waist, stimulates light pressure sensors just under her skin. The squished sensors send high-speed signals to her brain that tell her she is being touched. The waist has fewer receptors than the fingertips, so it is less sensitive.

3 HOLD AND FEEL
That milk bottle needs to be held to stop it from falling and breaking. Our model's skin receptors feel the hardness of the bottle, sense the coldness of the milk, and allow her fingers to apply just enough pressure to hold the bottle without dropping it.

4 AT A STRETCH
Does this hurt? Pinching or pulling the volunteer's skin tells deep-down receptors that something wrong is going on. They fire off messages to the skin-sensation part of her brain so that she knows which parts of her cheeks are being squeezed and which stretched

6 SOFT OR SMOOTH?

Lips and fingertips are covered with touch and pressure sensors that distinguish between different textures. Both the tickling softness of the feather duster on the volunteer's lips and the contrasting roughness of sandpaper on her fingertips are being put to the test.

7 HEAVY PRESSURE

Feel the weight of these suitcases. That's exactly the job of large receptors located deep beneath the skin's surface that react to deep, heavy pressure. As they get squashed, they signal to her brain, and she feels the pulling power of her luggage.

8 HOT OR COLD?

Is the model hot headed or does she have cold feet? The way she finds out is through heat and cold receptors near the surface of her skin. They tell her brain whether what she's touching or is close to is chilly or roasting and if it's cooling down or warming up.

9 OUCH! THAT HURTS!

They might seem minor, but paper cuts really hurt. When the edge of paper slices into her skin, it triggers pain receptors that send signals to her brain. What's more, it makes skin cells release "alarm" chemicals that make the pain even more intense.

10 DRESSED COMFORTABLY

Imagine if, from the moment she put her clothes on in the morning until she took them off, our volunteer could feel her clothes rubbing against her skin. Fortunately she can't, because skin receptors "turn off" automatically as soon as she's dressed.

Nerve carries
signals to brain

Nasal cavity

Watery mucus

Smell receptor
detects odors

SMELLS GOOD

Your sense of smell helps you enjoy foods and drinks, and to be aware of other smelly things around you. It can also warn you of danger!

SMELL MENU

We have thousands of delightful odors for you to sample with your sense of smell. Odor molecules in the air will be drawn into your nose. High up in your nasal cavity, the molecules will dissolve in watery mucus and be individually detected by smell receptors.

MIX 'N' MATCH

Why not try both senses together? Mix and match smells and tastes to fully appreciate the flavors of everything on offer at the diner.

PIZZA CHOICE

Our pizzas offer a cornucopia of mouthwatering odors. Whether it's cheese, chilies, pepperoni, or herbs, each smell will be picked out by your smell receptors. Saliva will pour into your mouth, ready for that first bite.

POPCORN

Why not dip into some popcorn? When you smell it, does it remind you of a trip to the movies? It probably will, because odors commonly trigger memories that are closely associated with them.

MOVIE MEMORIES!

STINKY CHEESE

All the cheeses we have on offer have a strong smell because they have been ripened using bacteria and, sometimes, fungi, too. Many people like that, but some people think cheese smells stinky.

BURNED FOOD

Back to the kitchen for this burned offering! Long before you see the charred remains, you can smell the smoke coming from the food. That's why your sense of smell is really useful to warn you of dangers, such as fire.

WARNING!

ROSE

A small token of our appreciation for our guests. As well as delighting in the shape and beauty of its flower, you can smell the rose's delicate perfume. But watch out for those thorns!

DINER MENU

Papilla on tongue

Taste bud

Nerves from taste buds

TASTES GOOD

Your sense of taste works with smell to identify the flavors in food. It will also pick out anything nasty!

Nerves carry signals from tongue to brain,

TASTE MENU

Here at the diner our menu provides all five of the tastes that your tongue can detect. The little bumps, or papillae, on your tongue contain tiny taste buds. Each has receptors that detect taste molecules in saliva-dissolved food.

SWEET THINGS

Everyone loves our fantastic selection of candy and chocolate. It's the sugars in them that make them taste sweet. And, just like our ancestors, we crave sweetness because sugars give us the energy we need to do everything—including eat!

FRIES, WITH SALT

Because the body cannot make salt, you need a little on your food to ensure the required intake. We are pleased to provide a salty taste to the menu with our hand-cut French fries, garnished with ground sea salt.

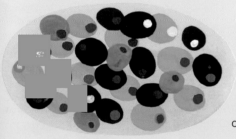

OLIVES

Many customers enjoy the bitter taste of olives. But humans are naturally wary of bitterness because many poisonous substances taste bitter. Our tastes buds detect that, giving us time to spit out the offending material. But not here, please!

MEATY MOUTHFUL

To sample the most recently discovered taste, dig into a juicy steak. That will give you the savory taste known as umami. If you don't eat meat, you can savor the umami taste in cheese or mushrooms.

LEMONS

Here at the diner, we don't recommend sucking on lemons. But if you do, your taste buds will immediately pick out the sour taste. It's produced by the acids in citrus fruit such as lemons, limes, and oranges.

TASTE-TEST SPECIAL

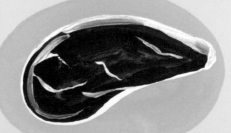

TURN OFF SIGHT AND SMELL

Try this experiment. Cut some apple, potato, onion, and chocolate into bite-size pieces. Get a friend to put on a blindfold and nose clip. Can they identify each food by taste alone? Probably not. You need to smell AND taste to detect food flavors.

TASTY TRIVIA

★ There are five million smell receptors in your nasal cavity (dogs have 250 million!).

★ Your sense of smell is 10,000 times more sensitive than your sense of taste.

★ You can detect and distinguish between 10,000 odors but only five tastes.

★ The tongue houses about 10,000 taste buds, although that number decreases with age.

At **TASTEGOOD™**, we're always on the lookout for people to join our trained team of professional food tasters—or "sensory evaluators," as we prefer to call them. They're here to ensure that each of the company's range of food and drink products meets the high standards of flavor and consistency expected by our customers.

AS A MEMBER OF OUR TEAM, YOU MAY BE ASKED TO TEST ANY PRODUCT, FROM CHOCOLATE AND CHEESE TO BREAKFAST CEREAL, CANNED SOUP, AND POTATO SNACKS. BELIEVE IT OR NOT, SOME OF OUR TEAM EVEN TASTE DOG FOOD FOR US!

THE TASTE OF SUCCESS

Do you have the perfect palate to join our team of supertasters? For a truly mouth-watering job, read on . . .

TASTY FACTS

☞ Taste buds are tiny sense organs scattered all over the mouth cavity.

☞ Each one contains receptor cells that pass on information to the brain about the taste of the food we are eating.

☞ Taste buds identify five basic taste sensations—bitter, sour, salty, sweet, and umami (described as meaty or savory).

☞ 80 percent of the sensations we get from food comes from its aroma.

For more information, contact us at TasteGood@sweetsour.com

HERE'S WHAT WILL HAPPEN:

You'll be asked to fill in a questionnaire and be given some simple tests to do. For example, you could be given a row of numbered containers filled with a sugar solution and asked to rank them for intensity of sweetness. If we think you'll make the grade as a sensory evaluator, we'll send you on an intensive training course, all expenses paid.

WHAT THEN?

Enjoyment of food involves all the senses. On our course you'll learn to assess different products for looks (Is the color attractive? Does it have a glossy sheen?), texture (Is it too chewy? Does it make a nice crunchy sound?), and smell (Tempting or off-putting?) as well as taste (Is it bitter or salty, sweet or sour?).

 # iEye

Introducing iEye, the unique human visual system. To view your surroundings, simply open the fully lubricated eyelids and iEye will do the rest! Its unique features detect light from outside the body and turn it into electrical signals. The brain (included free with every purchase) processes those signals to create a unique color movie that only you can see. And there's more. The brain compares the different viewpoints of each of iEye's twin eyeballs to make that movie 3-D.

AUTOFOCUS

Whether an object is near or far, iEye's autofocus always produces a sharp image on its retina. The cornea carries out the initial focusing of light rays reflected from the object. The shape of the elastic lens is automatically altered by the ciliary body—"fat" for near objects, "thin" for distant—to focus light rays on the fovea.

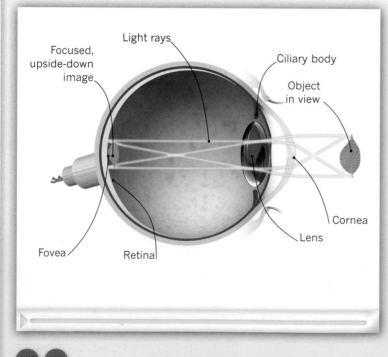

Focused, upside-down image

Light rays

Ciliary body

Object in view

Cornea

Lens

Fovea

Retina

LIGHT SENSORS

iEye's retina is equipped with a unique array of light sensors called rods and cones that send signals to the brain. The 120 million rods work best in dim light and are found all over the retina. Six million cones, concentrated in and around the fovea, provide detailed color vision in bright light.

FOVEA is area of retina, packed with cones, that receives light from directly in front of eye (see LIGHT SENSORS)

OPTIC DISK (blind spot) lacks light sensors and is where nerve fibers enter optic nerve

OPTIC NERVE carries nerve signals at high speed from iEye to brain (see WHAT YOU GET)

RETINA is layer of receptors that turns light rays into nerve signals (see LIGHT SENSORS)

Jellylike VITREOUS HUMOR shapes iEye and aids focusing

WHAT YOU GET

Every iEye has twin eyeball units (including muscles, eyelids, and eyelashes) and peripherals (optic nerves) that plug into a standard 500-terabyte central processor, or brain. The brain's visual cortex sorts and interprets signals from iEye to create a full-color, 3-D, real-time video stream from the outside world.

CHOROID'S BLOOD VESSELS provide oxygen for retina and sclera

Elastic **LENS** focuses light on retina *(see AUTOFOCUS)*

iEYE TECH SPECS

- Fully coordinated twin eyeballs
- Blink and wipe-clean function
- Automatic ligh-level control
- Automatic focusing
- Analogue (light) to digital (electrical signal) conversion
- Full-color operation
- High-speed link to brain
- Multidirectional in-socket movement
- Bony socket and fat-padding protection package
- Irises available in several colous including blue, green, and brown
- Accessory range includes colored contact lenses and false eyelashes

EYELIDS blink every few seconds to wipe clean front of iEye

CILIARY BODY controls thickness of lens *(see AUTOFOCUS)*

IRIS automatically adjusts pupil size according to light levels

CORNEA is clear layer that focuses light entering iEye

PUPIL is adjustable opening that allows light into rear section of iEye

SUSPENSORY LIGAMENT fibers attach lens to ciliary body

SCLERA is tough outer coat that protects iEye from damage

SCAN FUNCTIONS

Six small straplike muscles give iEye full mobility. They move it up and out **(1)**, out to the side **(2)**, up **(3)**, down and out **(4)**, inward **(5)**, or down **(6)**. iEye swivels smoothly in its socket to track moving objects. It also makes tiny movements to scan faces.

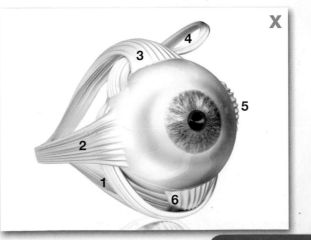

X

YOUR EYES IN MOTION

LARGE, SMOOTH EYE MOVEMENTS HELP YOU LOOK AT DIFFERENT PARTS OF A SCENE OR FOLLOW A BIRD AS IT GLIDES ABOVE YOU.

SMALLER, JERKY EYE MOVEMENTS SCAN FINER DETAILS, LIKE THE NOSE ON A PERSON'S FACE.

TINY, INVOLUNTARY EYE MOVEMENTS HELP FIX YOUR GAZE ON ANY STATIONARY OBJECT AND KEEP THE IMAGE IN FOCUS.

NEAR-SIGHTED

Visual problems are very common but can easily be fixed with the use of glasses or contact lenses. In nearsightedness, or myopia, the eyeball is too long, so light rays from all but nearby objects are focused not on the retina but in front of it. This means that any distant objects appear blurry.

CARE AND DEFENSE

Eyes are delicate organs, but fortunately the body has some built-in defenses. Tough, bony sockets protect the eyeballs and hairy brows direct sweat away from the eyes. Supersensitive eyelashes warn when an irritant is near the eyes, causing the eyelids to shut. When we blink, our eyelids wipe our eyes and keep them clear of dust.

TEAR TYPES

Feeling a bit weepy but no eye-dea why? There are three types of tears:

Basal tears lubricate the front of the eyeball, washing away dust and destroying bacteria.

Reflex tears are produced in response to irritants, such as the vapors released when you cut an onion.

Emotional tears are unique to humans. They have a different chemical makeup to the other two types of tears, including encephalins, chemicals that act as natural painkillers—that's why a good cry often makes you feel better.

COLOR IN YOUR EYES

Eyes come in an array of colors, from pale blue and green to hazel and dark brown. Overlaying the background color are flecks, rays, and splotches of browns, blues, ambers, and greens. The color depends on the amount of melanin pigment contained in the iris (the ring surrounding the pupil), and this is determined by the genes we inherit from our parents.

FAR-SIGHTED

In farsightedness, or hyperopia, the eyeball is too short and light rays from nearby objects focus behind the retina, so they appear blurred, although distant objects are clear. It is important to get your vision checked regularly by an optician.

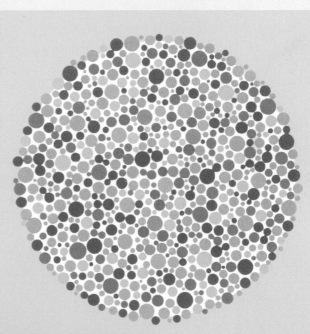

SEEING RED, SEEING GREEN

Light-sensing cells called rods and cones line the retina, converting light into electrical impulses. The cones enable us to see colors. There are three kinds, and each responds best to a particular wavelength, or color, of light: red, green, or blue. If one of these cone types is missing, it causes a condition called colorblindness. The pattern above is designed to test for colorblindness. People who cannot see the number "7" hidden among the dots may have red-green colorblindness, which means they are unable to tell the difference between the two colors.

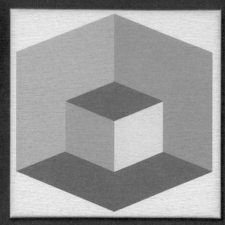

CHANGING CUBES

Is this a small cube in the corner of a larger cube or a big cube with one corner taken out? Both interpretations are possible—it's all in the way the lines are drawn parallel to one another.

ART OF ILLUSION

Enter the House of Visual Tricks, where nothing is quite what it seems. Patterns appear to be moving when they're not. Dots come and go. Colors change before your eyes. These things—called optical illusions—happen in most cases because the brain is confused. It has to make sense of signals from the eyes to create the images you see. And, in some cases, those signals are ambiguous and the brain is tricked.

MAKING TRACKS

The converging railroad tracks give a false sense of distance, tricking the eye into thinking that the yellow line at the top is longer than the one below. In fact, they're the same length.

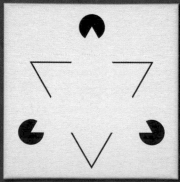

MYSTERY TRIANGLES

Two triangles or one? There are none! The brain interprets the three Pac-Man shapes and the three broken lines to see something that isn't there—one triangle lying above another.

SPOTS BEFORE YOUR EYES

When you look at the white circles between the black squares, you'll find that dark spots appear and disappear randomly. They go away when you tilt your head to either side. This effect is created by light receptors in the eyes.

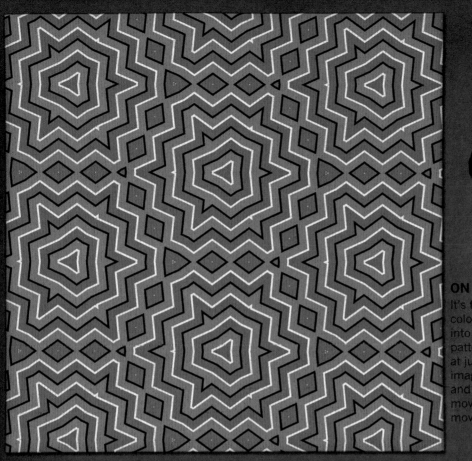

ON THE MOVE
It's the contrast of colors that fools your eyes into thinking that these patterns are moving. Look at just one part of the image for a few seconds and the pattern stops moving. When your eyes move on, it starts again.

BLUE OR RED?
Stare hard at the blue dot for 30 seconds then look away to a white surface. You'll find that the blue dot now appears red. What you see is actually an "afterimage" of the dot, imprinted on the back of the eye.

IDENTICAL COLORS
Although the green squares on the left look darker than those on the right, they are exactly the same color. The blue stripes mute the color tones of the green, and the yellow ones enhance them.

EAR FLAP

A flexible shape of cartilage, visible on either side of the head, the ear flap, or pinna, gathers sound waves, which it directs into the ear.

OUTER EAR CANAL

A wax-lined tube that tunnels through the skull bone, the ear canal carries sound waves to the middle ear.

EARDRUM

Located at the end of the ear canal, the taut tissue that makes up the eardrum, or tympanic membrane, vibrates as it is struck by sound waves.

OSSICLES

Three tiny connected bones are located within the air-filled space of the middle ear. The hammerlike malleus is attached to the eardrum and moves with each vibration. Each movement is then passed on to the incus, an anvil-shaped bone, and finally to the stirrup-shaped stapes (the smallest bone in the body), which transmits vibrations to the inner ear.

OVAL WINDOW

The moving stapes pushes against the oval window—a thin layer of tissue that forms the way for any quivering quavers to enter the fluid-filled inner ear.

COCHLEA

The oval window's movement produces vibrations in the channels of fluid within the spiralling cochlea. The ripples in the fluid are picked up by tiny hairs in the organ of Corti, which runs through the center of the cochlea. When the hairs move, the hair cells from which they sprout generate nerve impulses.

COCHLEAR NERVE

The impulses, or electrical signals, carry sound messages along the cochlear nerve to the brain. Here they are interpreted as sounds that we can "hear" as part of life's noisy soundtrack.

SEMICIRCULAR CANALS

Three fluid-filled ducts form part of the inner ear not involved in hearing. These semicircular canals work with other organs to transmit messages to the brain about the body's position. These are what the brain uses to help us keep our balance.

EUSTACHIAN TUBE

Linking the middle ear to the back of the nose, this airway helps control pressure in the ear. Closed muscles on the end of the tube normally separate the middle ear from the atmosphere, but when the outside pressure level changes, the muscles open and your ears "pop."

Messages sent to the brain

MUSIC TO OUR EARS

Listen up! Sound is all about movement—when something moves, it disturbs the air around it, creating a sound wave. The vibrations from a strummed guitar or a person singing send ripples through the air that are detected by hearing organs within your ears. The complex structures that make up the inner ears convert the vibrations into nerve impulses. These, in turn, are interpreted as tuneful sounds and recognized as music or words by the brain.

LOOKING AROUND
Constantly on the lookout, the eyes send messages to the brain about the body's position—such as if it's leaning forward, backward, or to the side and if it's upside down or not, as well as how far away the other performers are.

NECK CHECK
Muscles in the neck hold the head upright and stop it from lolling to the side. But if the head does turn, stretch receptors inside the neck muscles tell the brain what's going on. Messages then go to the neck muscles to keep the head in the right position.

SENSITIVE FEET
Whether standing on a trapeze or firmly on the ground, the soles of the feet provide a mine of information for the brain. Touch and pressure receptors tell the brain about the position of the feet and also what's underneath them.

BUSY BRAIN

Input from the ears, muscles, eyes, feet, and neck arrive nonstop to the brain. In a flash, the brain analyses all this information and sends out messages to the muscles telling them how to move the body, maintain its balance, and keep its posture.

EARS ON ALERT

Inside the ears are the body's balance sensors. Some detect whether the head is upright, leaning to one side, or upside down. Others detect movements of the head, either forward, backward, up or down, or when it rotates. All send their findings to the brain.

MOVING MUSCLES

Miss Demeanor's powerful thigh muscles house stretch receptors that measure how tense they are and send messages to the brain. It responds by tweaking the contraction (pulling) of the thigh muscles to maintain balance.

BALANCING ACT

Marvel at Miss Demeanor's death-defying display of equilibration (staying balanced, if you were wondering). Be amazed when you discover how she achieves her aims as an aerialist (someone who performs above the ground on a trapeze). Then admire the fact that the human body can stay upright, figure out its position, and avoid falling.

MISS DEMEANOR & THE FLYING FANDANGOS

BALANCE

How food and oxygen fuel the body, and how the body uses that fuel to perform all the processes that keep you alive.

FUELING YOUR BODY

Food fest

It was a great party. You've chomped on pizza and guzzled pitchers full of juice, so what happens next? After chewing and swallowing, it takes only ten seconds for the food to reach your stomach. But from that point on it will take at least another 24 hours or more for the solids and liquids to be sifted, processed, and absorbed until the pieces that the body doesn't want are dumped at the other end. Here's a blow-by-blow account of what happens at every stage of the digestive system.

INTO THE BAG

Food now enters the muscular bag that is your stomach, where it is churned and mashed by muscular walls and mixed with gastric juices. Once it has turned into a gloppy liquid, it is ready to progress to the small intestine. The flow of food from the stomach is controlled by a ring of muscle known as the pyloric sphincter.

DOWN THE HATCH

This first part of the digestive system works like a conveyor belt, carrying food from the throat to the stomach. Muscles in the wall of the esophagus contract to squeeze food toward the stomach—a process known as peristalsis.

NOT SMALL AT ALL

Your small intestine is actually much longer than your large one. It is divided into three sections—the duodenum, the jejunum, and the ileum—each with its own special role in processing food. A carpet of tiny fingerlike villi covers the inside of the small intestine. As liquid food swirls past, enzymes on the surface of the villi break down food into simple nutrients and absorb the glucose, amino acids, and fatty acids.

FIRST PART

The first, and shortest, section of the small intestine is the duodenum, which receives part-digested stomach contents known as chyme. The pancreas and liver are both linked to the duodenum. Digestive juice from the pancreas contains enzymes that break down starches, proteins, and fats in the food, while bile from the liver emulsifies the fat into tiny droplets so that it can be more easily digested and absorbed. Yum.

The wall of the stomach is lined with three layers of strong muscle.

Hydrochloric acid in gastric juices destroys bacteria swallowed with food.

The oesophagus is about 30 cm (12 in) long.

The large intestine is 4.9 ft (1.5 m) long.

The small intestine is longer, but narrower, than the large intestine.

SECOND PART

The middle section of the small intestine—the jejunum—is where enzymes attached to the lining complete digestion by breaking food into its simplest forms.

LAST, BUT NOT LEAST

Food then passes into your ileum, the final, and longest, stretch of the small intestine. Its main function is to absorb any products of digestion that were not absorbed by the jejunum. Waste not, want not.

THE FINAL STRETCH

At last, your barely recognizable meal (unless you have eaten corn!) arrives in your large intestine, the last section of the digestive system. It is now watery waste containing indigestible food. Water is absorbed through the walls of the intestine and into the bloodstream so that it's not lost by the body. As this happens, the liquid waste is changed into the more solid waste we know as feces, or poo. The end.

Undigested food spends 12–36 hours in the large intestine.

Trillions of bacteria in the last leg of the large intestine break down pieces of undigested food, releasing gases that make us . . .

The small intestine is 21.3 ft (6.5 m) long.

Food spends between 3–6 hours in the small intestine.

Break wind!

APPENDIX (NOT VERY USEFUL . . . OR IS IT?)

This appendage is used by herbivores (planteaters) to break down cellulose from plants, but for years was thought to have no purpose for humans. It is now known to play a part in our body's defense and is a reservoir of friendly bacteria.

02. THE TEARERS

The aptly named canines are our fanglike, pointed dogteeth, which grip and tear food between them.

03. THE CRUSHERS

Premolars have broad crowns with raised edges called cusps. They assist their larger molar neighbors in crushing and tearing food.

04. THE GRINDERS

The four-cusped, double-root molars at the back of the jaw hammer down on food with great force. They act like a mortar and pestle to grind the food pieces into a paste.

01. THE CHOPPERS

Flat, sharp, and chisellike, the incisors on the top and bottom jaw work together to slice through food and chop it up into smaller pieces.

Chop chop

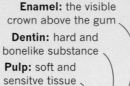

Enamel: the visible crown above the gum

Dentin: hard and bonelike substance

Pulp: soft and sensitve tissue

DENTAL KIT

Anchored in our jaws and held in place by the gums, teeth are the body's hardest organs. Each tooth type has its own job description; as one of 16 pairs of healthy and hard-working teeth, it chops, lears, crushes, or grinds up food into small pieces, ready for swallowing.

TOOTH STRUCTURE

Each tooth has a protective crown of enamel over the live tissue underneath. Dentin makes up the tooth's bulk including the root, held fast in the gum with a natural cement. The pulp cavity contains blood vessels and nerves that enable the tooth to sense heat, cold, and pain.

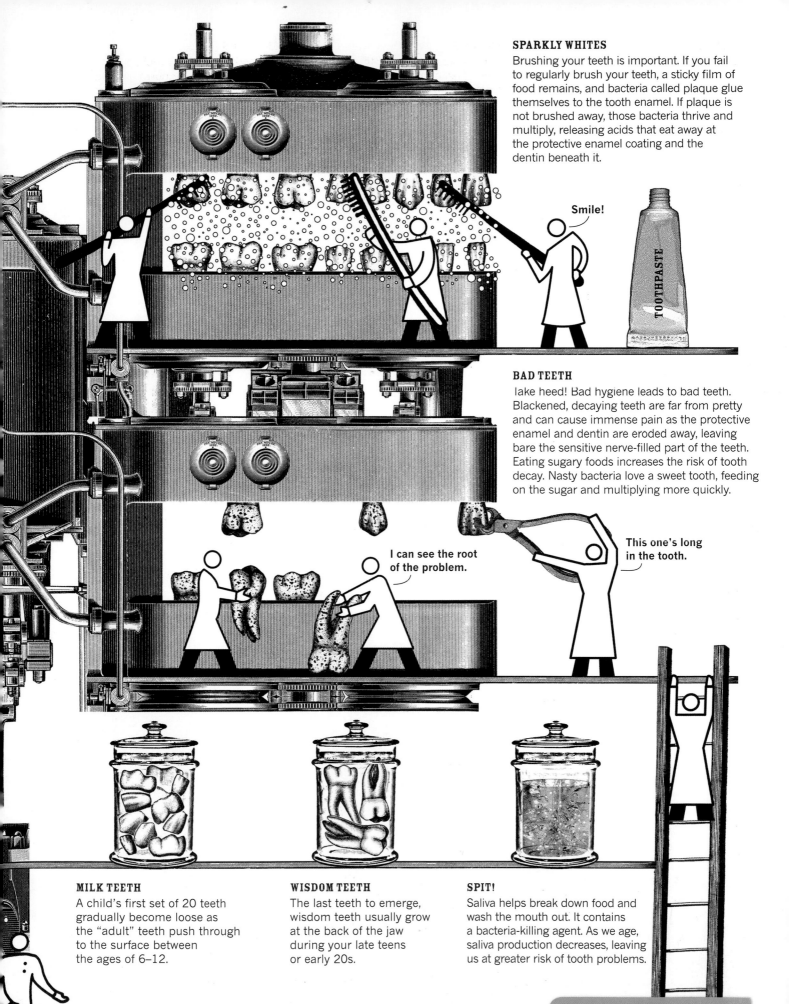

SPARKLY WHITES

Brushing your teeth is important. If you fail to regularly brush your teeth, a sticky film of food remains, and bacteria called plaque glue themselves to the tooth enamel. If plaque is not brushed away, those bacteria thrive and multiply, releasing acids that eat away at the protective enamel coating and the dentin beneath it.

Smile!

TOOTHPASTE

BAD TEETH

Take heed! Bad hygiene leads to bad teeth. Blackened, decaying teeth are far from pretty and can cause immense pain as the protective enamel and dentin are eroded away, leaving bare the sensitive nerve-filled part of the teeth. Eating sugary foods increases the risk of tooth decay. Nasty bacteria love a sweet tooth, feeding on the sugar and multiplying more quickly.

This one's long in the tooth.

I can see the root of the problem.

MILK TEETH

A child's first set of 20 teeth gradually become loose as the "adult" teeth push through to the surface between the ages of 6–12.

WISDOM TEETH

The last teeth to emerge, wisdom teeth usually grow at the back of the jaw during your late teens or early 20s.

SPIT!

Saliva helps break down food and wash the mouth out. It contains a bacteria-killing agent. As we age, saliva production decreases, leaving us at greater risk of tooth problems.

FOOD, GLORIOUS FOOD!

Calling all food lovers! Our awesome food pyramid is not just a foodie's dream but the blueprint for a balanced diet. Each step of the pyramid is built from a different food type, categorized according to what mix of nutrients each food contains. Macronutrients—carbohydrates, proteins, and fats—make up most of what we eat, providing energy and the material for growth and repair. Micronutrients—vitamins and minerals—are needed in small amounts, but are essential for general well-being. For a balanced diet, eat less of the food types near the top of the pyramid, and more of those near the bottom.

SWEETS

These tasty treats should be indulged only in small quantities. They may provide the body with plenty of energy, but they give little in terms of nutrition, being made up of mostly sugars and fats.

CONTRARY DAIRY

These foods, made from animal milk, provide the body with the bone-building mineral calcium and varying amounts of protein. Some dairy foods, such as butter, have a high fat content and so should be eaten only in small amounts, while others, like some types of yogurt, contain almost no fat at all.

ROOTS, SHOOTS, AND FRUIT

This colorful step of the pyramid is an important source of micronutrients, providing a whole host of vitamins and minerals that your body needs to function properly. Both fruit and vegetables are high in dietary fiber, which helps in digestion, and the sweet, sugary carbohydrates in fruit serve as a quick energy boost—a perfect snack before exercising.

These are berry good.

HAPPY AND HEALTHY

A healthy, nutritious diet helps maintain the body and reduces the risk of developing diseases such as cancer and heart disease. The World Health Organization recommends that each person eats at least five portions of fruit and vegetables every day. So stock up on the good stuff!

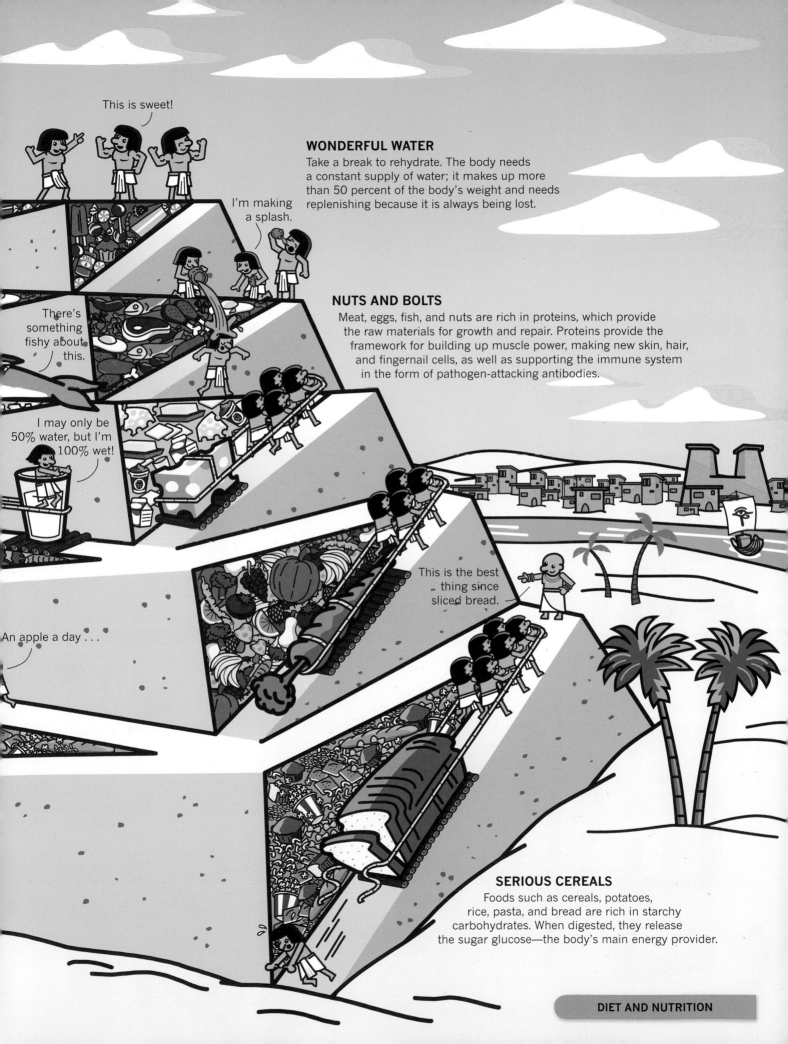

WONDERFUL WATER

Take a break to rehydrate. The body needs a constant supply of water; it makes up more than 50 percent of the body's weight and needs replenishing because it is always being lost.

NUTS AND BOLTS

Meat, eggs, fish, and nuts are rich in proteins, which provide the raw materials for growth and repair. Proteins provide the framework for building up muscle power, making new skin, hair, and fingernail cells, as well as supporting the immune system in the form of pathogen-attacking antibodies.

SERIOUS CEREALS

Foods such as cereals, potatoes, rice, pasta, and bread are rich in starchy carbohydrates. When digested, they release the sugar glucose—the body's main energy provider.

LEMONAID

Just a glass a day keeps scurvy away

"I wouldn't leave port without Lemonaid. Much tastier than my old pickled cabbage remedy!" Captain James Cook

Healthy benefits
What's Lemonaid's secret ingredient?

People have recognized the benefits of eating lemons since ancient times. It seems these yellow fruit contain a substance that keeps the body fit and healthy, though our 18th-century doctors don't yet know what that substance is. One day, medical science will come up with a name for it—vitamin "C" for "cure" might go down well. . . .

Miracle cure
Fights the symptoms of scurvy

On long sea voyages, sailors go for months without fresh fruit and vegetables. Many suffer from scurvy—a condition that leaves them with swollen and bleeding gums, loose teeth, and stiff joints. Medical tests have proved that lemon juice guarantees protection against this terrible and often fatal disease.

"Since starting the Lemonaid diet, my life has been transformed. I've gotten my good looks back again, so all you ladies better watch out! I'll always keep Lemonaid in my sea locker from now on, and I'll be recommending it to all my shipmates. Avast there, my hearties!"
Sailor Joe

Lind's superior remedy

In 1747, naval surgeon James Lind carried out a clinical trial on a group of sailors suffering from scurvy. He treated two sailors with cider, two with vinegar, two with seawater . . . and then two were given orange and lemon juice. THEY WERE THE ONLY ONES TO RECOVER. In 1795, the British Royal Navy finally agreed to supply all ships with lemon juice. A result for Lemonaid and, more importantly, sailors!

Before

After

Slice, squeeze, swallow: my motto for a healthy life.

If you don't immediately feel better I'll eat my hat!

Endorsed by the Royal Navy (though it took them 40 years).

Also good for coughs and colds, fevers, constipation, and more . . .

We'd like to thank Mrs Mendip Brown for this month's Lemonaid recipe.

An oh-so-soothing cure for a seriously sore throat: Add the juice of a lemon and one teaspoon of honey to a cupful of just-boiled water. Stir and allow to cool before drinking.

PITHY FACT I
Lemons are one of the richest sources of vitamin C (ascorbic acid)—an antioxidant that helps repair damaged cells. Vitamins (first named in the 1900s) form an essential part of our diet, although we need only tiny amounts to keep our bodies functioning normally.

PITHY FACT II
Other important vitamins are A, B group, D, E, and K. Vitamin D, found in liver and fatty fish, aids healthy bone growth, while lack of vitamin B1 causes beriberi—a disease of the nervous system.

PITHY FACT III
This is what an average-size lemon contains: 16mg phosphorus, 2mg sodium, 26mg calcium, 138mg potassium, 53mg vitamin C, 0.6g iron. No wonder they do you nothing but good!

BODY FUEL

Game Objective: Stay Alive!

Your body needs energy to keep you in the game of life. You can't see energy, but without it, you couldn't move a muscle or think a thought. Food provides all of the energy you need to survive. Your mission is to stay alive. How well you thrive depends on how well you balance your fuel choices with your activity levels. Should you fail, it's game over!

JUMP

KICK ━━━━ BLOCK

CROUCH

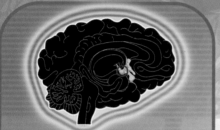

HYPOTHALAMUS ALERT

Your body gets energy mostly from the sugar glucose. The liver keeps blood glucose levels fairly steady, 24/7. After meals, your liver stores extra glucose as glycogen. Between meals, it tops up blood glucose levels by releasing glucose from glycogen. But if you don't eat for many hours, that limited store runs out and glucose levels drop. This makes the part of your brain called the hypothalamus go on red alert, triggering hunger so that you eat to get glucose levels back to normal.

CHANGE YOUR CHARACTER

Several factors are at play in determining how much energy a person needs each day. Your age, gender, and level of activity all affect your daily energy needs. A child's energy needs rocket when he or she reaches puberty as the body craves fuel to help it grow and change. A pregnant or breastfeeding woman needs extra energy to pass along to her baby. But whatever your energy needs, be careful: if you take in more energy than you need, your body may convert it to store as fat. If you are in it to win it, you will aim for a balanced diet that meets your energy needs.

8-YEAR-OLD BOY

A child needs an average of 7,760 kJ (1,853 kcal) a day to meet energy requirements.

15-YEAR-OLD GIRL

You will need 9,240 kJ (2,207 kcal) per day to power this girl through puberty.

ADULT WOMAN

An inactive woman needs 8,025 kJ (1,917 kcal), while an active one may consume 9,000 kJ (2,150 kcal).

ADULT MAN

Busy men run on approximately 12,560 kJ (3,000 kcal) a day, while an inactive man needs 10,530 kJ (2,515 kcal).

RESTORE YOUR ENERGY LEVELS

Different foods contain different amounts of food energy. These used to be measured in units called kilocalories (kcal), but today most dieticians use kilojoules (kJ) to measure energy levels. Whichever you use, choose your food with care. Too much fat-laden, energy-rich food like pizza and you will exceed your daily energy requirement. Aim for balance in your diet to ensure you get the nutrients you need.

1,115 KJ (266 KCAL)

339 KJ (81 KCAL)

837 KJ (200 KCAL)

CHOOSE YOUR MOVE

Match the foods you choose with your activity levels. If you are very active, you'll need to take in more calories in order to give you plenty of energy.

ENERGY LEVEL: LOW

When you are less physically active—such as when you're planning your next move—your body needs less energy.

ENERGY LEVEL: MEDIUM

When you spring into action, your body will oxidize, or "burn," glucose faster. Warning: keep a watch on your energy levels.

ENERGY LEVEL: HIGH

The glucose burns much faster with a high-energy move. You must replenish the energy you burn to stay in the game.

JUMP

KICK — BLOCK

CROUCH

ENERGY BALANCE

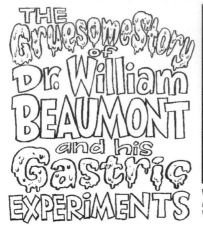

THE Gruesome Story of Dr William BEAUMONT and his Gastric EXPERIMENTS

WILLIAM BEAUMONT, AN AMERICAN ARMY SURGEON BASED AT FORT MACKINAC ON LAKE HURON, WAS CALLED IN TO TREAT A FUR TRADER WHO'D BEEN SHOT AT SHORT RANGE WITH A MUSKET.

THE MAN, ALEXIS ST. MARTIN, RECOVERED BUT WAS LEFT WITH A PERMANENT OPENING (FISTULA) INTO HIS STOMACH.

AT THAT TIME (1823), LITTLE WAS KNOWN ABOUT HOW THE STOMACH DIGESTED (BROKE DOWN) FOOD.

BEAUMONT FED PIECES OF FOOD THROUGH THE HOLE IN ALEXIS'S STOMACH AND PULLED THEM OUT A FEW HOURS LATER SO THAT HE COULD COMPARE THE LENGTH OF TIME TAKEN TO DIGEST DIFFERENT FOODS.

HE SIPHONED OFF THE JUICE IN ALEXIS'S STOMACH THROUGH A TUBE AND POURED IT ONTO DIFFERENT TYPES OF FOODS TO TEST THE RESULTS.

ALEXIS GREW TIRED OF HIS LIFE AS A HUMAN GUINEA PIG. IN 1833, HE WENT BACK TO HIS FAMILY IN CANADA. THE TWO MEN NEVER MET AGAIN.

BEAUMONT PUBLISHED HIS FINDINGS IN A BOOK. IT WOULD CHANGE MODERN UNDERSTANDING OF HUMAN DIGESTION.

BEAUMONT BECAME FAMOUS. HE LEFT THE ARMY, WENT INTO PRIVATE MEDICAL PRACTICE, AND DIED IN 1853 AFTER SLIPPING ON SOME ICE . . .

. . . ALEXIS SURVIVED TO THE RIPE OLD AGE OF 86. WHEN HE DIED, HIS FAMILY PILED HEAVY ROCKS ON HIS COFFIN AND PLACED IT IN AN UNMARKED GRAVE.

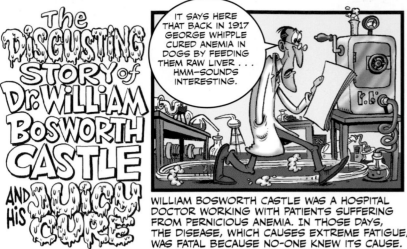

The Disgusting Story of Dr. William Bosworth Castle and his Juicy Cure

IT SAYS HERE THAT BACK IN 1917 GEORGE WHIPPLE CURED ANEMIA IN DOGS BY FEEDING THEM RAW LIVER... HMM—SOUNDS INTERESTING.

WILLIAM BOSWORTH CASTLE WAS A HOSPITAL DOCTOR WORKING WITH PATIENTS SUFFERING FROM PERNICIOUS ANEMIA. IN THOSE DAYS, THE DISEASE, WHICH CAUSES EXTREME FATIGUE, WAS FATAL BECAUSE NO-ONE KNEW ITS CAUSE.

RAW LIVER = ANTI-PERNICIOUS ANEMIA FACTOR

WE MADE OUR HUMAN PATIENTS EAT THE LIVER! LIKE WHIPPLE'S DOGS, THEY RECOVERED...

...GENTLEMEN, WE HAVE A CURE FOR PERNICIOUS ANEMIA!

THEY ALL DESERVE A NOBEL PRIZE.

RAW LIVER! YUCK! I FEEL SICK.

HMM...

CASTLE ATTENDED A LECTURE GIVEN BY GEORGE MINOT, A LEADING DOCTOR WHO HAD BEEN RESEARCHING PERNICIOUS ANEMIA WITH A COLLEAGUE, WILLIAM MURPHY.

EUREKA!

HOSPITAL

SOMETHING WAS BUGGING CASTLE. HE KNEW THAT PATIENTS WITH PERNICIOUS ANEMIA WERE LOW IN STOMACH JUICE. WAS THAT WHY THEY GOT SICK?... THEN HE HAD A BRAIN WAVE.

FEELING SQUEAMISH? READ NO FURTHER.

IT GETS WORSE!

STAN STOMACH

CHEW CHOMP CHOMP CHEW

TICK TOCK TICK TOCK

AAK AAK BLURGH

CASTLE'S ROOM WAS NEXT TO THE HOSPITAL KITCHEN. EVERY MORNING, HE SNEAKED IN AND FED HIMSELF RAW BEEF HAMBURGER... AN HOUR LATER, HE MADE HIMSELF THROW UP.

DON'T SAY YOU WEREN'T WARNED!

FUNNY-LOOKING LEMONADE.

THIS WILL PERK YOU UP, OLD BOY!

THE BOSWORTH CASTLE SPECIAL SMOOTHIE

THE REGURGITATED RAW BEEF HAD BEEN WELL DRENCHED IN CASTLE'S STOMACH JUICE. CASTLE STRAINED OFF THE JUICE AND SECRETLY FED IT TO SOME OF HIS PATIENTS.

WHAT D'YOU CALL THAT MIRACLE CURE OF YOURS, DOC?

THE INTRINSIC FACTOR.

BOSTON GENERAL HOSPITAL

HE'S ONE SICK MEDIC!

THE PATIENTS WHO HAD CASTLE'S MIXTURE MADE A BETTER RECOVERY THAN THOSE WHO HAD RAW LIVER ALONE. HIS GRUESOME EXPERIMENTS SHOWED THAT GASTRIC JUICE CONTAINS A SUBSTANCE THAT HELPS THE BODY ABSORB THE "ANTIPERNICIOUS ANEMIA FACTOR" IN FOODS.

CASTLE WENT ON TO A LIFETIME OF PIONEERING RESEARCH INTO ANEMIA AND WON MANY HONORS DURING HIS LONG CAREER. HE DIED IN 1990.

WHIPPLE, MINOT, AND MURPHY WON THE NOBEL PRIZE FOR MEDICINE IN 1934.

VITAMIN B12 WAS ISOLATED AND NAMED IN 1948.

I NAME THIS VITAMIN B12!

WE NOW KNOW THE "ANTIPERNICIOUS ANEMIA FACTOR" IN LIVER IS B12.

FOUND IN MEAT, FISH, EGGS, AND MILK, IT IS ESSENTIAL FOR MAKING RED BLOOD CELLS.

MILK

CASTLE'S "INTRINSIC FACTOR" WAS FINALLY IDENTIFIED AS A TYPE OF PROTEIN NEEDED FOR ABSORBING B12 IN THE 1970S.

CASTLE'S SNEAKY METHODS WOULD NOT BE PERMITTED TODAY—BUT HE GOT THE RIGHT RESULTS!

DIGESTION BREAKTHROUGHS

THE SMELLIEST GAS EMISSIONS ARE THOSE THAT CONTAIN EXCESSIVE AMOUNTS OF HYDROGEN SULFIDE, WHICH SMELLS LIKE ROTTEN EGGS. CERTAIN FOODS ARE RICH IN SULFUR, WHICH PRODUCES GREATER AMOUNTS OF HYDROGEN SULFIDE. SOME OF THE WORST OFFENDERS ARE BEANS AND CABBAGE.

... so remember to take something good to read.

Englishman John Harrington invented the first water closet in 1594. When he showed it off to his godmother, Queen Elizabeth I, she tried it out and was so impressed that she ordered one for herself. Talk about a royal flush!

You will spend approximately three years of your life on the toilet seat ...

People call it the toilet, bog, lavatory, restroom, bathroom, can, washroom, water closet, the facilities, john ... The list goes on and on! What do you call it?

About three-fourths of your average excrement is water, while the rest is a mixture of both dead and live bacteria, indigestible food remains, fats, dead cells, mucus from the lining of the intestines, and some proteins.

TOILET TRUTHS

It's not all embarrassing noises and unpleasant smells. Behind this door, the body is undergoing a crucial process of expelling urine and disposing of food waste in the the form of feces. This helps keep the body balanced and healthy. Not something to pooh-pooh.

Certain foods can change the smell of urine. When asparagus, onion, or garlic is broken down in the digestive system, a byproduct is released that causes urine to smell bad.

In 1857, American Joseph Gayetty invented the first packaged toilet paper. Before this, anything from leaves (ewww!) to stones (ouch!) were used! The Ancient Romans reportedly used sponges on sticks!

The bile duct carries bile—a fluid to aid digestion—from the gallbladder (where bile is stored) to the small intestine. Digested bile pigments are also what gives feces (poo) its brown color.

THE TOTO INTELLIGENCE TOILET CAN ANALYSE BLOOD SUGAR LEVELS, BODY WEIGHT, BLOOD PRESSURE, AND FAT PERCENTAGE. IT THEN WIRELESSLY SENDS THESE RESULTS TO YOUR COMPUTER. OUTSMARTED . . . BY A TOILET!

If you have eaten any corn lately, it is likely that you will see it again pretty soon . . . in the toilet. But what may look like a whole kernel is really just the indigestible outer coating of the corn. The inside part is where all the nutrients are, and it's broken down and absorbed by the body.

A day dedicated to the humble toilet? Yep, really! World Toilet Day—held each year on November 19—is an annual event that celebrates the importance of the toilet. This day also emphasizes how increased toilets around the world can lead to a more hygienic society.

IT'S ALL ABOUT WATER. NOT ONLY DOES WATER MAKE UP MORE THAN THREE-FOURTHS OF FECES AND MORE THAN NINE TENTHS OF URINE, A SINGLE PULL OF A TOILET CHAIN FLUSHES AROUND 1.6 GALLONS (6 LITERS) OF DRINKING WATER.

A heavyweight organ that's the biggest of all organs inside the body, with an equally big number of jobs! And so it is our pleasure to announce . . .

the Human Body Lifetime Achievement Award

goes to that champion of blood regulation . . .

THE LIVER

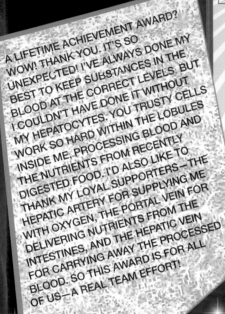

A LIFETIME ACHIEVEMENT AWARD? WOW! THANK YOU. IT'S SO UNEXPECTED! I'VE ALWAYS DONE MY BEST TO KEEP SUBSTANCES IN THE BLOOD AT THE CORRECT LEVELS. BUT I COULDN'T HAVE DONE IT WITHOUT MY HEPATOCYTES. YOU TRUSTY CELLS WORK SO HARD WITHIN THE LOBULES INSIDE ME, PROCESSING BLOOD AND THE NUTRIENTS FROM RECENTLY DIGESTED FOOD. I'D ALSO LIKE TO THANK MY LOYAL SUPPORTERS—THE HEPATIC ARTERY FOR SUPPLYING ME WITH OXYGEN, THE PORTAL VEIN FOR DELIVERING NUTRIENTS FROM THE INTESTINES, AND THE HEPATIC VEIN FOR CARRYING AWAY THE PROCESSED BLOOD. SO THIS AWARD IS FOR ALL OF US—A REAL TEAM EFFORT!

THE LIVER'S MAJOR LIFETIME ACHIEVEMENTS

Glucose control
Always one to keep an eye on glucose levels, the liver stores glucose—the body's main fuel—when there's a lot in the blood and releases it when there isn't enough.

Fat metabolism
Eager to offer a helping hand to visitors, the liver houses fats, arranges for their transportation around the body, and breaks down fatty acids to release energy.

Protein metabolism
In the liver, many blood proteins—important elements for blood well-being—are made. The liver also breaks down excess amino acids—protein building blocks—that can't be stored.

Vitamin and mineral storage
The liver acts as a major storage facility for vitamins A, B12, and D, as well as iron, which it releases to make red blood cells.

Detoxification
A huge campaigner for a clean body inside and out, the liver removes any drugs, poisons, or other unwanted chemicals in the blood.

Bile
The liver is a lifelong bile and bile-salt producer for aiding digestion in the small intestine.

Hormones
Change the record! The liver breaks down these chemical messengers so that they don't keep delivering the same message again and again and again . . .

RED BLOOD CELL
We know the fate that awaits us when we get old. You're going to break us down and get rid of our bad pieces into bile. We just try not to think about it because we are big fans of all the good stuff you do for us, recycling the oldies' useful pieces and generally keeping the blood in tiptop condition. So a big thanks from us—you deserve this award.

LIVER AWARDS

Heartfelt congratulations, Liver, old friend.

Let's hear it for the liver!

What a story. I was gripped!

STAYING COOL WHEN IT'S HOT

A built-in thermostat in the brain regulates body temperature, working to maintain a constant 98.6°F (37°C) to keep the body running smoothly. When we begin to overheat, the thermostat kick-starts a series of heat-loss tactics.

CEREBRAL CORTEX

The "thinking" part of the brain is alerted to the fact that the body is too warm. The now-aware person embarks on a variety of activities, such as removing clothes, seeking shade, or sipping a cold drink, to help the body cool down.

SKIN RECEPTORS

Temperature receptors in the skin note an increase in the external temperature.

BLOOD TEMPERATURE

The body's internal temperature increases along with its external one, causing the blood temperature to rise.

BLOOD VESSELS

Warm blood rushes to blood vessels near the skin's surface, which widen and radiate the heat out of the body.

HYPOTHALAMUS

Using information from temperature receptors in the blood and skin, the hypothalamus (the body's thermostat) in the brain registers that the body's core temperature is too high. It sends messages to different parts of the body to initiate heat loss.

NORMAL BODY TEMPERATU 98.6°F (37°

HEAT STROKE

If the body remains overheated for too long, the heat regulation system begins to struggle. Sweating ceases and the body's temperature increases. If the body is not quickly cooled, multiple organ failure can lead to death.

SWEAT GLANDS

The body's sweat glands receive the hypothalamus's message, triggering sweating. Sweat then evaporates from the skin's surface to cool the body.

ADRENAL GLANDS

The hypothalamus puts a cap on the adrenal glands, which release the hormones adrenaline and noradrenaline into the bloodstream.

BODY CELLS

With a reduced amount of adrenaline and noradrenaline reaching the body's cells, their rate of working slows down. The speed at which the chemical reactions inside the cells take place (the metabolic rate) is decreased, reducing the amount of heat that the body creates.

When we begin to lose too much heat, our natural thermostat initiates a heat-gain strategy to maintain a temperature of 98.6°F (37°C)—the optimum temperature for the chemical reactions that keep us alive to take place in our cells.

STAYING WARM WHEN IT'S COLD

CEREBRAL CORTEX
By processing the information that the body is too cold, the "thinking" part of the brain decides to act to increase body temperature. The person may dress in warmer clothes, move closer to a heat source, or start moving around more.

SKIN RECEPTORS
Temperature receptors in the skin register a decrease in the external temperature.

BLOOD TEMPERATURE
The body's internal temperature decreases along with its external one, causing the blood temperature to fall.

BLOOD VESSELS
Blood vessels near the skin's surface narrow to reduce the amount of blood flowing through them, thus reducing the amount of heat lost through the skin.

HYPOTHALAMUS
The body's thermostat registers its chilly state from the temperature receptors in the skin and blood. It then starts the ball rolling to warm the body up again.

NORMAL BODY TEMPERATURE 98.6°F (37°C)

FROSTBITE
If the body stays too cold for a prolonged period of time, the narrowed blood vessels deprive the body's skin cells of oxygen and food for too long, causing them to die in a condition known as frostbite.

MUSCLES
The body's skeletal muscles receive messages from the hypothalamus to contract. This involuntary shivering creates extra heat.

ADRENAL GLANDS
The adrenal glands act on instructions from the hypothalamus to release extra adrenaline and noradrenaline into the bloodstream.

BODY CELLS
The extra hormones (adrenaline and noradrenaline) in the bloodstream trigger an increase in the body's metabolic rate, speeding up the chemical reactions in the body's cells to generate more heat.

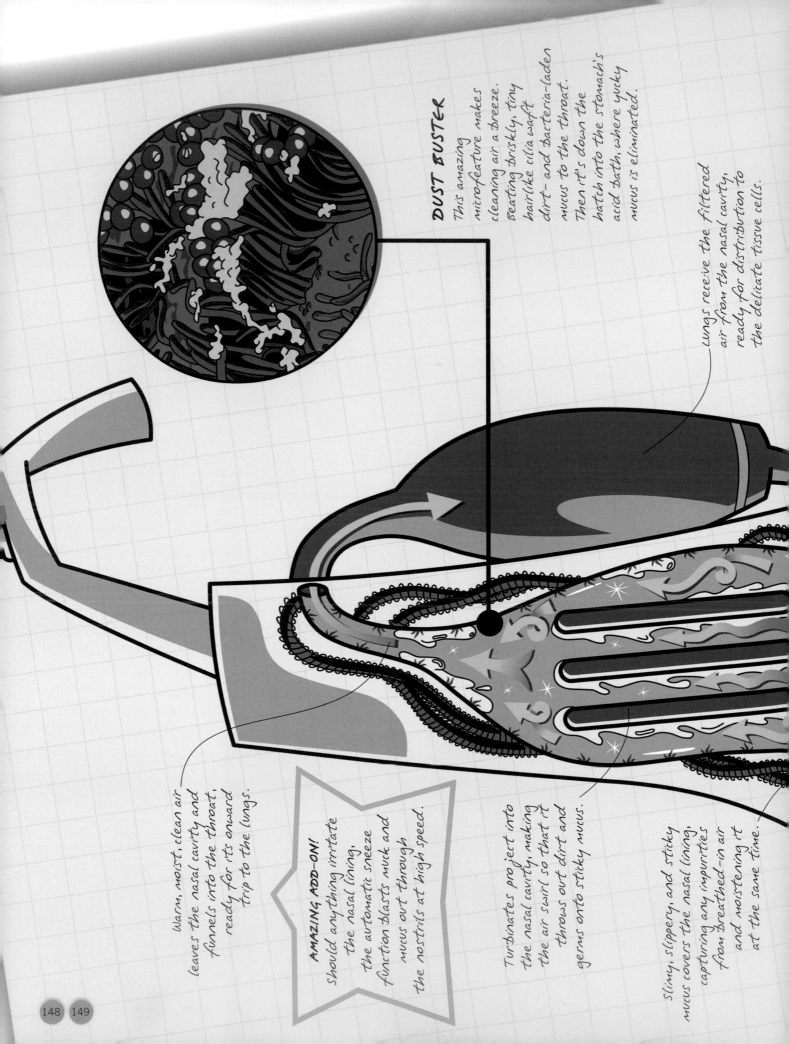

DUST BUSTER

This amazing microfeature makes cleaning air a breeze. Beating briskly, tiny hairlike cilia waft dirt- and bacteria-laden mucus to the throat. Then it's down the hatch into the stomach's acid bath, where yucky mucus is eliminated.

Lungs receive the filtered air from the nasal cavity, ready for distribution to the delicate tissue cells.

Warm, moist, clean air leaves the nasal cavity and funnels into the throat, ready for its onward trip to the lungs.

AMAZING ADD-ON!
Should anything irritate the nasal lining, the automatic sneeze function blasts muck and mucus out through the nostrils at high speed.

Turbinates project into the nasal cavity, making the air swirl so that it throws out dirt and germs onto sticky mucus.

Slimy, slippery, and sticky mucus covers the nasal lining, capturing any impurities from breathed-in air and moistening it at the same time.

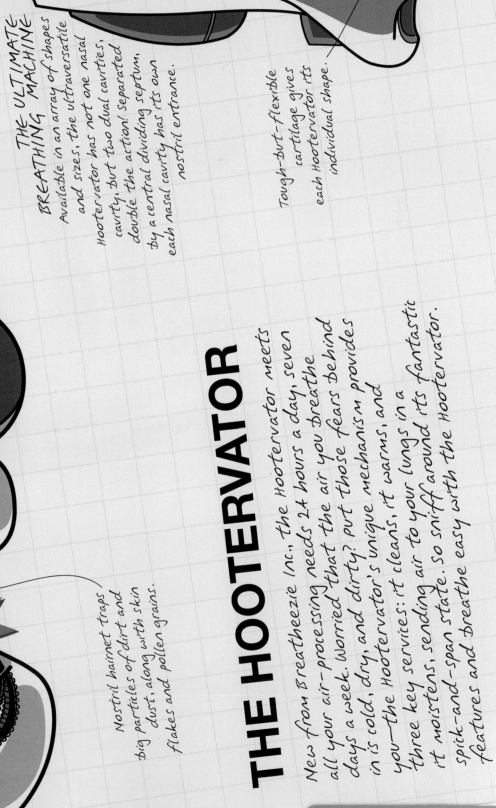

Blood vessel radiators release heat that warms air, even on the coldest days.

THE ULTIMATE BREATHING MACHINE

Available in an array of shapes and sizes, the ultraversatile Hootervator has not one nasal cavity, but two dual cavities, separated double the action! separated by a central dividing septum, by a central dividing septum, each nasal cavity has its own nostril entrance.

Tough-but-flexible cartilage gives each Hootervator its individual shape.

Nostril hairnet traps big particles of dirt and dust, along with skin flakes and pollen grains.

THE HOOTERVATOR

New from Breatheezie Inc., the Hootervator meets all your air-processing needs 24 hours a day, seven days a week. Worried that the air you breathe in is cold, dry, and dirty? Put those fears behind you—the Hootervator's unique mechanism provides three key services: it cleans, it warms, and it moistens, sending air to your lungs in a spick-and-span state. So sniff around its fantastic features and breathe easy with the Hootervator.

BREATHING

Every second, oxygen passes from your lungs into your blood. Breathing ensures that oxygen supplies are constantly replenished by pumping fresh air into your lungs and stale air out. Lungs lack muscles, so your diaphragm and rib muscles do the hard work.

AIR IN

When you breathe in, the diaphragm—a sheet of muscle that separates the chest and abdomen—and intercostal rib muscles contract to increase the space inside the chest cavity. The elastic lungs expand into the space, sucking air in through the nose, throat, and trachea.

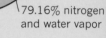

20.8% oxygen

79.16% nitrogen and water vapor

0.04% carbon dioxide

Throat links the nasal cavity, through which air enters and leaves the body, to the trachea

Trachea carries oxygen-rich air to the lungs

Ribs form a cage around the delicate lungs, protecting them from damage, as well as playing a part in breathing

Rib cage surrounding the lungs consists of the movable curved ribs, along with the backbone and, at the front, the sternum

Air is a mixture of the gases oxygen (red), carbon dioxide (blue), and nitrogen (green), with a dash of water vapor. The air you breathe out contains less oxygen and more carbon dioxide and water vapor than the air you breathe in.

Intercostal muscles connecting neighboring ribs contract to pull the rib cage upwards and outward, making the chest expand

Lungs passively follow the movements of the rib cage and diaphragm, sucking in air as they expand

Diaphragm—normally dome shaped—contracts and flattens, further increasing the space inside the chest cavity

AIR OUT

During breathing out, the diaphragm relaxes, curves upward, and resumes its dome shape. The intercostal muscles also relax so that the chest shrinks. This decreases the space inside the chest cavity, squeezing the lungs so that the oxygen-depleted air is forced out through the nose and mouth.

Breathing is controlled automatically by the respiratory center in the brain stem. It monitors levels of oxygen and carbon dioxide in your blood. When you exercise, it increases the rate and depth of your breathing to get extra oxygen to the muscles.

Cerebrum—the "thinking" part of the brain—can consciously control breathing, necessary for playing a wind instrument or singing a song, for example

80.4% nitrogen and water vapor

15.6% oxygen

4% carbon dioxide

Air passing up the trachea when a person breathes out contains waste carbon dioxide, produced by the body's cells as they release energy

Intercostal muscles relax to stop pulling neighboring ribs together, so the rib cage moves downward and inward

Lungs act like elastic bags, so the decreasing space inside the chest cavity makes them shrink, forcing stale air out

Diaphragm relaxes and is pushed upward from below by organs in the abdomen, decreasing the space inside the chest cavity

BODY TOUR

Oxygen is the body's lifeline. Without it, cells would be unable to do what they do, day in and day out, to keep you alive and kicking.

MY TRAVEL BLOG

They call me oxygen, O_2 for short owing to my dual-atom makeup. There's a bunch of us jostling through the world—me and my kind make up 20.8 percent of air. We love to travel, and one of my favorite trips is inside a human body. Just check out the incredible itinerary . . . .

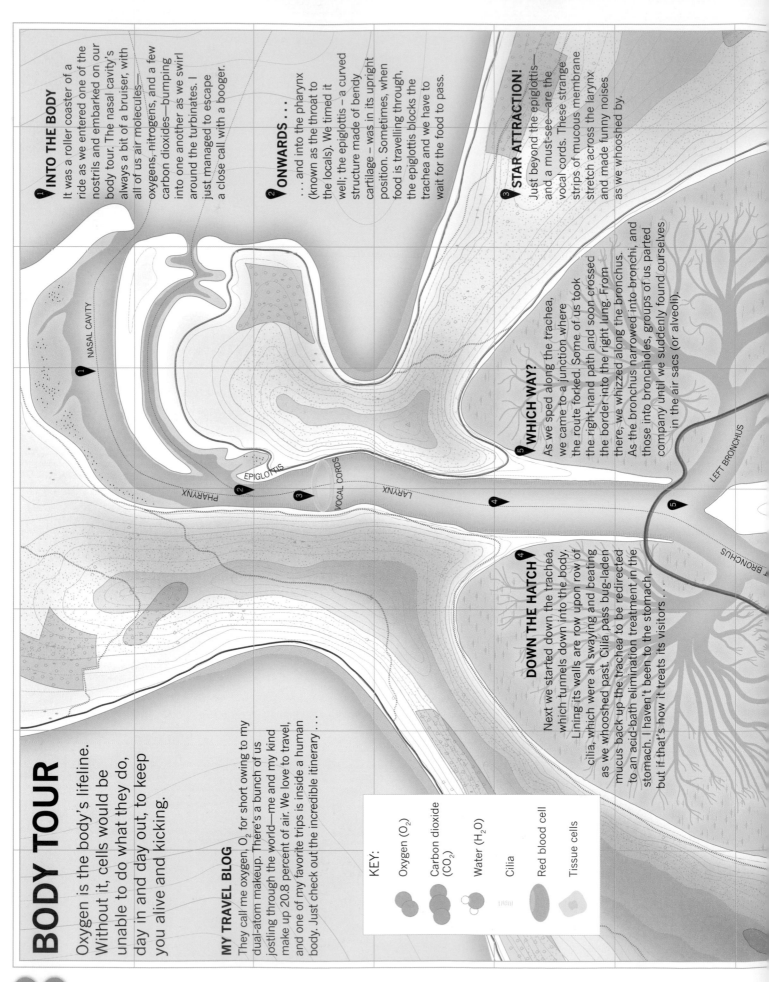

1 INTO THE BODY

It was a roller coaster of a ride as we entered one of the nostrils and embarked on our body tour. The nasal cavity's always a bit of a bruiser, with all of us air molecules— oxygens, nitrogens, and a few carbon dioxides—bumping into one another as we swirl around the turbinates. I just managed to escape a close call with a booger.

2 ONWARDS . . . .

. . . and into the pharynx (known as the throat to the locals). We timed it well; the epiglottis – a curved structure made of bendy cartilage – was in its upright position. Sometimes, when food is travelling through, the epiglottis blocks the trachea and we have to wait for the food to pass.

3 STAR ATTRACTION!

Just beyond the epiglottis— and a must-see—are the vocal cords. These strange strips of mucous membrane stretch across the larynx and made funny noises as we whooshed by.

4 DOWN THE HATCH

Next we started down the trachea, which tunnels down into the body. Lining its walls are row upon row of cilia, which were all swaying and beating as we whooshed past. Cilia pass bug-laden mucus back up the trachea to be redirected to an acid-bath elimination treatment in the stomach. I haven't been to the stomach, but if that's how it treats its visitors . . .

5 WHICH WAY?

As we sped along the trachea, we came to a junction where the route forked. Some of us took the right-hand path and soon crossed the border into the right lung. From there, we whizzed along the bronchus. As the bronchus narrowed into bronchi, and those into bronchioles, groups of us parted company until we suddenly found ourselves in the air sacs (or alveoli).

NASAL CAVITY

PHARYNX

EPIGLOTTIS

VOCAL CORDS

LARYNX

LEFT BRONCHUS

RIGHT BRONCHUS

KEY:

Oxygen (O_2)

Carbon dioxide (CO_2)

Water (H_2O)

Cilia

Red blood cell

Tissue cells

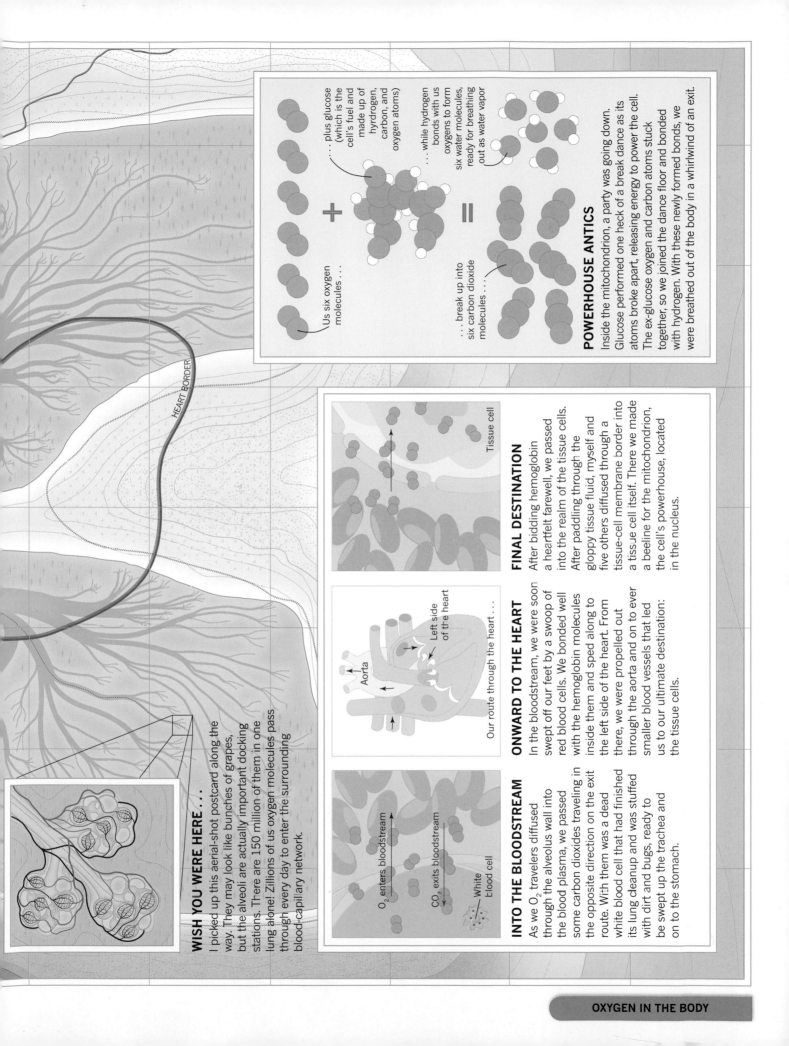

WISH YOU WERE HERE . . .

I picked up this aerial-shot postcard along the way. They may look like bunches of grapes, but the alveoli are actually important docking stations. There are 150 million of them in one lung alone! Zillions of us oxygen molecules pass through every day to enter the surrounding blood-capillary network.

HEART BORDER

POWERHOUSE ANTICS

Inside the mitochondrion, a party was going down. Glucose performed one heck of a break dance as its atoms broke apart, releasing energy to power the cell. The ex-glucose oxygen and carbon atoms stuck together, so we joined the dance floor and bonded with hydrogen. With these newly formed bonds, we were breathed out of the body in a whirlwind of an exit.

Us six oxygen molecules . . .

+

. . . plus glucose (which is the cell's fuel and made up of hydrogen, carbon, and oxygen atoms)

. . . while hydrogen bonds with us oxygens to form six water molecules, ready for breathing out as water vapor

=

. . . break up into six carbon dioxide molecules . . . .

INTO THE BLOODSTREAM

As we O_2 travelers diffused through the alveolus wall into the blood plasma, we passed some carbon dioxides traveling in the opposite direction on the exit route. With them was a dead white blood cell that had finished its lung cleanup and was stuffed with dirt and bugs, ready to be swept up the trachea and on to the stomach.

O_2 enters bloodstream

CO_2 exits bloodstream

White blood cell

ONWARD TO THE HEART

In the bloodstream, we were soon swept off our feet by a swoop of red blood cells. We bonded well with the hemoglobin molecules inside them and sped along to the left side of the heart. From there, we were propelled out through the aorta and on to ever smaller blood vessels that led us to our ultimate destination: the tissue cells.

Aorta

Left side of the heart

Our route through the heart . . . .

FINAL DESTINATION

After bidding hemoglobin a heartfelt farewell, we passed into the realm of the tissue cells. After paddling through the gloppy tissue fluid, myself and five others diffused through a tissue-cell membrane border into a tissue cell itself. There we made a beeline for the mitochondrion, the cell's powerhouse, located in the nucleus.

Tissue cell

If you hold your breath for a little while, your body will eventually take over and start breathing again. But there are times when your body is the one that "holds" your breath. As strange as it may seem, certain movements in your body require it to close off your airways for a short time. As you will discover, that's nothing to sneeze at.

coughing

If something gets in your respiratory passage that shouldn't be there, from a speck of dust to a piece of food that's gone down the wrong way, you cough to clear the airways. When coughing, your vocal cords close for a moment and then reopen as air blasts out, carrying the offending object with it out of your mouth. Got the all clear?

sneezing

A sneeze is similar to a cough, but the rush of air exits through your nostrils. If something irritating gets inside your nose, your brain alerts the necessary muscles that you need to sneeze. After a quick, deep breath, the vocal cords close and open quickly to release air, your eyes shut, and your tongue presses against the roof of your mouth to force the air out of your nose. Bless you!

hiccuping

Sometimes your diaphragm contracts suddenly to suck in a breath. When the air hits the closed vocal cords, you make a "hic" sound. Hiccups are a reflex action, and they are beyond your control. People swear by different ways to stop hiccups, from being startled to chugging a glass of water. But most bouts last only a few minutes.

breathtaking////

yawwwwwww
wwwwwwww
wwwwwwww
wwwwwwww
wwwwwwww
wwwwwwww
wwwwwwwwn

zzzz zzzzz zzzz
zzzz zzzzz zzzz
zzzzz zzzz

boooo hoooo
sob sob
sniffle wail

blubber blubber
boooo hooooo

yawning

When you yawn, your mouth opens wide and your jaw drops so that you can fill your lungs with air. As your diaphragm pushes downward, your lungs expand to draw in air, and then a tiny bit of air blows out. No one knows why we yawn, although we tend to do it more often when we're tired. And yawning really is contagious—even reading about yawning makes you yawn . . . did it?

snoring

At night, some of the muscles that keep your airways open relax while you snooze. This causes the airways to narrow. Air passing over the floppy muscles can make them vibrate, creating the sound of snoring. Loud or infrequent snoring can indicate a condition called sleep apnea, when the relaxed muscles block the airway and cause breathing to stop several times a night.

crying

Are you having a laugh? Or are you crying your eyes out? Sometimes it's difficult to distinguish between the two. When you cry, you take in a deep breath and let it back out in short bursts. As the air crosses your vocal cords, crying sounds are made. When sobbing, you take in many shallow breaths and let the air out in one burst. The movements used to laugh are very similar. You can even laugh yourself into tears.

WHEEL BASE
JOURNALS

T.12-3. 1

172–173 SAILING THROUGH LIFE
Early blood transfusions and the discovery of blood types

180–181 SPECIAL BREW
The urinary system and how it removes excess water and wastes from the blood

168–169 DRAIN AND DESTROY
The lymphatic system and how it functions to drain excess fluid from the tissues and destroys pathogens

174–175 SLICE OF LIFE
How blood clots seal leaks in blood vessels and skin so that healing can take place

164–165 RESUMÉ: RED BLOOD CELL
The role of red blood cells in the body

176–177 HEART-TO-HEART
A step-by-step guide to performing a heart transplant

158–159 TUBE NETWORK
How the circulation of blood around the body, pumped by the heart, provides cells with oxygen and removes waste products

How the body's transportation networks nourish cells and defend against invading pathogens and how medical advances can sometimes help.

MAINTENANCE AND TRANSPORTATION

TUBE NETWORK

Every day, blood journeys through 93,205 miles (150,000 km) of tube network that branches out to link every part of your body. Driven by a pumping heart, blood delivers oxygen and nutrients to cells and organs and collects their waste products. This circulatory system is our body's lifeline and is just the ticket for keeping cells alive.

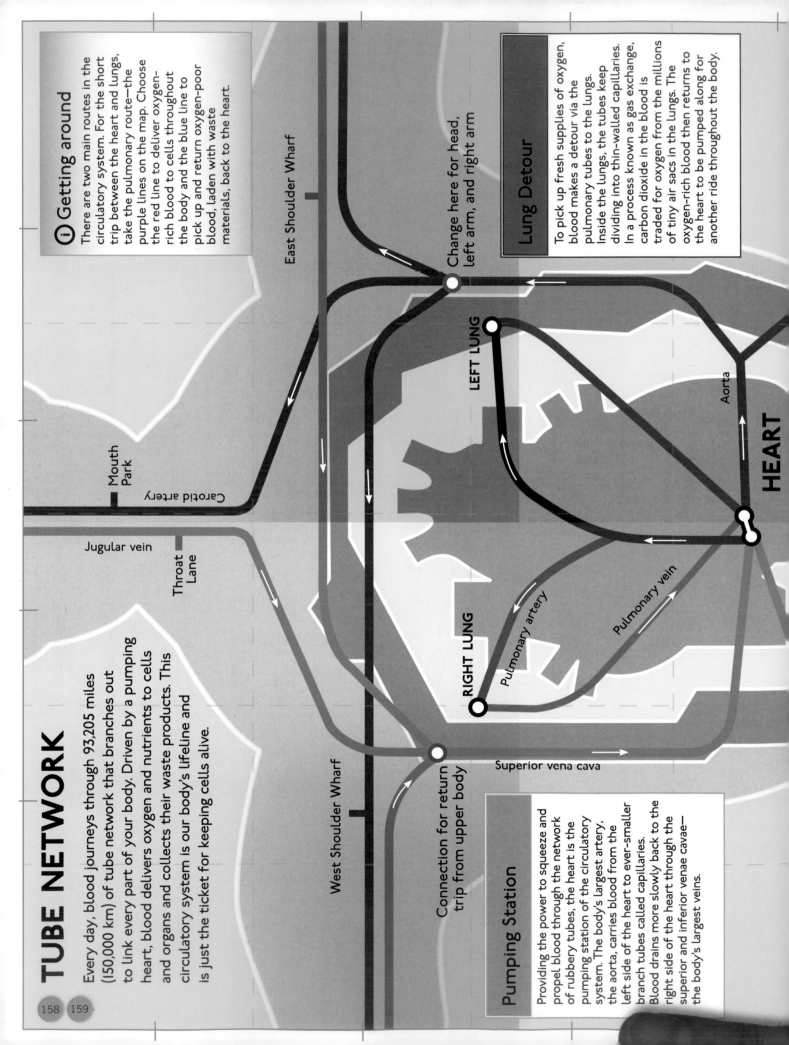

There are two main routes in the circulatory system. For the short trip between the heart and lungs, take the pulmonary route—the purple lines on the map. Choose the red line to deliver oxygen-rich blood to cells throughout the body and the blue line to pick up and return oxygen-poor blood, laden with waste materials, back to the heart.

Lung Detour

To pick up fresh supplies of oxygen, blood makes a detour via the pulmonary tubes to the lungs. Inside the lungs, the tubes keep dividing into thin-walled capillaries. In a process known as gas exchange, carbon dioxide in the blood is traded for oxygen from the millions of tiny air sacs in the lungs. The oxygen-rich blood then returns to the heart to be pumped along for another ride throughout the body.

Pumping Station

Providing the power to squeeze and propel blood through the network of rubbery tubes, the heart is the pumping station of the circulatory system. The body's largest artery, the aorta, carries blood from the left side of the heart to ever-smaller branch tubes called capillaries. Blood drains more slowly back to the right side of the heart through the superior and inferior venae cavae—the body's largest veins.

East Shoulder Wharf

Change here for head, left arm, and right arm

Mouth Park

Carotid artery

Jugular vein

Throat Lane

LEFT LUNG

Aorta

HEART

RIGHT LUNG

Pulmonary artery

Pulmonary vein

West Shoulder Wharf

Connection for return trip from upper body

Superior vena cava

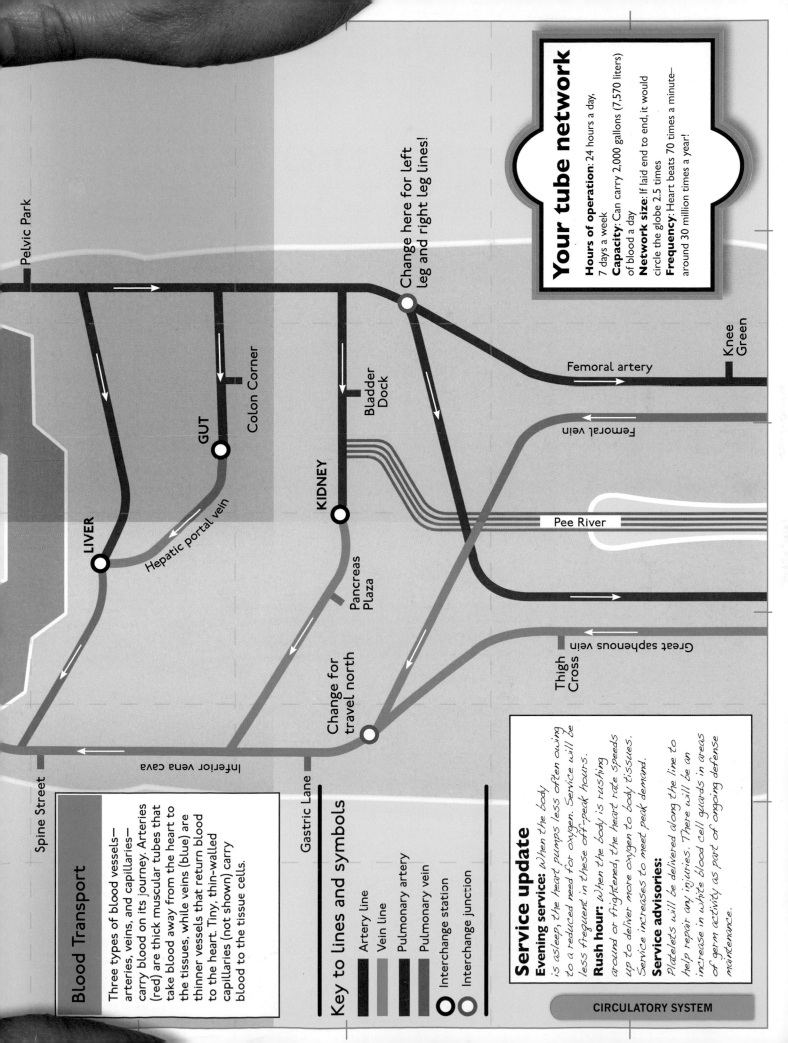

Blood Transport

Three types of blood vessels—arteries, veins, and capillaries—carry blood on its journey. Arteries (red) are thick muscular tubes that take blood away from the heart to the tissues, while veins (blue) are thinner vessels that return blood to the heart. Tiny, thin-walled capillaries (not shown) carry blood to the tissue cells.

Key to lines and symbols

- Artery line
- Vein line
- Pulmonary artery
- Pulmonary vein
- ◯ Interchange station
- ◯ Interchange junction

Service update

Evening service: When the body is asleep, the heart pumps less often owing to a reduced need for oxygen. Service will be less frequent in these off-peak hours.

Rush hour: When the body is rushing around or frightened, the heart rate speeds up to deliver more oxygen to body tissues. Service increases to meet peak demand.

Service advisories:

Platelets will be delivered along the line to help repair any injuries. There will be an increase in white blood cell guards in areas of germ activity as part of ongoing defense maintenance.

Your tube network

Hours of operation: 24 hours a day, 7 days a week

Capacity: Can carry 2,000 gallons (7,570 liters) of blood a day

Network size: If laid end to end, it would circle the globe 2.5 times

Frequency: Heart beats 70 times a minute—around 30 million times a year!

Pelvic Park

Change here for left leg and right leg lines!

Femoral artery

Knee Green

GUT

Colon Corner

Bladder Dock

Femoral vein

KIDNEY

Hepatic portal vein

Pee River

LIVER

Pancreas Plaza

Thigh Cross

Great saphenous vein

Change for travel north

Inferior vena cava

Spine Street

Gastric Lane

A BLOODY REBELLION

Up until the 1600,s, doctors believed that blood was made from food in the liver. From there, it was carried by veins to body organs, where it was consumed. Some of the blood was sucked into the heart, brought into contact with air, and then carried away by arteries. At least, these were the teachings of Greek physician Claudius Galen (200-129 B.C.), which no one dared challenge for 1,400 years . . . Until 1628, when a certain English physician named William Harvey published a book called On the Motion of the Heart and Blood. In it he explained how blood is pumped by the heart, through arteries and veins, along a single circular route. Harvey had discovered circulation.

A gifted student

Born in 1578, William Harvey studied medicine in
Padua, Italy. There he was taught by anatomist
Hieronymus Fabricius, who had described valves in veins
but had no idea of their function. In 1602, Harvey returned
to England, becoming a prestigious doctor and the physician
to the king. Through his research, Harvey discovered
the function of the valves that had so puzzled his teacher.

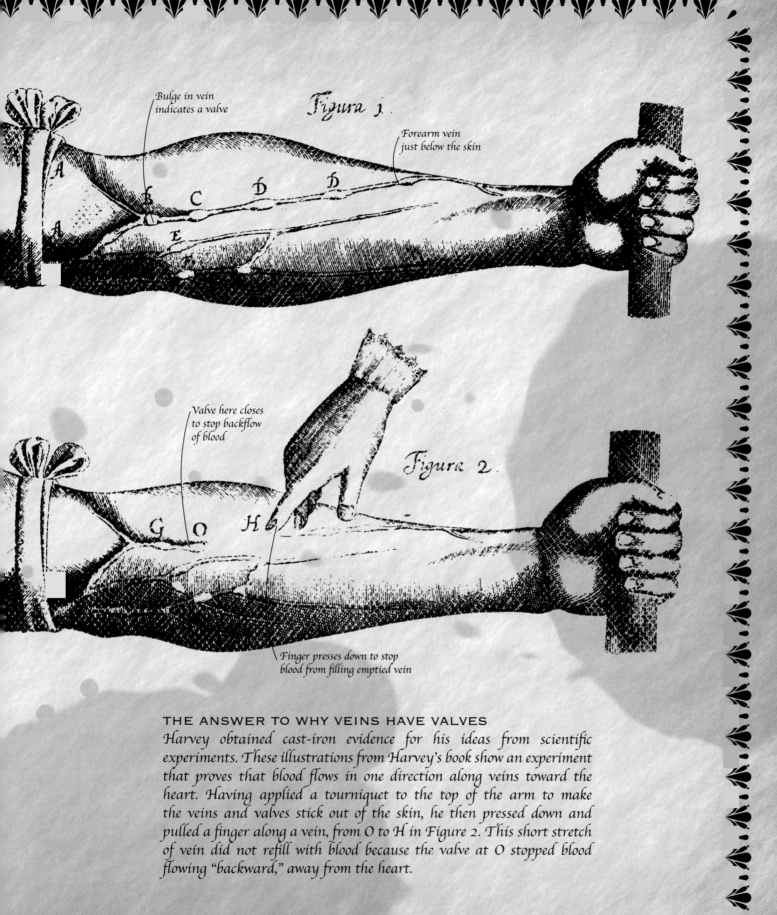

Bulge in vein
indicates a valve

Figura 1

Forearm vein
just below the skin

A

B C D D

E

Valve here closes
to stop backflow
of blood

Figura 2

G O H

Finger presses down to stop
blood from filling emptied vein

THE ANSWER TO WHY VEINS HAVE VALVES

Harvey obtained cast-iron evidence for his ideas from scientific experiments. These illustrations from Harvey's book show an experiment that proves that blood flows in one direction along veins toward the heart. Having applied a tourniquet to the top of the arm to make the veins and valves stick out of the skin, he then pressed down and pulled a finger along a vein, from O to H in Figure 2. This short stretch of vein did not refill with blood because the valve at O stopped blood flowing "backward," away from the heart.

heartbook

Heart

is beating away as per usual

Updated 2 minutes ago

Gender:	Other (I'm a muscle, actually)
Age:	Same as you, duh!
Last active:	Online now (which is why you are able to read this)
Profile views:	2.5 billion hits, baby (that's how often I'll pump in my lifetime)
Share the luv:	❤ THIS ANNOYS ME, okay? I look nothing like that
Hometown:	Smack bang in the middle of Chest

View Photos of Heart (23)

View Videos of Heart (1)

Send Heart a Message

Prod Heart

▼ **Friends:**

36 friends   See All

Coronary Arteries
I need blood, too, but I can't just steal it from a ventricle. This network of blood vessel buddies fills my muscles up with oxygen and food. Arteries, you'll always be a part-a-me!

Personal info:

About me:

I heart you, and I mean that wholeheartedly. Call me Heart. I'm kind of a big deal around here. Want to get to know me better? Let's start off with a little heart-to-heart. I'm not a cute red blob like you see on those Valentine's Day cards. And love? Meh! That's not what I'm about. All that stuff about broken hearts? Not me, amigo. I'm made of tougher stuff. Solid muscle. (You probably guessed from my photo that I work out. A lot.) I beat 72 times a minute, in fact, pumping blood all the way around your body and back again. Nonstop, 24/7. The blood delivers the goods that keep you alive. So you can thank me from the bottom of your heart.

Are You Interested?

See All

4 friends are…

① **Right atrium:** oxygen-low blood is in da house!

② **Right ventricle:** blood pours in and gets pumped through the pulmonary artery to the lungs . . . whoosh!

③ **Pulmonary vein:** newly oxygenated blood spills through this tunnel to the left atrium . . . fresh!

④ **Left atrium:** oxygen-rich blood is in da house!

⑤ **Left ventricle:** oxygen-rich blood goes via the mitral valve into this chamber. Ready to pump up the jams?

⑥ **Aorta:** the aortic arch delivers the blood to the upper body and head, and the descending aorta takes the blood down low. Job done.

Messages

Displaying 4 out of 15 messages

Write a message…:

Send

A Red Blood Cell wrote
at 8:00 P.M. today

Hey there, do you have to pump so fast? It's cool that you can send blood all around the body in just under a minute, but I'm getting a little bit tired of all this rushing around.

Reply   Forward

Inferior Vena Cava wrote
at 6:29 P.M. today

I'm writing to complain about Superior Vena Cava. I know it's only a word, and that in medical terms superior is just the name for the upper of two parts, but it still bothers me.

Reply   Forward

Septum wrote
at 3:15 P.M. yesterday

I'm sorry if it seems like I'm always coming between you, I really am. It's just that I am supposed to be the wall that divides the heart into its left and right halves. It's what I do.

Reply   Forward

The Heart Valves wrote
at 9:43 A.M. yesterday

You know how when we open and close 100,000 times a day we make that lubDUBlub sound? Well, it's getting a little repetitive. Would you mind if we changed it to dubLUBdub?

Reply   Forward

Pericardium

You're a wrap star, a snug double layer of tissue and fluid around me. You stop excess friction as I pump to the beat. With you wrapped around me, I can't overheat.

Cardiac Muscle

Hey, tough stuff! You're what makes me me: long fibers of muscle found only in the heart. You don't need a brain to tell you what to do—you just do it—and you don't get tired.

Best Friend

Add

Lungs

What can I say? Left Lung and Right Lung, so glad you're around me (literally). You give me the oxygen-rich blood I need . . . and you're right next door! We'll be BFF.

Be Best Friends Forever

See All

Photos

2 of 8 albums

Awesome giant sculpture of yours truly in a museum!
Created today

Shots of supposedly heart-shaped things that look nothing like me at all :-(
Created about a month ago

RESUMÉ: RED BLOOD CELL

O RH POSITIVE

7 80750 250467

NAME

Red Blood Cell
(Also known as: Erythrocyte, RBC, Red Cell)

DATE OF BIRTH

100 days ago (only 20 more days left until I wear out, so please reply soon)

PLACE OF BIRTH

Inside the red bone marrow. My "parents" are stem cells. When they split (in a good way) and divided, I was created (along with millions of other red blood cells).

CONTACT INFORMATION

I am constantly on the move as I whoosh through the arteries at top speed, but I do slow down a little when picking up oxygen in the lungs, so write to me at:

ADDRESS

Red Blood Cell, Lower Lobe, Left Lung
(NB: when I get older and less flexible, I might be hanging around the capillaries of the spleen, where blood cells past their prime tend to congregate. But try the lungs first.)

TELEPHONE NUMBER

As a home phone is impractical, please contact me on my cell phone. (NB: the reception is poor in the extremities; leave a message or text me and I will get back to you.)

To: Anybody, Inc.
From: Red Blood Cell

Dear Anybody, Inc.,

I am writing about potential employment opportunities within your bloodstream. I am a capable and experienced red blood cell that can deliver on all aspects of the job, just as I deliver oxygen around the body. My current employer, AN Other, values me not only as a highly skilled individual worker but also as a cooperative member of a vast team. After 100 days here, however, I feel I have come full circle through this circulatory system and am looking for a new challenge.

I know that the oxygen-delivery industry has quite a high turnover of workers, so I am eager to make my mark while I am at the top of my game. Please find enclosed my resumé, setting out my qualifications and experience. I would be more than happy to come in for an interview, if only I could figure out a way to get out of here.

Yours sincerely,

Red Blood Cell

PERSONAL STATEMENT

A highly competent one of a kind seeking a challenging and vital role in the oxygen-transportation-and-delivery industry.

KEY STRENGTHS

An essential part of the human-body team. My main function—carrying oxygen from the lungs to the body tissues—is vital to life.

One hundred percent committed to a job I am perfectly created to do. My large surface area makes it easy for me to pick up and deposit oxygen.

I'm a great team player. Hemoglobin (a bright red, iron-rich protein packed inside me) and I work together to deliver the goods.

Extremely flexible, I am able to change shape to squeeze through even the tiniest capillaries. I'm bendable and twisty enough to get through any tight spots but can pop myself back into my usual puffy, dented-pillow shape when there's more room.

I'm a self-starter who picks up new skills very quickly—within just a few days on the job here, I had already matured into a fully operational red blood cell.

There may be 25,000,000,000,000 of me in one human body, but I am unique.

EMPLOYMENT HISTORY

For references, please contact hemoglobin, white blood cells, stem cells, or lungs (NB: I would steer clear of the macrophages, though. These white blood cells wait until I am past my peak then gobble me up, recycling the iron I contain and sending it to the liver for storage. Nasty.)

JOB TRAINING

I spent my first three or four days making hemoglobin and filling myself up with it. (This is the stuff that gives me my red coloring.) I lost my nucleus (I'm the only cell in the body without one) and became a reticulocyte (immature red blood cell). At five days old, I was released from the bone marrow into a capillary along with two million other newly qualified red blood cells . . . And two million more follow suit each and every second of the day. You can see why I'm keen to set myself apart!

JOB TITLE

A fully fledged red blood cell

RESPONSIBILITIES

See above for oxygenating tasks. I can also take on additional jobs, such as carrying waste carbon dioxide away from tissue cells.

HOBBIES AND INTERESTS

I am an avid swimmer who enjoys circulating around the body. I love to travel, which is a good thing, because I'm always moving. I stay in shape by pumping iron (through the body).

RED BLOOD CELLS

Peaks and pulses

Right atrium fills with oxygen-poor blood from the body

STAGE 1: DIASTOLE

The muscular walls of the heart's chambers—the two upper atria and the larger, lower ventricles—are relaxed. This allows oxygen-poor blood to flow into the right atrium and oxygen-rich blood into the left atrium. The semilunar valves close to stop blood pumped in the last cycle from flowing back into the heart.

Right atrium contracts to push blood into the right ventricle

Left atrium

Left ventricle

Right ventricle

Left atrium fills with oxygen-rich blood from the lungs

Semilunar valves close to prevent backflow of blood from leaving the heart

Valves between the atria and ventricles open

HEARTBEAT CYCLE

A heartbeat is not a single event. Each beat consists of three stages that together make up the heartbeat cycle. During these stages, the heart's chambers relax and then contract, aided by one-way valves, to pump blood to the lungs and the rest of the body.

During a person's lifetime, the heart beats billions of times without taking a break. Each of those beats is cleverly orchestrated to ensure that blood is pumped efficiently around the body. Doctors have many techniques for checking how well the heart and circulatory system are working, from taking a pulse to reading the peaks on an ECG.

HEART ECHOES

Very high-pitched sounds called ultrasounds are used to produce images of babies inside their mothers. Echocardiography uses the same technique to produce images of the heart, called echocardiograms. They help doctors find out how well the heart is pumping and to spot valve problems or any damage to heart muscle.

SOUND IT OUT

Simple but effective, the stethoscope enables doctors to clearly hear heart sounds. During every heartbeat cycle two sounds, called "lub" and "dup," can be picked out. Lub is produced when the valves between the atria and ventricles close, dup when the semilunar valves snap shut. Swishing sounds, called murmurs, may indicate leaky valves.

Left atrium contracts to push blood into the left ventricle

Oxygen-rich blood flows to the body

Valves between the atria and ventricles slam shut

Left ventricle contracts to pump blood to the rest of the body

Right ventricle contracts to pump blood to the lungs

STAGE 2: ATRIAL SYSTOLE

A natural pacemaker in the right atrium sends out electrical signals that instruct the muscular walls of both the right and left atria to contract. This contraction squeezes blood into the ventricles through the now-open valves. The semilunar valves guarding the exits from the ventricles remain closed.

STAGE 3: VENTRICULAR SYSTOLE

Finally, the two powerful ventricles contract together, forcing open the semilunar valves. This allows blood to flow from the right ventricle along arteries to the lungs to pick up oxygen and from the left ventricle to the rest of the body to deliver oxygen. At the same time, the valves between the atria and ventricles close, preventing blood from flowing back into the atria. And now to do it all over again …

PRESSURED NETWORK

A bit of a mouthful of a name, a sphygmomanometer is a device for measuring blood pressure— the pressure generated in arteries each time the heart beats. It consists of an inflatable cuff that wraps around the arm and a pressure gauge. Persistently high blood pressure is dangerous and needs to be treated.

FEEL THE BEAT

With every heartbeat, blood surges along arteries, making their walls bulge outward and then spring back. This surge can be felt as a pulse wherever an artery runs close to the body's surface, such as in the wrist. Counting the number of pulses in a minute provides an easy way of measuring and monitoring heart rate.

ELECTRO HEART

Each heartbeat is coordinated by electrical signals. By attaching electrodes to the skin, these signals can be detected by a machine called an electrocardiograph, which produces a trace called an electrocardiogram (ECG). By "reading" the peaks on an ECG, a doctor can see whether or not the heart is beating normally.

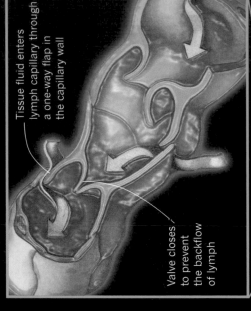

Tissue fluid enters lymph capillary through a one-way flap in the capillary wall

Valve closes to prevent the backflow of lymph

LYMPH CAPILLARIES

Lymph is drained from the body's tissues by the tiniest branches of the lymphatic system. These are the dead-end lymph capillaries that reach into every tissue. Fluid enters capillaries through flaps that act like one-way swing doors to prevent backflow. Lymph then flows in one direction into larger lymph vessels.

THYMUS GLAND

Most important in childhood, your thymus gland, found in the chest, "trains" lymphocytes to become pathogen killers.

DRAIN AND DESTROY

Your body's lymphatic system is a network of vessels. It drains surplus fluid (lymph) from your tissues and returns it to the bloodstream so that the volume of your blood always stays the same. At the same time, it filters the fluid and destroys any pathogens it carries, thus protecting you from disease.

TONSILS

These tiny lymph organs, located around the entrance to your throat, trap and destroy bacteria in food and air.

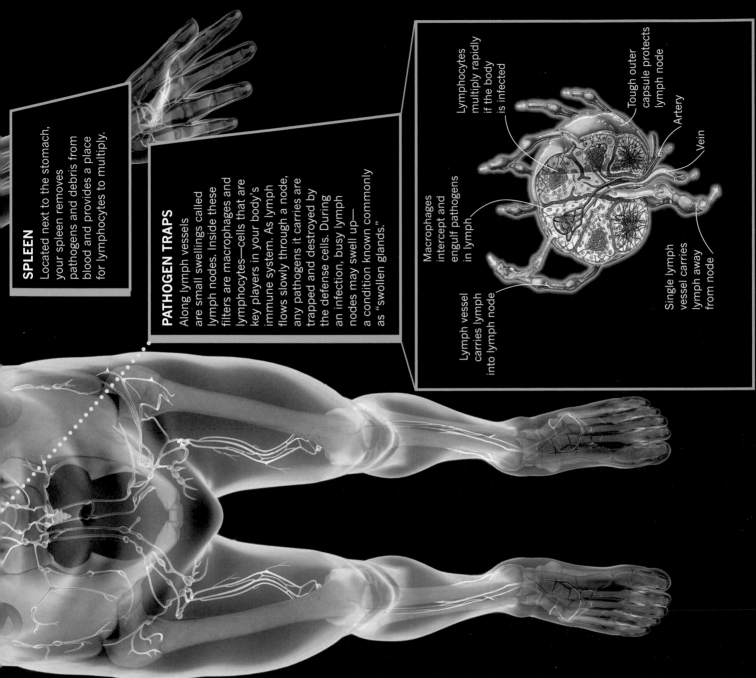

SPLEEN

Located next to the stomach, your spleen removes pathogens and debris from blood and provides a place for lymphocytes to multiply.

PATHOGEN TRAPS

Along lymph vessels are small swellings called lymph nodes. Inside these filters are macrophages and lymphocytes—cells that are key players in your body's immune system. As lymph flows slowly through a node, any pathogens it carries are trapped and destroyed by the defense cells. During an infection, busy lymph nodes may swell up—a condition known commonly as "swollen glands."

Lymphocytes multiply rapidly if the body is infected

Tough outer capsule protects lymph node

Artery

Vein

Macrophages intercept and engulf pathogens in lymph

Lymph vessel carries lymph into lymph node

Single lymph vessel carries lymph away from node

Large vein receives fluid from lymphatic duct

LUNG

FLUID RETURN

Lymph vessels (green) eventually drain into one or other of the two large lymphatic ducts in your chest, or thorax. Like an opened tap, these ducts pour their lymph into two large veins, returning the excess fluid left behind in the tissues to its rightful home in the blood.

PEYER'S PATCHES

These clusters of lymph tissue in your small intestine destroy harmful bacteria that could cause infections.

BLOOD SOLDIERS

Meet the white blood cells—a band of brave and noble warriors with one single objective: to identify and attack enemy pathogens. Be they bacteria, parasites, or viruses, pathogen invaders that successfully breach the body's outer defenses are soon tracked down and destroyed. White blood cells—we salute you!

SERGEANT NEUTROPHIL

My army of neutrophils is always on red alert. As soon as we are alerted to an inflammation or infection, we zoom on down to the battle zone to round up the enemy. We are loaded with enzymes (proteins that cause chemical reactions) to destroy enemy bacteria invaders.

SELECT YOUR SOLDIER

CLEAN-UP SQUAD	LOGISTIC CORPS	ARMORED DIVISION	GUZZLER GROUP	SPECIAL OPERATIONS
SERGEANT NEUTROPHIL	CAPTAIN BASOPHIL	MAJOR EOSINOPHIL	COLONEL MACROPHAGE	GENERAL LYMPHOCYTE

Once we have fixed on an infected target, we release cytotoxic (cell-killing) granules to destroy the infected cells. We don't always shoot to kill; sometimes we fire Y-shaped protein molecules called antibodies, which lock onto enemy antigens and disable them.

KNOW YOUR ENEMY

BACTERIA
These one-celled organisms can cause disease. A rapid response is required to reach a border breach in time to prevent mass invasion.

PARASITES
These pesky organisms will make the body their home given half a chance. They must be stopped at all costs.

VIRUSES
Left unchecked, viruses can unleash deadly germ warfare on the body, infecting cells and causing all sorts of nasty diseases.

MAJOR EOSINOPHIL
As well as patroling the bloodstream, my army is also stationed in the gut lining. Our primary purpose is to protect the body from pesky parasites.

COLONEL MACROPHAGE
We may be large, but we macrophages can get all around the body, even leaving blood vessels to enter body tissues. Our speciality is ingesting large foreign particles and debris. BURP! Pardon me—those dead cells I consumed earlier keep repeating on me.

CAPTAIN BASOPHIL
Our main role is supporting the efforts of the other white blood cells. If a toxin enters the body, we release a chemical called histamine. This makes the blood vessels wider and leakier, allowing an increased flow of blood and more neutrophils to reach the enemy target—vital in the war on pathogens.

SAILING THROUGH LIFE

In 1628, William Harvey showed that a river of blood runs around the body through arteries and veins, pumped by the heart. His findings launched a wave of speculation. Was it possible to treat someone who had lost blood by giving them someone else's blood? Could a transfusion (or transfer) of blood from a healthy person heal a sick person? Listen to the incredible tales of those who pushed the boat out, allowing us to find out how blood can help and heal.

1

FIRST TRANSFUSION

Ahoy, matey! Arthur Coga's the name. In 1667, I volunteered for a medical experiment. This English doctor Richard Lower put some sheep blood into me. Baaaaad idea? Who knows? I'm a bit fuzzy about why he did it. Anyway, I survived, but I now feel a little sheepish about the whole incident.

2

FIRST HUMAN TRANSFUSION

My wife here lost a great deal of blood while giving birth in 1818. I begged Dr. Blundell to bail her out. He drew some of my blood and gave it to her, and it worked—the first human blood transfusion! Blundell then went on to invent tools to help other doctors do transfusions. These made him rich. His ship certainly came in!

Glass funnel
Syringe

James Blundell's transfusion instruments

3

Red blood cell

A

A antigen

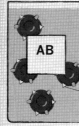

B

Anti-A antibody rejects "foreign" blood with A antigens, binding to the A antigen and marking the cell for destruction

AB

B antigen
A antigen

Anti-B antibody

O-type red blood cell has no antigens for antibodies to attack

Anti-A antibody

O

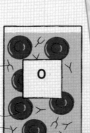

BLOOD TYPES

I'd be sunk without Dr. Reuben Ottenberg. In 1901, Austrian biologist Dr. Karl Landsteiner was trying to figure out why so many transfusions failed. He noticed that red blood cells from some people had a substance called an antigen attached, and others didn't. Based on this, he divided blood into four types: A, B, AB, and O. In 1907, I needed blood, and Doc Ottenberg figured out that my friend here and I were in the same boat, blood-type wise that is. The transfusion went swimmingly.

RHESUS FACTOR

It's me, Karl Landsteiner—yes, the one and only. I've been very patient, but it is time for a doctor to do some talking. In 1937, I was working in the lab with this little fellow, a rhesus monkey. I injected some of his red blood cells into a rabbit, and the rabbit's allergic reaction led me to discover an antigen I named the Rhesus factor. Some people have it—they're Rh-positive. Others don't—they're Rh-negative. A blood transfusion between the dos and don'ts simply will not do.

6

5

4

Group O recipient

Group B recipient

Group B recipient

Group AB recipient

STORING BLOOD

You might notice I'm all by myself here. No, my donor didn't miss the boat. In 1915, American physician Richard Lewisohn showed that adding sodium citrate to blood stops it from clotting. This meant blood could be stored, and people could donate it without ever encountering the recipient. That certainly floats my boat.

THE POWER OF "O"

Ottenberg's work made a splash. People understood how important it was to cross match donors and recipients, as a mismatch could cause death. For example, if a patient's blood had antibodies against antigens in the donor's blood, the antibodies could attack those blood cells, well and truly rocking the boat. In 1912, my doctor, Roger Lee, showed that it was safe to give blood type O to anyone, of any blood type, because its red blood cells don't have any antigens for the antibodies to attack. Oh yes.

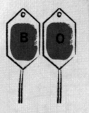

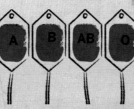

Slice of life

The body tackles any damage to its tissues quickly and efficiently to minimize the chances for nasty pathogens to invade it. As soon as a part of the body is damaged, local tissue cells spring into action, releasing the chemical histamine. This causes blood vessels near the wound to widen, bringing an influx of clotting and healing ingredients to the damaged site.

CLOTTING INGREDIENTS

Just as sticky strawberry jam can fill and hold together the layers of a cake, so platelets in blood plasma fill and hold together the damaged tissue in a wound. Circulating the body in blood, these tiny oval cell fragments play a key role in clotting by transforming into swollen, spiky, sticky versions of themselves that group together to plug a wound.

Menu

CAKE 1: INJURY

When an injury causes a cut in the skin and blood vessel just below its surface, white blood cells spring immediately into action to hunt down any pathogen invaders. At the same time, platelets in the blood oozing out of the cut start to become sticky and clump together.

CAKE 2: PLUGGING THE WOUND

The sticky platelets and damaged tissue release chemicals that turn the soluble blood protein, fibrinogen, into insoluble fibrin and attract more platelets to the wound site. These form a plug that stops more blood from leaking out of the wound and prevents more pathogens from entering the body—no unwanted ingredients in this mixture!

CAKE 3: CLOTTING

The fibrin strands make the watery blood jellylike as they mesh together to form a net that traps red blood cells into a clot. This reinforces the platelet plug and tightens eventually to gradually pull the edges of the cut together.

CAKE 4: SCAB FORMATION

Finally, the clot near the skin's surface dries to form a protective scab—the frosting on the cake—while underneath, the clot shrinks as the damaged blood vessel and tissue cells divide to produce new cells to repair the damage. Eventually, when healing is complete, the scab falls off, revealing the new skin underneath. Piece of cake.

Cake 2

Cake 1

sticky platelet

fibrin strands

cut in skin

scab

skin cells

Cake 4

Cake 3

platelet

red blood cell

blood vessel

blood plasma

net of
fibrin threads

A heartfelt gift

There is no more precious gift to give than your heart. Anyone who plans to donate their heart and other organs in the event of their death can carry a donor card or sign up to an online registry. This selfless act can literally be a lifesaving one.

HEART-TO-HEART

Fifty years ago, most people would not have believed it possible for surgeons to replace a diseased heart with a healthy one from another person. And yet today, thousands of people undergo heart-transplant surgery every year. Although the risks are high, more than one half of them live for ten years or more after receiving their new hearts.

The first heart transplant

It was once the unbelievable stuff of science fiction, but on December 3, 1967, pioneering South African heart surgeon Christiaan Barnard made heart transplantation a science fact. At Groote Schuur Hospital in Cape Town, he transplanted the heart of a car accident victim into 59-year-old Louis Washkansky, who had incurable heart disease. Washkansky survived the surgery but, sadly, died 19 days later from pneumonia.

Four steps to a new heart

It is a race against the clock getting the donor heart into the recipient patient. The donor heart must be implanted within five or six hours of the donor being declared brain dead. The patient receiving the heart is attached to a heart/lung bypass machine, which allows blood to circulate around the body during the lengthy surgical procedure, and is given medication to prevent him or her from rejecting the new heart.

STAGE 1

The surgeon exposes the recipient patient's chest cavity through a cut in the rib cage. The heart is stopped, and the surgeon carefully removes it, leaving only the back part of the patient's left atrium (the left upper chamber of the heart) in place.

Diseased heart removed

STAGE 2

The donor heart is taken out of the special cold fluid in which it has been kept and is trimmed, ready for insertion. The first step is to sew the left atrium of the donor heart to the patient's old atrium.

Blood vessels tied to stop blood flow

Patient's old atrium

Left atrium of donor heart

STAGE 3

Working as quickly as possible over several hours, the surgical team sutures (stitches) the blood vessels in place. The final blood vessel to be attached is the aorta, which carries blood from the heart to the rest of the body.

Aorta

Blood vessels are sutured into place

STAGE 4

The new heart starts beating as blood circulation and oxygen are restored. Once the blood is flowing normally, the heart-lung machine is disconnected and the chest incision is closed. The patient is taken to the recovery room and, after 10–14 days, is ready to leave the hospital.

MAKING A SPLASH

Where would we be without water? More than one half of your body is made up of the stuff. Inside cells, the chemical reactions that keep you alive take place in water. Watery blood carries materials around your body. And all tissues, even bones and fat, contain water. Mechanisms in your body maintain its water balance so that, day by day, the water you take in equals the amount of water you lose.

WATER OUT

URINE 60%

Several times a day, you make a trip to the bathroom to release the urine made by your kidneys. Urine is almost completely made up of water, with a dash of dissolved wastes, and contributes the most to your body's water-loss.

WATER MAKES UP 90–95% OF BLOOD AND TISSUE FLUID

25% OF BONE TISSUE IS WATER

HEALTHY MALE 60% WATER
If he's in good shape, he's water-rich — plenty of water and skeletal muscle and relatively high... relatively high... water content.

WATER IN

WATER INSIDE THE BODY

How much water your body contains depends on your sex, age, and weight. Also, different body tissues contain different amounts of water. Blood plasma, for example, contains a lot of water, while fat has relatively little.

70–80% OF ORDINARY TISSUE IS MADE UP OF WATER

SKELETAL MUSCLE CONSISTS OF 65–70% WATER

DRINKS 60%

Most water taken into your body comes from drinks. Whether it's fruit juice, tea, a smoothie, milk, or soda, all drinks consist mostly of water. Except water, of course, which is 100 percent water! To maintain your bodily water balance, you need to drink around 0.4 gallons (1.5 liters) of water every day.

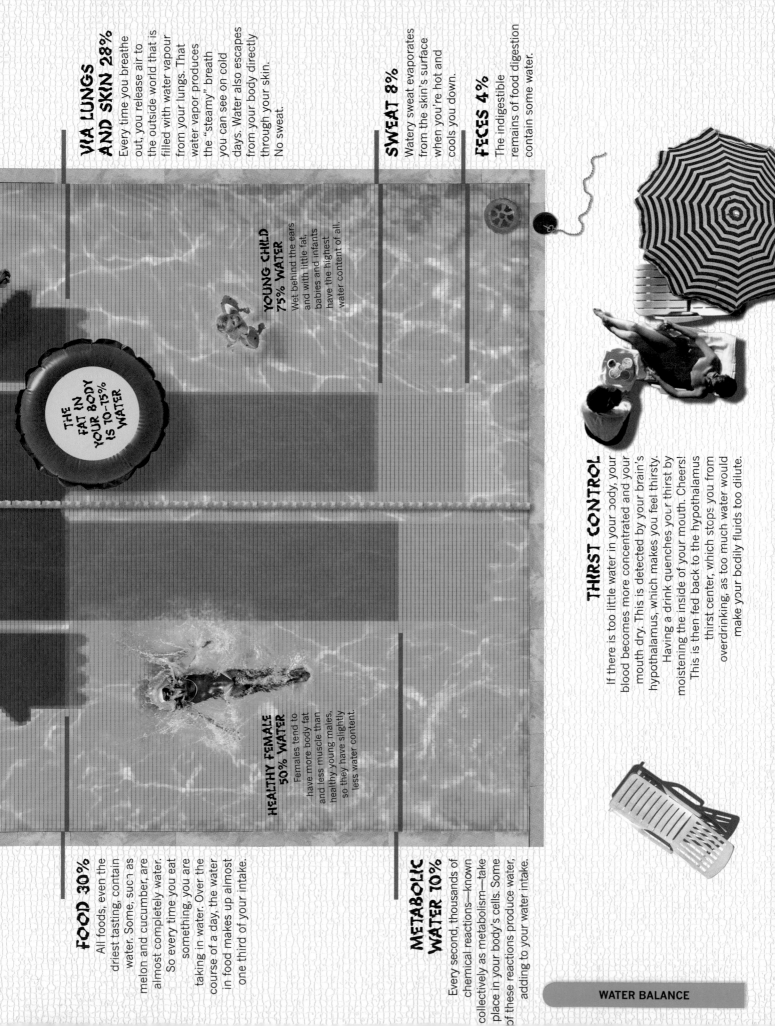

VIA LUNGS AND SKIN 28%

Every time you breathe out, you release air to the outside world that is filled with water vapour from your lungs. That water vapor produces the "steamy" breath you can see on cold days. Water also escapes from your body directly through your skin. No sweat.

SWEAT 8%

Watery sweat evaporates from the skin's surface when you're hot and cools you down.

FECES 4%

The indigestible remains of food digestion contain some water.

YOUNG CHILD 75% WATER

Wet behind the ears and with little fat, babies and infants have the highest water content of all.

THE FAT IN YOUR BODY IS 10–15% WATER

HEALTHY FEMALE 50% WATER

Females tend to have more body fat and less muscle than healthy young males, so they have slightly less water content.

FOOD 30%

All foods, even the driest tasting, contain water. Some, such as melon and cucumber, are almost completely water. So every time you eat something, you are taking in water. Over the course of a day, the water in food makes up almost one third of your intake.

METABOLIC WATER 10%

Every second, thousands of chemical reactions—known collectively as metabolism—take place in your body's cells. Some of these reactions produce water, adding to your water intake.

THIRST CONTROL

If there is too little water in your body, your blood becomes more concentrated and your mouth dry. This is detected by your brain's hypothalamus, which makes you feel thirsty. Having a drink quenches your thirst by moistening the inside of your mouth. Cheers! This is then fed back to the hypothalamus thirst center, which stops you from overdrinking, as too much water would make your bodily fluids too dilute.

SPECIAL BREW

Today's special blend is a liquid mix of excess water and salts and potentially harmful wastes removed from the blood—a concoction we call urine. We make up to 0.4 gallons (1.5 liters) a day, enough to fill half a dozen coffee cups. It's always fresh—as soon as you empty the pot through urination, we're already filtering down some more. But what's really special about this is that it's brewing right inside of you.

HOW TO OPERATE URINARY SYSTEM

urine-o-matic 5000

Unit contains a pair of coffee-bean-shaped kidneys, two tubes called ureters, the baglike bladder, and the urethra exit point. Assemble as shown and ensure a steady flow of blood (from which waste will be removed) through the kidneys. Unit functions automatically. We(e) guarantee it.

KIDNEY FILTERS

The kidneys (most people have a pair, but you can live with one) filter out unwanted byproducts from our blood.
They also remove excess water to ensure that we have just the right amount in order to function. Every minute of the day, about 1 quart (1 liter) of blood passes through the kidneys to be filtered and cleaned. It takes less than one hour to clean our entire blood supply.

Ureter

Renal vein

THE BLADDER

A stretchy muscular bag in the lower abdomen, the bladder receives a constant trickle of urine from the

THE NEPHRONS

Blood gushes through the renal artery to enter the kidney. The artery branches into smaller vessels that wrap around the nephrons. These filtering units—one million of them in each kidney—are where salts and wastes are removed.

Tubule receives liquid from the glomerulus and separates out waste matter for the urine

A cluster of tiny branching blood vessels, collectively called a glomerulus, filter out liquid from the blood

Renal vein returns anything "good" that can be recycled, along with the filtered blood, to the rest of the body

COLOR AND AROMA

Since urine is mostly water, it doesn't usually smell much. But its odor may be stronger if you are dehydrated, causing other ingredients to become more concentrated. Some foods like asparagus can affect the smell, while others, such as beets, affect its color. Urine usually has a yellow tint owing to a chemical left over in the bloodstream from worn-out blood cells, which is then extracted by the kidneys. It's the same chemical that makes bruises yellow.

TESTING URINE

Your doctor might request a sample cup of your urine blend to help diagnose certain disorders. In earlier times, doctors would perform a taste test—sweet-tasting urine, for example, indicates diabetes. Today, doctors prefer to dip a strip of special paper into the urine. If something is in there that shouldn't be, the stick changes color.

Bladder full

Bladder empty

URINE DELIVERY

The sphincter muscle keeps the bladder shut tight (thankfully) until a person is ready to go. Then the muscle relaxes, and the urine exits the body through the urethra. Muscles in the bladder walls contract to help push urine out of the body. Your special blend, hours in the making, is finally dispensed.

URINE MAKEUP

95% water –
urea and uric acid –
(nitrogen-containing wastes)
creatinine –
salts, including sodium, –
potassium, phosphate, and
sulfate ions
calcium –
magnesium –
bicarbonate ions –

wall signal to the brain to suggest a bathroom break, ASAPee!

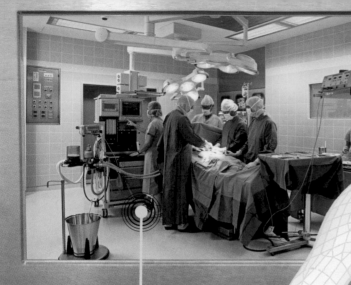

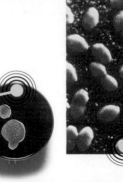

204–205 MIRACLE MOLD
How penicillin was discovered accidentally

212–213 NURSING
The story of how nursing developed into the modern profession

214–215 UNDER THE KNIFE
Contrasting surgery in the 1700s with modern operations

184–185 PATHOGEN PARADE
A lineup of the main disease-causing organisms

190–191 ENEMY WITHIN
What cancers are, how they develop, and how they can be treated

218–219 MEDICAL TIMELINE
From Hammurabi to the Human Genome Project

202–203 PANDEMIC
The horrors of the global 1918–1919 influenza epidemic

186–187 SPREADING DISEASE
Why European diseases killed many in the New World

188–189 MALARIA
The vicious cycle of a global killer

206–207 FIRST AID
How basic emergency care can save lives

198–199 HIV
How HIV infects cells and how it can be treated

196–197 VACCINATE AND PROTECT
The risky, pioneering experiment to prove that vaccinations work

When the body is injured or invaded by pathogens, built-in defenses kick in, but sometimes medical help is needed.

192–193 HUMAN ZOO
Creatures that set up home—or dine— on humans

194–195 ANCIENT REMEDIES
Unusual treatments from the past

208–209 ALTERNATIVE THERAPIES
Herbalism and other alternatives to Western medicine

210–211 MAKING A DIAGNOSIS
How a doctor uses signs, symptoms, and tests for diagnosis

216–217 THROUGH THE KEYHOLE
How endoscopes and video pills are used to see inside the body

200–201 DISEASE DETECTIVES
The research that proved that polluted water was the cause of a deadly cholera epidemic

MALFUNCTIONS AND MEDICINE

PATHOGEN PARADE

Hey, kid. Have a look-see at this bunch of mugs. The usual suspects . . . viruses, bacteria, protists, fungi . . . It's enough to make you sick, isn't it? These tough guys run in a gang called the pathogens. (That's germs to you and me.) Pathogens specialize in breaking and entering the human body, causing disease. Your body can defend itself and rub some of these bad guys out. Medicine can also stop these clowns in their tracks. But the especially unpleasant characters can do some serious damage.

Hey, buddy, invite me in already! I promise I won't stay long.

VIRUSES

These chemical packages are real home wreckers. They spread through human contact, invite themselves in, and take over a host cell, where they grow and reproduce. And whaddya think these unwanted guests bring? Measles, mumps, chickenpox, flu, and HIV, that's what. It's an outrage.

BACTERIA

Don't let the fact that these microorganisms consist of a single cell fool you into thinking that they can't do you much harm. Get this: some bacteria can cause tuberculosis, food poisoning, typhoid fever, tetanus, and pneumonia. Of course, they don't all deserve a bum rap. Most bacteria in your body are harmless, and some are even helpful. But those pathogenic types, releasing toxins into the body to mess with cell functions, are nasty.

Most Wanted

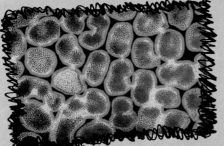

INFLUENZA

Lemme tell you, I get the chills just looking at this influenza-causing virus. Flu viruses bring fevers, headaches, sore throats, muscle pain (and sometimes death) to millions every year.

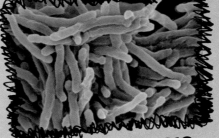

TUBERCULOSIS

This here's the brutal bacteria behind the potentially deadly disease TB. When an infected person sneezes or spits, the bacteria whooshes through the air. If you breathe it in, the disease may attack your lungs. Not good.

MALARIA

Talk about a tropical terror: this parasite spreads deadly flulike malaria when an infected female mosquito gives you a bite. (It's always the dames you've got to watch out for.)

> Who are you calling creepy? Ask anyone. I'm a real fun guy.

PROTISTS

These are the misfits of the pathogen group. The protists are a large bunch of single-celled organisms that tend to hang around water or damp places. A few of these characters are parasites (that means they sponge off a host) that can cause you some serious harm. We're talking diseases like malaria, sleeping sickness, and diarrhea.

FUNGI

These creepy cousins of mushrooms and mold can cause a lot of trouble. The diseases they cause—ringworm, athlete's foot, jock itch, and thrush—are rarely fatal, but they aren't pretty either. A fungal infection can last a lifetime and can really irritate an infected individual.

PATHOGENS

Spreading disease

Listen to my story and you will learn how infectious diseases spread from person to person and why it was that the coming of Europeans to North America brought great misery and distress to our people.

Long, long ago, in the age of ice, our ancestors crossed into North America from Asia. Later the seas rose, and they were cut off from other humans. Left on their own, they had space to roam freely.

Meanwhile, in other parts of the world, people gave up living as hunters and gatherers and became farmers. They domesticated animals such as sheep and cattle and grew crops in fields next to their villages, where they lived close to their animals and other people.

This way of life created ideal conditions for diseases to spread and multiply. Humans picked up diseases from their cattle, pigs, and chickens. Sick people passed on germs to their neighbors every time they coughed or sneezed.

Over time, humans developed immunities that made them more resistant to infection. People still got sick, but they were better at fighting the organisms that spread the diseases, and not all of them died. It was very different for our people when the first Europeans arrived here.

Our people had never come into contact with white people's diseases before, so they had no natural defenses against them. Measles, smallpox, even the common cold spread rapidly among us, killing thousands.

Now I must tell you about an incident that happened back in 1763, when a number of our people joined an uprising led by a warrior named Pontiac.

They attacked a fort where some white people were lying sick in the hospital with smallpox.

The British commander, General Henry Amherst, hated our people. He sent a letter to the officer defending the fort, Colonel Jeffrey Bouquet. "Could it not be contrived to send smallpox among these tribes," he wrote. Bouquet came up with a plan to infect them with blankets taken from the smallpox hospital.

Bouquet arranged for two blankets to be given to a group of warriors who had come to the fort to talk peace terms. Soon afterward people in the surrounding villages began to get sick and die.

Whether the story is true or not, I cannot say, but it is known for a fact that smallpox killed many, many Native Americans at the time of Pontiac's Rebellion. Many of our people perished from the European diseases they had no immunity to.

MALARIA

IT'S NAME COMES FROM THE ITALIAN "MALA ARIA", MEANING "BAD AIR"—A REFERENCE TO THE UNWHOLESOME AIR AND STAGNANT WATER THOUGHT FOR CENTURIES TO CAUSE THE DEADLY DISEASE THAT RAVAGES TROPICAL REGIONS. WE NOW KNOW THAT MALARIA IS SPREAD BY MOSQUITOES. THIS IS ITS CYCLE OF DESTRUCTION . . .

REGIONS AFFECTED BY MALARIA

TOGO

IT IS THE MIDDLE OF THE NIGHT IN A VILLAGE IN TOGO, A COUNTRY IN WEST AFRICA, AND 13-YEAR-OLD KODJO IS FAST ASLEEP IN A HOME HE SHARES WITH HIS MOTHER, FATHER, BABY SISTER . . . OH, AND A BLOOD-SUCKING KILLER.

BUZZING AROUND THE ROOM IS A FEMALE ANOPHELES MOSQUITO. THE AIRBORNE PEST IS HUNGRY AND IS LOOKING FOR SOME TASTY HUMAN BLOOD TO FEAST ON.

THE MOSQUITO LANDS ON KODJO'S ARM AND BITES DOWN, SUCKING UP KODJO'S BLOOD.

HOW ANNOYING! I'VE BEEN BITTEN DURING THE NIGHT. IT IS A BIT RED AND ITCHY, BUT I'M SURE IT WILL GO AWAY AFTER A FEW DAYS. NOTHING TO WORRY ABOUT!

BUT THIS MOSQUITO HAD PREVIOUSLY FED ON A PERSON WITH BLOOD CONTAINING MALARIA PARASITES. THESE MIXED WITH THE MOSQUITO'S SALIVA AND WERE INJECTED INTO KODJO WHEN HE WAS BITTEN.

KODJO IS COMPLETELY UNWARE THAT HIS LIFE IS IN DANGER. HE DOESN'T FEEL SICK SO HE CARRIES ON WITH HIS NORMAL DAILY ROUTINE. HE STUDIES HARD AT SCHOOL, PLAYS WITH HIS FRIENDS, AND MAKES SURE HE DOES ALL HIS CHORES AT HOME SO THAT HE DOESN'T GET IN TROUBLE WITH HIS MOTHER.

ALL THE WHILE, THE MALARIA PARASITES ARE TRAVELING THROUGH KODJO'S BLOOD SYSTEM.

WHEN THEY REACH KODJO'S LIVER, THE PARASITES GROW AND DIVIDE.

SEVERAL DAYS LATER, THE PARASITES EXIT THE LIVER, ENTER THE BLOODSTREAM, AND INVADE RED BLOOD CELLS. HERE THEY MULTIPLY AND THEN BURST OUT.

KODJO STARTS TO FEEL VERY SICKS. HE GETS A FEVER, HEADACHE, AND THE CHILLS.

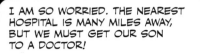

I AM SO WORRIED. THE NEAREST HOSPITAL IS MANY MILES AWAY, BUT WE MUST GET OUR SON TO A DOCTOR!

THE DOCTOR REALIZES IMMEDIATELY THAT KODJO HAS MALARIA—THE HOSPITAL GETS MANY CASES EVERY DAY. TOO MANY.

MANY PEOPLE ARE NOT AS FORTUNATE AS KODJO. MALARIA CLAIMS TWO MILLION LIVES WORLDWIDE EVERY YEAR.

KODJO, WE ARE GIVING YOU INTRAVENOUS QUININE SULFATE— A MEDICINE THAT KILLS THE MALARIA PARASITE.

KODJO IS LUCKY. HE WILL LIVE. HIS FAMILY GETS NETS TREATED WITH MALARIA REPELLENT TO SLEEP UNDER SO THAT NO INFECTED MOSQUITOES WILL GET NEAR THEM AGAIN.

WHILE KODJO WAS SICK, HE WAS BITTEN BY ANOTHER MOSQUITO. THE MOSQUITO INGESTED A MALARIA PARASITE FROM KODJO'S BLOOD . . .

. . . THE PARASITE DEVELOPED AND REPRODUCED IN THE MOSQUITO'S GUT AND SPREAD TO ITS SALIVARY GLAND, READY FOR THE NEXT VICTIM . . .

MALARIA

ENEMY WITHIN

Cancers are diseases that attack the body from within. There are many different types, but all start in the same way. Over a period of time, the genes that control cell division mutate (change), either under the influence of carcinogens (cancer-causing agents) such as tobacco smoke or because faulty genes were inherited from a parent. Uncontrolled cell division produces a cancerous growth, or tumor, that exploits the body's resources and, left untreated, spreads elsewhere in the body.

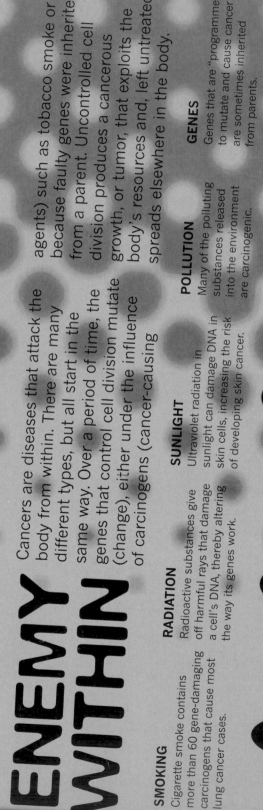

SMOKING
Cigarette smoke contains more than 60 gene-damaging carcinogens that cause most lung cancer cases.

RADIATION
Radioactive substances give off harmful rays that damage a cell's DNA, thereby altering the way its genes work.

SUNLIGHT
Ultraviolet radiation in sunlight can damage DNA in skin cells, increasing the risk of developing skin cancer.

POLLUTION
Many of the polluting substances released into the environment are carcinogenic.

GENES
Genes that are "programmed" to mutate and cause cancer are sometimes inherited from parents.

HOW CANCER DEVELOPS

ONE
Body cells normally divide and replace themselves in a controlled way, just as these epithelial cells have done to maintain a layer that covers the inside or outside of an organ.

Normal epithelial cells

Basement membrane separates epithelium from underlying tissue

Blood vessels carry blood through tissues

Lymph vessel drains excess fluid from tissues

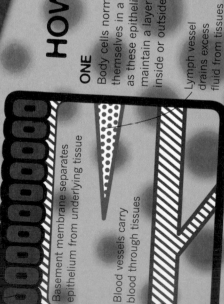

TWO
An abnormal cell with mutated genes appears in the epithelial layer. Normally, such cells are identified and destroyed by the immune system. But, undetected, this one starts to divide.

Abnormal cells in epithelial layer

Cancerous tumor breaks through into underlying layer

FOUR

The mass of cancerous cells forms a primary tumor that expands into neighboring tissues and "hijacks" blood vessels in order to supply it with the food and oxygen it needs for further growth.

Rapidly dividing abnormal cells change shape of epithelial layer

THREE

Out of control, the abnormal cancerous cells divide rapidly and protrude upward from the organ's surface. They are bigger than the normal epithelial cells, which they push to one side, and have larger nuclei.

Original primary cancer is where abnormal cells first appeared

Cancerous cells have invaded neighboring tissues

Lymph and blood vessels carry cancerous cells away from the primary tumor to other sites

Tumor grows its own blood supply

METASTASIS

Cancerous cells from the primary tumor spread to other parts of the body, where they establish secondary tumors, through a process called metastasis. Cancerous tumors demand vast amounts of nutrients, causing the body to waste away.

DIAGNOSIS AND TREATMENT

Diagnosis
The sooner a diagnosis is made, identifying the type and location of the cancer, the better.

Screening
Routine screening procedures—such as mammograms (breast x-rays)—help detect cancers early.

Biopsy
A biopsy is performed to remove a sample of tissue to see if it contains cancerous cells.

Imaging
Techniques such as CAT and MRI scanning identify the size and position of tumors.

Staging
Doctors determine whether and how much the cancer has spread, how it should be treated, and the chances of survival.

Surgery
Many cancers are treated surgically. A surgeon operates on a patient to remove the tumor or tumors.

Radiotherapy and chemotherapy
Radiation (radiotherapy) and anticancer drugs (chemotherapy) are often used to destroy any cancer cells remaining after surgery or to slow the growth of tumors.

Lifestyle
Certain factors, including smoking, obesity, poor diet, and lack of exercise, increase the risks of developing cancer. Lifestyle improvements, such as taking exercise and eating a healthy diet, can reduce that risk.

Scan shows cancers in prostate gland and bones

Human Zoo

Ladies and gentlemen! Assembled here for your irritation and plight is an incredible collection of critters that call the human body home (or dinner).

Ascaris roundworm
Especially prevalent in tropical regions, these worms can grow up to 12 in (30 cm) long. The gutsy parasites anchor themselves to the walls of human intestines.

Bedbugs
They may be only 0.1 in (4 mm) long, but these nocturnal insects have a nasty nip. They like the warmth of a cozy bed and will dine on your blood while you sleep.

Head louse
The size of a sesame seed, a head louse uses its claws to cling to a human hair, and it feeds on blood from the scalp. These itchy pests often pass from one head to another.

Dust mite
Millions of microscopic dust mites feed on the dead skin flakes that fall from your body. It may sound like a handy cleaning service, but their droppings can trigger asthma attacks.

Tick
Don't get too close! This bloodsucker will attach itself to you given half a chance. It will bite your skin and gorge on your blood until full.

Guinea worm
The larvae of this parasite lurk inside microscopic plankton in dirty drinking water. Once inside a human, they grow up to 3 ft (1 m) and then try to exit through the skin.

Harvest mite chigger
The larvae of this microscopic mite like to dine on human skin. Instead of biting, they use digestive fluid to break down skin cells and then suck up the contents.

Scabies mite
This mite is especially irritating. The female uses her piercing mouth to tunnel under the skin and then lays her eggs in the newly dug burrow—causing a lot of itchiness for the host!

Sand flea chigger
As its name suggests, this chigger thinks life's a beach. It hides in the sand, ready to pounce and burrow into exposed skin, where it will lay its eggs.

Tapeworm
Tapeworms have set up homes in the digestive tracts of some 50 million people worldwide. The symptoms they cause are often misdiagnosed—until parts of the worm crop up in your feces!

Eyelash mite
It may be too small to see with the naked eye, but this midget mite is no doubt hanging out in your eyelash hair follicles right now, feeding on the dead skin cells.

Flea
To reach a tasty piece of skin to bloodsuck, the flea will launch into an impressive 12-in (30-cm) leap. Sounds easy? It's the same as you jumping over a 60-story building!

ANCIENT REMEDIES

This catalog brings you a range of cures and treatments from all around the world and all ages of the past. Some are based on traditional old wives' remedies, while others come backed by the top medical opinions of the ancient Egyptians, Greeks, and Romans. Considered good science at the time, many of them now seem weird and wacky; others, like trepanning and cupping, are still occasionally used today. Browse its pages and see what you think.

HEAD PAINS?
EVIL SPIRITS?
BLOOD CLOTS?
TREPANNING
IS AHEAD OF THE COMPETITION . . .

Ever thought that drilling a hole in your skull could stop your headaches? We can assure you that it's completely safe (it has been practiced since prehistoric times). We use a boring tool to make a small round hole in the top of your head so that whatever or whoever's causing your convulsions or migraines can escape . . . And afterward the round disk of bone we remove is yours to keep as a lucky charm. Guaranteed satisfaction—some clients even come back for more!

PLAGUE POMANDERS

Does the stench of plague-ridden bodies in the streets put you off from going shopping? You need one of our special medieval pomanders. Shaped like an orange, you fill each segment with sweet-smelling herbs and spices, and it purifies the air of deadly vapors. To keep death at bay, make sure you don't leave home without it. Available in gold or silver, or choose our book-shaped model.

HURRY WHILE STOCKS LAST!

A SPOT OF BALDNESS?

HEDGEHOG AMULETS

Guard against unwanted hair loss by carrying one of our ancient Egyptian hedgehog amulets. A concealed cavity in the base contains extract of hedgehog spine, which will hopefully return your bristles to full growth. And that's not all! Hedgehogs are known to attack and kill snakes, so this lucky hedgehog amulet also protects the wearer against snakebites.

ANIMAL OINTMENTS

If all else fails, we recommend rubbing an ancient Egyptian ointment of ibex fat into your scalp just before you go to bed. Customers tell us that their hair grows after a single application. It's the latest in our range of ointments, which includes fat of lion, hippo, crocodile, cat, and snake.

IBEX
OINTMENT

BLOODLETTING

Are your humors out of balance? Feeling liverish, melancholic, or in a fever? In the words of Claudius Galen, the great Greek doctor, "There's nothing a nice bit of bloodletting won't cure." Our steel lancets, razors, and scrapers are made to the very highest standards—one nick in the arm and all the bad blood flows out. As practiced by barbers pretty much everywhere.

DELUXE TRAVEL SET

HERBAL REMEDIES

No home is complete without a mortar and pestle for pounding your own syrups, balms, and elixirs from throughout history. Ours is the best available.

We also supply camphor, myrrh, ginger, cloves, and other spices for making medicines. Write today for our complete book of herbal recipes.

BLACK EYE

FAT LIP

MEAT! IS THE ANSWER

Been in a fight? Got a real shiner? Try putting a piece of raw steak on it. People have done this since ancient Egyptian times. We don't know why it works—could be that the coldness helps to reduce the swelling or that the meat looks like the injury (sympathetic healing). But we won't blame you if you decide to eat the steak instead!

CURE ALL WITH MIRACLE CUPPING

Not everyone's cup of tea, this ancient healing technique is at least 3,000 years old. Simply heat a small glass vessel and place it on the skin. As it cools, the skin is sucked up inside, drawing poisonous substances from the body. Use for muscle stiffness, back pain, and chesty coughs. It's a treatment that really leaves its mark (round red ones, to be precise).

VACCINATE AND PROTECT

The most effective way of protecting against infectious disease is by vaccination—this is when a very small amount of infective agent that has been rendered harmless (called a vaccine) is introduced into the body, either by injection or through the mouth. As a result, the immune system starts producing antibodies against the disease, giving the body immunity (resistance) to it. The word *vaccine* comes from *vacca*, Latin for "cow." The story of how the first-ever vaccination eventually eradicated smallpox begins with a country doctor, milkmaids, and cows.

1

◄ DEADLY DISEASE

Smallpox was a deadly scourge in 18th-century Europe, killing up to 400,000 people a year. Victims were covered with pus-filled blisters on the face and body, which left survivors with terrible scars. Not everyone was so lucky—almost 60 per cent of those who got the disease died. Famous smallpox deaths included Queen Mary II of England and King Louis XV of France.

3

KILL OR CURE? ►

2

One way of preventing smallpox (called variolation) was to take pus from someone with a mild form of the disease and scratch it into someone else's skin. The hope was that it would make them slightly sick, but they would be safe from getting smallpox in the future. It was very hit and miss— often people died.

MOO-VING RESULTS ▶

Jenner had found a safer way than variolation to protect against smallpox. He called it vaccination. The public was scornful at first, and cartoons appeared in the press showing people with cows growing out of their bodies after being vaccinated. But Jenner gradually won support for his ideas.

5

4

◀ TEST CASE

In 1796, Jenner took some pus from the blisters of a milkmaid infected with cowpox and rubbed it into the arm of a young boy, James Phipps. Later, when Jenner rubbed smallpox material into James's arm, the boy did not become sick. As Jenner thought, the cowpox antibodies also worked against smallpox.

VACCINE RESEARCH ▶

19th-century French scientist Louis Pasteur continued Jenner's work. He developed vaccines against anthrax and rabies, using artificially weakened forms of the pathogens that cause the diseases. Vaccines are now successfully used to control infectious diseases ranging from the flu and measles to polio and cholera.

6

▲ SPOTTY MILKMAIDS

The cattle disease of cowpox belongs to the same family as smallpox but is much milder. It sometimes passed from cows to milkmaids, who got the blisters on their hands from milking infected animals. A doctor, Edward Jenner, noticed that milkmaids who'd had cowpox never got smallpox. It gave him an idea.

7

◀ END OF SMALLPOX

Smallpox is the only infectious disease to have been completely eradicated from the world, following a huge vaccination campaign in the 1970s. Only two specimens of the smallpox virus are known to survive, kept in top-security labs in Russia and the U.S.

HIV

and AIDS are terms that are familiar today. But that wasn't the case in the early 1980s when American doctors first reported seeing young patients dying from rare infections that shouldn't affect healthy people. All the patients had weakened immune (defense) systems that allowed opportunistic diseases to invade and destroy their bodies. In 1982, the new condition was given the name AIDs—acquired immune deficiency syndrome.

By 2008, more than 25 million people had died from AIDS, and 33 million people were living with HIV.

THE RACE WAS ON to discover its cause. The breakthrough came in 1984 at the Pasteur Institute in Paris, where scientists isolated the virus, later called HIV (human immunodeficiency virus), which causes AIDS. In the years that followed, many cases of HIV infection and deaths from AIDS were recorded around the world. By 2008, more than 25 million people had died from AIDS—with one third of the deaths in sub-Saharan Africa—and 33 million people were living with HIV. The disease spreads from person to person through sexual intercourse, blood transfusions, or from a mother to her baby.

HOW DOES HIV WORK? Like all viruses, it has to invade a living cell to reproduce, or replicate. The reason that HIV is so dangerous is that its target cell is the helper T cell, a key player in the body's immune system. HIV attaches itself to a helper T cell **[see box, right]** and injects its genetic material (RNA) into its host. There it is converted into DNA that, once inside the cell's nucleus, hijacks the cell's metabolism to produce the raw materials—proteins and RNA—to make thousands of new virus

HIV BUDDING
Colored microscopic image of budding HIV particles

particles. These are assembled in the host cell's cytoplasm and bud off from its surface **[see below]**, ready to invade other T cells. The whole process destroys helper T cells, thus weakening the immune system

CAN HIV BE CURED?

At present, no. But there are drugs available that slow the progress of the virus by targeting its replication inside the host cell. Some drugs stop RNA from being copied as DNA **[3]**. Others prevent the viral DNA from getting inside the cell's nucleus **[4]**. And yet others prevent HIV's proteins from being made properly **[5]**. To be effective, a combination of these drugs should be taken by people with HIV. Research for a cure continues.

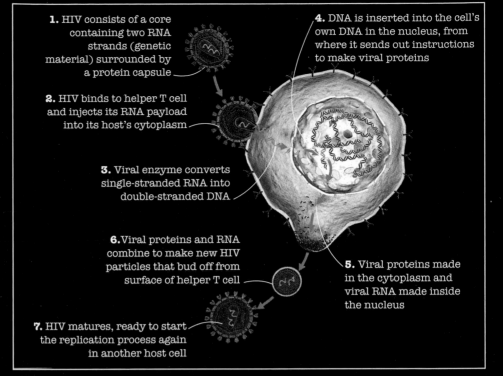

1. HIV consists of a core containing two RNA strands (genetic material) surrounded by a protein capsule

2. HIV binds to helper T cell and injects its RNA payload into its host's cytoplasm

3. Viral enzyme converts single-stranded RNA into double-stranded DNA

4. DNA is inserted into the cell's own DNA in the nucleus, from where it sends out instructions to make viral proteins

6. Viral proteins and RNA combine to make new HIV particles that bud off from surface of helper T cell

5. Viral proteins made in the cytoplasm and viral RNA made inside the nucleus

7. HIV matures, ready to start the replication process again in another host cell

HIV replication

CASE: Disease detectives

1854, SOHO

Summer 1854. Soho, in central London, England, is an area of decaying, overcrowded houses. There is no sanitation—the streets are filthy with a mix of sewage, dirty water, and animal feces. There is a heat wave, and the stench is terrible. People line up at water pumps to quench their thirst.

- Unsanitary conditions
- Hot weather
- Drinking cold water

August 31

The night of August 31. A violent outbreak of cholera sweeps through Soho. In the next three days, 127 people die in the Broad Street area alone. Most people believe that a miasma—a poisonous invisible cloud of air—is the cause of the disease.

WITNESS

Dr. John Snow, a well-known physician of the day, lives nearby on Frith Street. He has published a book disagreeing with the miasma theory and believes that contaminated water is responsible for spreading diseases like cholera. Now is his chance to investigate. He makes a map of the area, showing the location of the houses where victims of the outbreak have died, and notes that all of them get their water from the Broad Street pump.

Each red bar indicates a cholera death.

NOEL STREET

POLAND STREET

PORTLA

GREAT MARLBOROUGH STREET

POOR HOUSE

MARSHALL STREET

BROAD STREET PUM

CARNABY STREET

SILVER STREET

GOLDEN

SQUARE

A Just behind Broad Street is a poorhouse. Although cholera is raging all around, none of the inmates get sick. Snow notes that the poorhouse has its own water well.

Workers at the Broad Street brewery also escape the disease. Their employer gives them free beer to drink, and they do not use the pump.

B

Snow is sure that water from the Broad Street pump is helping spread cholera and persuades the authorities to put it out of action by removing its handle. He discovers that there is a crumbling cesspool close to the well that supplies the pump with water.

Dirty diapers infect water supply

A local priest visits a family on Broad Street. They tell him that their baby got sick just before the outbreak, and they threw the water from washing out the dirty diapers into the collapsed cesspool. It is the final clue Snow needs. He now knows how the well water became contaminated.

Today, Snow is recognized as a pioneer of modern epidemiology—the science of why, and how often, particular diseases affect different groups of people. The statistical evidence gathered by epidemiologists is used in campaigns to prevent illness and improve public health.

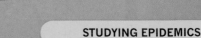
STUDYING EPIDEMICS

OUTBREAK!

Soldiers at Fort Riley in Kansas were the first to get sick, in March 1918. By April, 30 U.S. cities were infected. American troops fighting in World War I carried the deadly flu with them to Europe.

WORLDWIDE KILLER

Human carriers transmitted the virus along international rail and shipping routes. Nowhere in the world was safe. Spanish flu wiped out entire communities in Alaska, and it even spread to remote islands in the South Pacific.

Spanish flu virus

WHY SPANISH FLU?

As the flu raged through the trenches, the military authorities imposed a total news blackout. Spain was not involved in the war, so Spanish newspapers were the first to report the outbreak.

20% of world population infected by influenza = 500 million people

TAKING PRECAUTIONS

Flu vaccines were unavailable in those days. People wore gauze masks to prevent spreading the infection. They even tried eating boiled onions or rubbing themselves with kerosene, but nothing worked.

INFLUENZA PANDEMIC

KILLER DISEASE IS SPREADING—WHERE NEXT?

Fears are growing that Spanish flu, which has been raging in the U.S. for some months, is now sweeping right across the world.

Some experts forecast that the eventual death toll will climb into the millions.

There are terrible reports of citizens setting out to work in the morning and dying in the street before they reach home.

Symptoms include a blue tinge to the face and coughing up blood. Most people die from the secondary effects of pneumonia. Their lungs fill up with bloody fluid, and they literally drown.

HIGH DEATH RATE

Roughly 2.5 percent of people who caught the flu died from it, an unusually high death rate. The normal figure for flu epidemics is less than 0.1 percent.

I had a little bird.
Its name was Enza.
I opened a window
and in-flu-enza.

Skipping rhyme, 1918

HEALTHY VICTIMS

More than one half of the deaths were adults between 20 and 40 years old. The virus caused the body's immune system to overreact. People in good health with strong immune systems were especially vulnerable, while those with weak immune systems, such as young children and the very old, suffered fewer deaths.

pandemic

noun *pan-dem-ik*

A pandemic is a disease that spreads through a whole country, or around the entire world. The Spanish influenza (flu) pandemic of 1918–1919 was the most catastrophic ever known, killing at least 50 million people worldwide—more than twice the number who died in World War I. Some historians believe that the total death toll was closer to 100 million. Scientists now know that a type of avian flu virus was responsible.

GROUNDBREAKING RESEARCH

In recent years, scientists have sequenced the genome of the 1918 flu virus using DNA samples recovered from the bodies of buried victims, including the frozen corpse of a Native American woman.

AVIAN FLU

The H1N1 virus that caused Spanish flu belongs to a group of viruses that usually affect birds but sometimes jump across species to humans. The H5N1 avian (bird) flu virus, identified in 2005, belongs to the same group.

PANDEMICS

MIRACLE MOLD

"When I woke up just after dawn on September 28, 1928, I certainly didn't plan to revolutionize medicine by discovering the world's first antibiotic. But I guess that is exactly what I did."

British biologist Sir Alexander Fleming

St Mary's Hospital, London. Fleming's research lab, 1928: A tiny spore of fungal mold is carried on a wisp of a fall breeze into Fleming's deserted lab. The spore drifts silently, finally settling on a culture dish smudged with bacteria . . .

. . . In that small, seemingly insignificant moment, medical history is made . . .

. . . For that single rogue spore, taking root in a dish of staphylococcus bacteria, will trigger a chain reaction of events that will eventually save millions of lives around the world. This is the remarkable story of the discovery of penicillin.

The Western Front, World War I, 1917: Scottish-born Alexander Fleming, a promising young bacteriologist, fights to save the lives of the wounded in a battlefield hospital.

Confound it, woman! Yet another one lost to septicemia. These boys give their all in battle, only to lose the battle with infection. Like it or not, we're on the frontline here . . . against death.

Yes, Captain Fleming.

What I wouldn't give to have some weapon—any weapon— against bacteria!

After the war, Fleming resumes his research at St. Mary's, obsessed with finding an antibacterial agent capable of killing invading bacteria. Fleming is notoriously messy, often neglecting to clean up after his experiments.

Hmm, I wonder if nasal mucus has antibacterial properties . . . Oh no! My vacation! Must go. No time for cleaning up now. These dishes of staphylococcus bacteria will have to wait.

After his vacation, Fleming returns to the lab. Ready for a fresh start, he is about to chuck his dishes, covered in a thick carpet of yellow-green mold, into a sink full of disinfectant when he makes a startling discovery.

Hello, what's this? There seems to have a strange sort of halo around this bacteria that's stopping it from spreading. Could it possibly be? Has the mold released some sort of substance to inhibit bacterial growth?

Fleming grows the mold and tests it on a number of disease-causing bacteria. Eureka! He names the antibacterial superagent penicillin and tries to interest his colleagues.

Goodness, man, don't you see? If we can isolate it and produce it in quantity, we will have the absolute key to fighting deadly bacteria.

Don't get your necktie in a twist, dear boy. You yourself have said that it is quite difficult to grow, and you haven't managed to isolate it in all this time, have you now?

Even if you can isolate it, how do you know this "penicillin" malarkey will live long enough in the human body to fight anything?

Sorry, old boy, I simply don't see it. Now, where are my spectacles?

Fleming cannot achieve the breakthrough he needs. He abandons his investigation. Yet as one lab door closes, another opens . . .

It is finished. I must move on. I must!

Oxford University, 1939: Australian-born physiologist Howard Florey and his crack team, including brilliant chemist Ernst Boris Chain, a refugee from Nazi Germany, are hard at work.

All right gents, we have here a sample of Fleming's mold. We all think he was on to something. Now, let's find that something.

Once we isolate the bacteria killer, we will purify it. The race is on. Let's do this.

After a flurry of activity, Florey and his team produce enough pure penicillin to treat mice given lethally high doses of bacteria. Within a year, they publish their results, and this time, the scientific world listens.

Lucky old mouse. They say cats have nine lives. This penicillin has just saved yours.

Florey and his team deliver the news to the world: penicillin is a wonder drug. A single injection can cause miraculous recoveries from a range of maladies. As World War II rages, the U.S. and U.K. instruct drug companies to mass-produce penicillin.

Yes, sir. Right away, sir. We can fill that order in the next 24 hours.

Move it, now! That's another truckload before tomorrow.

By D-day in June 1944, there is enough penicillin available to treat every soldier who needs it. By the end of World War II, Fleming's miracle mold has saved millions of lives.

This will give you a fighting chance, my son.

We need more penicillin, stat!

In 1945, Fleming, Florey, and Chain are awarded the Nobel Prize for Medicine. Thanks to their work on penicillin, some 200 million lives will be saved. Their pioneering research will lead others to develop an array of different antibiotics, saving the lives of untold millions more . . . perhaps even yours.

DISCOVERY OF PENICILLIN

FIRST AID

Yikes! This is one accident-prone neighborhood! Fortunately, there are some first aiders on hand to administer lifesaving treatments. The first aiders have had special training, so they know exactly how to care for casualties until the emergency services arrive.

▲ CPR

When the first aider realized that this unconscious casualty wasn't breathing, she started CPR (cardio pulmonary resuscitation). She presses with her palms to compress his chest—this squeezes the heart and keeps blood pumping around the vital organs in his body.

▼ RECOVERY POSITION

This unconscious casualty is still breathing. The first aider checked for obvious injuries and then moved him into the recovery position, turning the casualty onto his side to prevent his tongue from blocking his airway and to allow any vomit or fluid to drain away.

▲ CHOKING

The diner couldn't cough up the food lodged in his airway so the first aider tried slapping him between the shoulder blades. This didn't work, so now she is performing abdominal thrusts to force air from the lungs through the airway, taking the obstruction with it.

◄ HEART ATTACK

Severe chest pains were an indicator to the first aider that this casualty might be having a heart attack. She positions him with head and shoulders raised and knees bent to assist breathing and circulation, and she reassures him until help arrives.

BURNS ▶

After extinguishing the flames on this casualty's clothes by smothering them with a blanket, the first aider will douse the burns with cold water to stop the burning process and to ease the pain.

▶ **WOUNDS**
A well-stocked first-aid kit in this workplace means that this first aider can apply a sterile bandage to the casualty's cut arm. The bandage applies pressure to the wound, stopping blood from escaping and encouraging clotting.

▼ **BROKEN BONES**
This unlucky man may have broken his arm. It is too painful to move, and there is swelling and bruising. Very gently, the first aider puts the arm in a sling to support the injury, but the casualty will need an x-ray and treatment at a hospital.

▲ **EMERGENCY HELP**
If a casualty is seriously ill or injured, he or she will need to go to a hospital for treatment. Every country has a special number to call to get emergency help, or you can call 112, which will connect you to the local emergency services wherever you are in the world. In the U.S. or Canada, dial 911.

ALTERNATIVE THERAPIES

Modern health care is rooted in the conventional method of seeing a traditional doctor who practices modern Western medicine. But there are also many branches of alternative therapies, designed to relieve pain and improve well-being. Some have been practiced for thousands of years, while others have sprouted more recently.

CHIROPRACTIC

Two of the core beliefs of chiropractic are that the body has a strong ability to heal itself and that the spine is the the key area of the anatomy. By aligning the spine, chiropractors hope to be able to reduce pain in other regions of the body as well as the back.

TRADITIONAL CHINESE MEDICINE

Practiced by millions of people around the world, traditional Chinese medicine combines a number of elements found in other therapies. As well as using herbs and acupuncture to relieve pain, it incorporates exercise techniques to promote general well-being.

AYURVEDA

With its origins stretching back to traditional Indian philosophy from 5,000 years ago, Ayurvedic medicine is made up of a number of strands that include herbal medicine, massage, exercise (in the form of yoga), breathing techniques, and meditation.

AROMATHERAPY

At the heart of aromatherapy is the use of natural plant oils to improve an individual's health and general well-being. The oils can be massaged into the skin, dropped into a bath, and heated as a room fragrance.

ACUPUNCTURE

First practiced more than 2,000 years ago, acupuncture is based on a Chinese procedure of applying needles to pressure points at specific points across the body, with the goal of relieving pain. It is now accepted as a valid method of pain relief by many practitioners of Western medicine.

HERBALISM

Plants and herbs such as aloe vera, garlic, mint, and dock leaves have been used to relieve the symptoms of illnesses for thousands of years. Herbalism remains popular with many people seeking a natural alternative to manufactured medicines.

HOMEOPATHY

Homeopathy is an alternative approach to medicine that is based on the belief that tiny extracts of natural substances can trigger healing within the body. It remains controversial because many studies have found that there are little or no health benefits to taking the extracts.

HYPNOTHERAPY

Practitioners of hypnotherapy believe that by placing patients in a hypnotic (deeply relaxed) state, they can be taught how to overcome worries, eating disorders, and even pain. This therapy is often used to help people conquer phobias such as the fear of flying.

REFLEXOLOGY

In reflexology, the foot is divided into separate areas that each represent a part of the body or a particular organ. The belief is that by applying pressure to these sections of the foot, ailments associated with these areas can be improved. Sometimes, hands and ears are also massaged.

REIKI

Originating in Japan, reiki is based on a belief that the body contains invisible energy fields that, when they get strong and weak, directly affect our health and the way we feel. Trained reiki practitioners claim to be able to raise energy levels by moving their hands over a patient.

MAKING A DIAGNOSIS

If you're feeling sick, it may be time to see a doctor to get an opinion. He or she will use logic and experience to weigh the evidence and make a diagnosis of what is wrong with you. That evidence includes symptoms (your experiences) and signs (family history, lifestyle, and the results of physical exams and tests).

1 SYMPTOMS

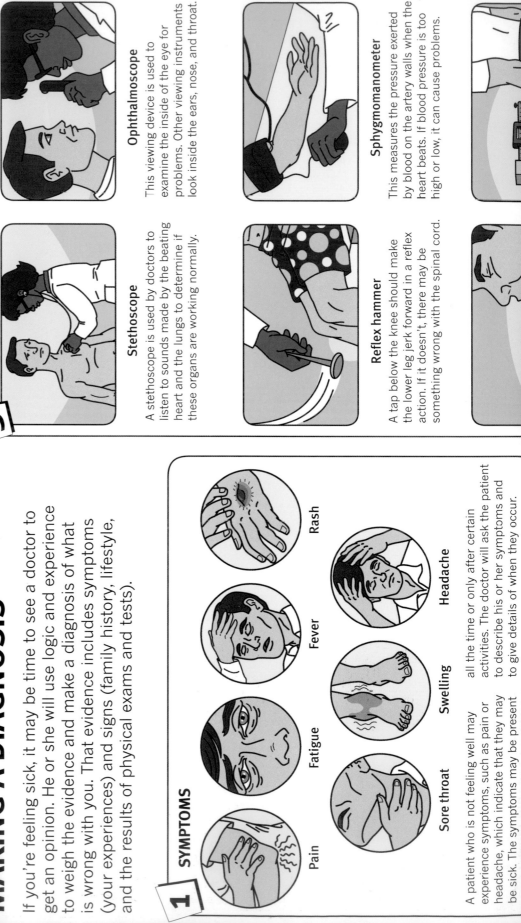

Pain

Sore throat

Fatigue

Fever

Swelling

Rash

Headache

A patient who is not feeling well may experience symptoms, such as pain or headache, which indicate that they may be sick. The symptoms may be present all the time or only after certain activities. The doctor will ask the patient to describe his or her symptoms and to give details of when they occur.

3 PHYSICAL EXAM

Ophthalmoscope

This viewing device is used to examine the inside of the eye for problems. Other viewing instruments look inside the ears, nose, and throat.

Stethoscope

A stethoscope is used by doctors to listen to sounds made by the beating heart and the lungs to determine if these organs are working normally.

Sphygmomanometer

This measures the pressure exerted by blood on the artery walls when the heart beats. If blood pressure is too high or low, it can cause problems.

Reflex hammer

A tap below the knee should make the lower leg jerk forward in a reflex action. If it doesn't, there may be something wrong with the spinal cord.

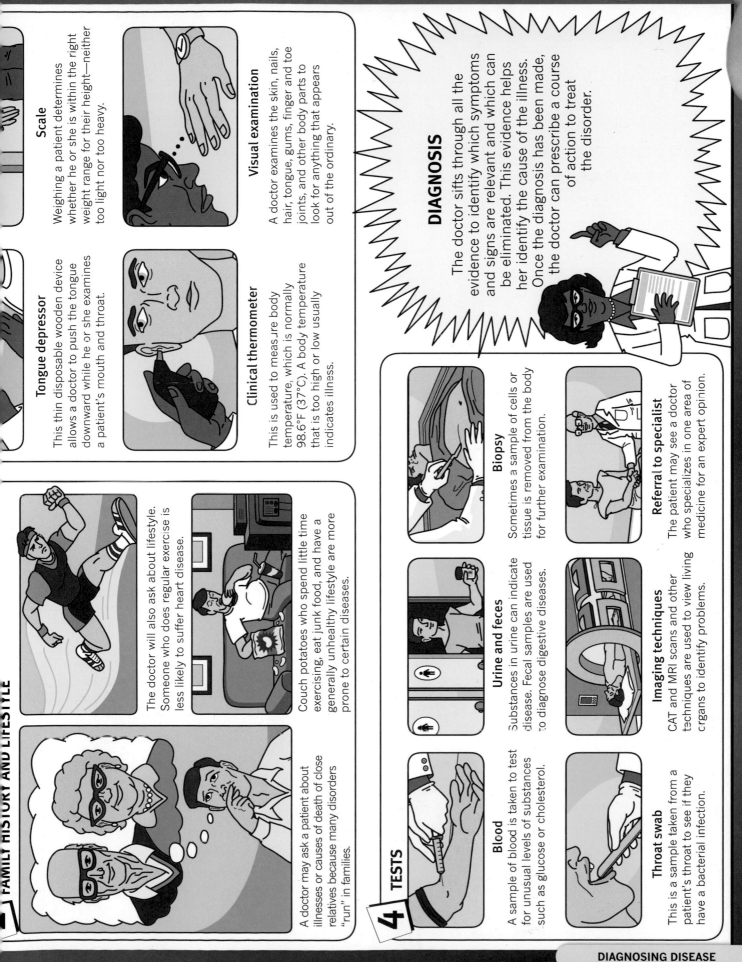

FAMILY HISTORY AND LIFESTYLE

A doctor may ask a patient about illnesses or causes of death of close relatives because many disorders "run" in families.

The doctor will also ask about lifestyle. Someone who does regular exercise is less likely to suffer heart disease.

Couch potatoes who spend little time exercising, eat junk food, and have a generally unhealthy lifestyle are more prone to certain diseases.

Scale

Weighing a patient determines whether he or she is within the right weight range for their height—neither too light nor too heavy.

Tongue depressor

This thin disposable wooden device allows a doctor to push the tongue downward while he or she examines a patient's mouth and throat.

Visual examination

A doctor examines the skin, nails, hair, tongue, gums, finger and toe joints, and other body parts to look for anything that appears out of the ordinary.

Clinical thermometer

This is used to measure body temperature, which is normally 98.6°F (37°C). A body temperature that is too high or low usually indicates illness.

DIAGNOSIS

The doctor sifts through all the evidence to identify which symptoms and signs are relevant and which can be eliminated. This evidence helps her identify the cause of the illness. Once the diagnosis has been made, the doctor can prescribe a course of action to treat the disorder.

4 | TESTS

Blood

A sample of blood is taken to test for unusual levels of substances such as glucose or cholesterol.

Throat swab

This is a sample taken from a patient's throat to see if they have a bacterial infection.

Urine and feces

Substances in urine can indicate disease. Fecal samples are used to diagnose digestive diseases.

Imaging techniques

CAT and MRI scans and other techniques are used to view living organs to identify problems.

Biopsy

Sometimes a sample of cells or tissue is removed from the body for further examination.

Referral to specialist

The patient may see a doctor who specializes in one area of medicine for an expert opinion.

WHEN PEOPLE ARE SICK IN A HOSPITAL, THEIR CONDITION MUST BE MONITORED, DRUGS ADMINISTERED, WOUNDS DRESSED, AND WORRIES EASED. IT'S THE JOB OF NURSES—HIGHLY SKILLED HEALTH PROFESSIONALS—TO AID THE RECOVERY OF SICK AND INJURED PEOPLE.

EARLY ORIGINS

Before the 1800s, most sick people were cared for at home by members of their family or someone in the neighborhood known to have healing skills. They were usually women, though men often worked as bonesetters (setting broken bones) or even as midwives, helping deliver babies. In Britain, women (and men) were employed in hospitals to wash and care for the sick, but no special training was needed. In Catholic countries, religious orders of nuns nursed the sick, which is why, in some countries today, senior nurses are sometimes called "sisters."

WAR AND NURSING

During the Crimean War (1853–1856), news reached Great Britain that thousands of soldiers sent to fight the Russians were dying of cholera far from home. Florence Nightingale, the daughter of a wealthy landowner who had fought her parents' opposition to become a nurse, headed a group of 38 nurses who traveled there to care for them. The soldiers were housed in filthy rat-infested barracks. Nightingale immediately scrubbed the place clean, improved sanitation, and reorganized patient care. The army at first opposed her efforts, but the soldiers loved her, calling her "the lady with the lamp." Death rates began to fall, and

MARY SEACOLE

Seacole opened a hotel for soldiers two miles (3.2 km) from the Crimean battlefront, where she sold food and drink. This helped pay for the medical care she gave the sick.

Nightingale became a national heroine. Another nurse in the Crimean War was Jamaican-born Mary Seacole, who had been turned down by Florence Nightingale, probably on grounds of race, and made her own way to the Crimea. She showed great courage in caring for wounded and sick soldiers just behind the enemy lines. A few years later, many American women volunteered to nurse the wounded in the American Civil War (1861–1864), most notably Dorothea Dix and Clara Barton. More than 3,000 women served as army nurses during the conflict.

NURSING BECOMES A PROFESSION

Once back in Britain, Florence Nightingale founded the Nightingale School of Nursing, which set new standards of training for nurses. Her *Notes on Nursing*, published in 1860, was an instant bestseller. In it, she spelled out her views on caring for the sick, stressing the need for light, airy rooms, cleanliness, and a good, simple diet. Her ideas were taken up all over the world. Nurses were expected to work 12 hours a day, with very little time off. Most of their day was spent scrubbing and cleaning the wards. They wore a uniform of starched apron, cap, and heavy "nonsqueak" shoes.

Pay was very low, and they had to live in barracklike nurses' homes. Yet there was no shortage of recruits. By the 1900s, nursing had become a popular career choice for women, many of them attracted by the idea of nursing as a "sacred trust."

MODERN NURSING

Nurses today are as committed as ever to caring for the sick, but their role and image have changed. They are no longer considered inferior to doctors but work side by side with them, giving different but equally important care. Between five and 10 percent of nurses are men. Training has expanded to meet the challenges of modern medical science, and nurses have varied jobs. Some give specialist care in premature baby units, emergency rooms, or intensive care units (ICUs); others may give cancer treatments or work as anesthetists or in medical labs. One very important area of nursing is in the community. Nurses head up health-care education programs and work with groups such as babies and children, people with disabilities or mental illness, and the old, giving support and care at home or in community clinics.

UNDER THE KNIFE

Not every disease and ailment can be combated with drugs, and sometimes surgery is the only option. Surgeons use special instruments to make incisions into the body in order to treat or remove body parts. Today, surgical procedures take place in sterile conditions, and the patient is usually kept unconscious throughout the operation. If you were in need of surgery before the mid-1800s, however, you could expect extreme pain, surgeons caked in the blood of previous patients, and an audience gawping at the entire spectacle. It wasn't called an operating "theater" for nothing!

Anesthesia won't be used until 1846, so this is going to really hurt! The patient has drunk some alcohol to numb the pain, but the surgeon will have to complete the operation in a matter of minutes to prevent shock from killing the patient.

Even if this man survives the operation, a bacterial infection in the wound could kill him soon after. It is not until the 1860s that British doctor Joseph Lister recognizes the importance of sterile conditions.

Students and other onlookers stand in specially constructed viewing platforms to enjoy a perfect view of this 18th-century leg amputation. Shame they are breathing their germs all over the patient.

As there is no anesthetic, the patient is conscious throughout. Assistants are required to hold him down while the surgeon cuts through the bone.

Surgeons take pride in having blood and gore from their previous operations dripping from their clothes. And there's no point washing their hands before the operation—they are just going to get dirty again!

A range of tools is used in surgery. They are designed to slice through tissue, saw through bone, clamp blood vessels, and ease tissues apart. The surgeon uses a saw to amputate this fellow's leg.

Bright angled lights give the surgical team a clear view, aiding more intricate procedures.

Everyone in the room has a clearly defined role. As well as the surgeon and anesthesiologist, there are nurses and surgical technicians who organize instruments and supplies during the operation. They make sure that the surgeon has the tools he needs and that the room is kept sterile.

Many of the surgical instruments are similar to ones used in previous centuries. There is one major improvement, though—they are sterile!

Doctors and nurses thoroughly scrub their hands and arms before entering the room. They wear disposable sterile gowns, headwear, masks, and latex gloves to reduce the risk of contaminating a patient's wounds.

A specialist doctor called an anesthesiologist administers drugs to keep the patient unconscious and pain free throughout the surgery. She also monitors the patient's vital signs, such as pulse and blood pressure.

The modern operating room is kept spotlessly clean and sterile, so it is pathogen free. This protects patients from infection.

SURGERY

THROUGH THE KEYHOLE

Doctors can operate without making large incisions by using keyhole surgery. A surgeon makes small cuts and inserts a tiny video camera mounted on a flexible tube into one opening. Surgical tools pass through the other openings. He or she can then operate, watching "live" on a camera monitor. But these days there is the option of asking the patient to swallow the camera: a video pill that travels the length of the digestive system, just like food.

Search

twitter

Login Join Twitter!

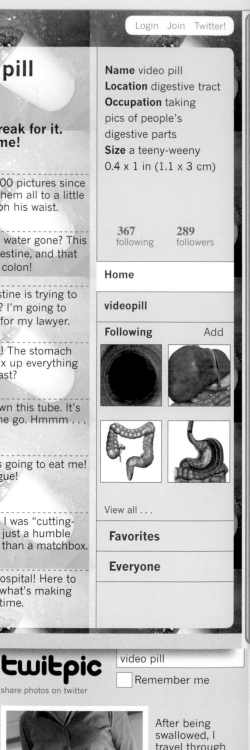

video pill

I am gonna make a break for it. Toilet bowl, here I come!

5 seconds ago

video pill I've taken 58,000 pictures since I've been in here and sent them all to a little box that the patient wears on his waist.

2 hours ago

video pill Where's all the water gone? This must be end of the long intestine, and that means . . . oh pooh, it's the colon!

8 hours ago

video pill The small intestine is trying to digest me. Isn't that typical? I'm going to take a bunch of picture . . . for my lawyer.

14 hours ago

video pill This is INSANE! The stomach muscles are churning to mix up everything in here. How long will this last?

18 hours ago

video pill I'm moving down this tube. It's squeezing me and letting me go. Hmmm . . . It must be the esophagus.

20 hours ago

video pill Holy moly, he's going to eat me! Look at the size of that tongue!

20 hours ago

video pill Mister MD said I was "cutting-edge technology." Little me, just a humble video camera weighing less than a matchbox.

22 hours ago

video pill Hi, I'm in the hospital! Here to help the doctors figure out what's making this guy's stomach hurt all time.

23 hours ago

Done

Name video pill
Location digestive tract
Occupation taking pics of people's digestive parts
Size a teeny-weeny 0.4 x 1 in (1.1 x 3 cm)

367 following   **289** followers

Home

videopill

Following   Add

View all . . .

Favorites

Everyone

The capsule endoscope, or video pill, is used to identify damage or disease in the digestive system. This avoids having to insert an endoscope through the anus and into the rectum and colon. The video pill has a tiny camera, light source, and transmitter.

START HERE TO CHECK OUT MY GUTSY ADVENTURE! ➘

twitpic

share photos on twitter

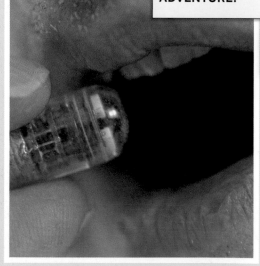

Down the hatch! See you in 24 hours!

Here I am traveling down the oesophagus; the journey has just begun!

Ouch! Just landed in the stomach. Whoa, the walls are solid muscle. This is creeping me out!

⊞ Put this photo on your website
Views 238
Tags
This photo has not been tagged. Be the first to tag it.

twitpic

share photos on twitter

video pill

☐ Remember me

After being swallowed, I travel through the digestive system, taking pictures that are transmitted to this outside receiver so that a doctor can view the images.

⊞ Put this photo on your website

Done

endoscope

That's me done. Wonder where I'll be exploring this afternoon?

5 seconds ago

endoscope With my help, so he can see what he's doing, the doc is going to fix the damage.

20 minutes ago

endoscope I think he's spotted the damage. Looks like something is there that shouldn't be and will need to be removed.

25 minutes ago

endoscope He puts the tools he needs for the examination through the opening and has a good poke around the knee.

35 minutes ago

endoscope My business end goes right through the opening, and I transmit images to the surgeon's monitor.

44 minutes ago

endoscope And I'm in!

45 minutes ago

endoscope The surgeon's got the scalpel ready. He's going to make a couple of tiny cuts on both sides of the patient's kneecap.

50 minutes ago

endoscope Looks like I'm going to be helping out with some keyhole surgery in the knee joint. Cool!

55 minutes ago

endoscope Everything's awesome. I'm nice and bendy, my lens is working fine, light bulb's A-OK, and I'm good to go.

1 hour ago

Done

Login   Join   Twitter!

Name endoscope
Location knee
Occupation getting up close and personal in surgical procedures
Worst job visiting the urinary tract—it was a little bit damp

142
following

265
followers

Home

endoscope

Following   Add

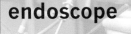

View all . . .

Favorites

Everyone

◀ **WANT THE INSIDE SCOPE ON KNEES? START HERE!**

Search

twitpic
share photos on twitter

endoscope

☐ Remember me

This is me in action. The surgeon carefully pokes around, and I send back the images.

➕ **Put this photo on your website**

Done

The endoscope consists of a flexible tube with a fiber optic system. There is also a light source to illuminate the organ or tissue it is inspecting.

Keyhole surgery of the knee involves inserting an endoscope through a small incision in the knee. This can not only identify a damaged part of the knee, but it can also provide an extra channel to allow surgical instruments to take tissue samples or to remove damaged tissue.

NONINVASIVE SURGERY

twitpic
share photos on twitter

☐ Remember me

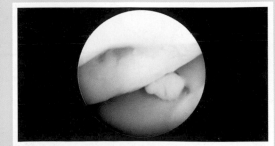

That's got to hurt! This poor person has a foreign object trapped inside the right knee. It is up to me to send back good images to the surgeon. It's a good angle, if I do say so myself.

➕ **Put this photo on your website**

Done

MEDICAL

From Hammurabi to the Human Genome Project

TIMELINE

c. 1760 B.C.
Babylonian King Hammurabi sets down written laws, some of which regulate the work of doctors—including cutting the arms off surgeons who make mistakes during surgery!

c. 420 B.C.
Hugely influential Greek physician Hippocrates establishes medicine as a distinct discipline, dependent on observation and diagnosis, moving it away from magic and myth.

1846
The first use of an anesthetic (ether) during an operation at a hospital in Boston, Massachusetts, paves the way for painless surgery.

1849
English-born Elizabeth Blackwell graduates from medical school in the U.S. and becomes the first female doctor. In 1859, she is the first woman to be included on the British medical registry.

1816
French doctor René Laennec invents the stethoscope, a tube he uses to listen to his patients' heart and breathing sounds. Later versions have two earpieces, as used by doctors today.

1853–1856
The work of Florence Nightingale and Mary Seacole during the Crimean War changes how wounded soldiers are nursed and leads to the establishment of modern nursing.

1860s
Pioneering French scientist Louis Pasteur (and later, German doctor Robert Koch) establish the germ theory, which proves that bacteria and other microorganisms cause infectious disease.

1865
In an attempt to reduce wound infections by bacteria, British surgeon Joseph Lister introduces antiseptic (germ-killing) sprays into his operating room, drastically reducing death rates.

1901
Austrian-American doctor Karl Landsteiner's team identifies blood types—later called A, B, AB, and O—enabling safe blood transfusions to take place.

1984
Three years after AIDS is recognized as a new disease, French scientist Luc Montagnier identifies HIV, the virus that causes it by weakening the body's defenses.

1980
Surgeons start using "keyhole" surgery to look inside the body and perform operations through tiny openings rather than large incisions.

2008
A Colombian woman has her damaged trachea replaced by one custommade using her own cells, so it won't be rejected by her body's defenses.

2003
Started in 1990, the Human Genome Project completes its goal of identifying the DNA sequence of a full set of human chromosomes and shows that humans have fewer than 25,000 genes.

C. A.D. 190
Claudius Galen describes, often wrongly, the body's anatomy and workings. His views remain unchallenged for 1,500 years.

1543
Flemish doctor Andreas Vesalius publishes *On the Structure of the Human Body*, the first accurate description of human anatomy, including the brain.

1614
Italian physician Santorio Santorio publishes a study of his own bodily functions after spending 30 years in a "weighing chair" measuring what went in and what came out!

c. 1000
Persian physician Avicenna (Ibn Sina) publishes *Canon of Medicine*, a book that combines Islamic medicine with Galen's ideas, and influences medicine for centuries.

1545
A pioneer of battlefield medicine, French surgeon Ambroise Paré publishes *The Method of Treating Wounds*, which describes new treatments (such as an ointment made of egg yolk and roses rather than the traditional wound remedy of boiling oil).

1792
Austrian doctor Franz Gall develops his flawed theory of phrenology, which involves feeling the shape of the head to determine different aspects of someone's personality.

1667
The first-ever blood transfusion, from a sheep to a student named Arthur Coga, is carried out by English physician Richard Lower. Amazingly, Coga survived.

1796
English doctor Edward Jenner carries out the first vaccination against an infectious disease, protecting a young boy from smallpox.

1674–1677
Dutch amateur microscopist and textile merchant Anton van Leeuwenhoek observes red blood cells, sperm, and bacteria for the first time using a homemade microscope.

1628
English physician William Harvey publishes *On the Motion of the Heart and Blood*, proving that blood circulates around the body, pumped by the heart.

1921
Canadian scientists Frederick Banting and Charles Best isolate the hormone insulin. This controls how much glucose is in the blood and is absent in people with diabetes.

1954
American doctor Jonas Salk introduces a vaccine against polio, an epidemic disease that can cause paralysis or death in children.

1928
British doctor and bacteriologist Alexander Fleming discovers penicillin, the first antibiotic drug, when he notices a substance released by mold-killing bacteria.

1954
The first successful kidney transplant—the transfer of a healthy kidney to a person with a diseased kidney—is performed in Boston, Massachusetts.

1978
On July 26, Louise Brown—the world's first test-tube baby—is born in Britain. She was conceived by IVF (in vitro fertilization) nine months earlier in a laboratory.

1972
Computerized axial tomography (CAT) scanning, which uses X-rays and computers to produce images of living tissues and organs as "slices" through the body, is used for the first time.

1977
The killer infection smallpox becomes the first disease to be eradicated by a coordinated vaccination program.

TIMELINE OF MEDICINE

222–223 PUBERTY
The changes that take place when the sex hormones kick in and the reproductive organs start working

226–227 BEING MALE
The male reproductive system and what it means to be a man

236–237 TWINS
Multiple births, how they happen, and why scientists study twins

**246–247
THE NEXT STEP**
How will humans evolve in the future?

240–241 THE END
What happens when the body dies

**242–243 BODY
PRESERVATION**
Natural and artificial ways to preserve a body after death

234–235 DIFFERENT FEATURES
Examples of features, such as free hanging ear lobes, that are caused by single gene differences

244–245 BODY PARTS
How the body could be modified with replacement organs and brain chips

Explore the journey through life from conception and birth to adulthood, and death. Plus what the future may hold for the human species.

230–231 NINE MONTHS
A peek inside the uterus to see a developing fetus

224–225 BEING FEMALE
The female reproductive system and what it means to be a woman

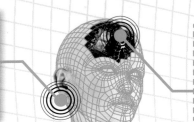

228–229 MISSION: CONCEPTION
The epic journey of competing sperm to fertilize an egg

238–239 LIFETIME
The different stages of life, from childhood to old age

232–233 BABY TALK
The first year of human life

LIFE STORY

PUBERTY

BOY TO MAN

PUBERTY BEGINS

Hey dude! I've recently been noticing changes. My testicles have gotten a little larger and my penis is longer. Do you think this is the start of puberty? It kicks off in boys between the ages of 9–14.

BODY CHANGES

Thanks to testosterone (the male sex hormone), I'm really shooting up—I grew a whopping 4 in (10 cm) in the last year. And hairs are starting to sprout around the base of my penis and under my arms.

VOICE DEEPENS

I was reading aloud at school when, midsentence, out came a high-pitched squeak! Everyone laughed! My voice box is growing bigger, so random squeaks are normal as deeper adult vocal cords develop.

GIRL TO WOMAN

PUBERTY BEGINS

Big news! I'm growing tall super fast. Hormones from my pituitary gland and ovaries have gone into overdrive, triggering puberty. It's nothing freaky—it happens to all girls between the ages of 7–13.

BODY CHANGES

Eww! First my breasts started to grow and I had to shop for a bra. Then hairs started to appear in my armpits and between my legs. Pubic hair is totally gross!

BODY ODOR

Pooh! What a stink! Large sweat glands have formed around my armpits and genitals. If I don't wash regularly and use deodorant, sweat and bacteria on my skin get together and cause bad body odor.

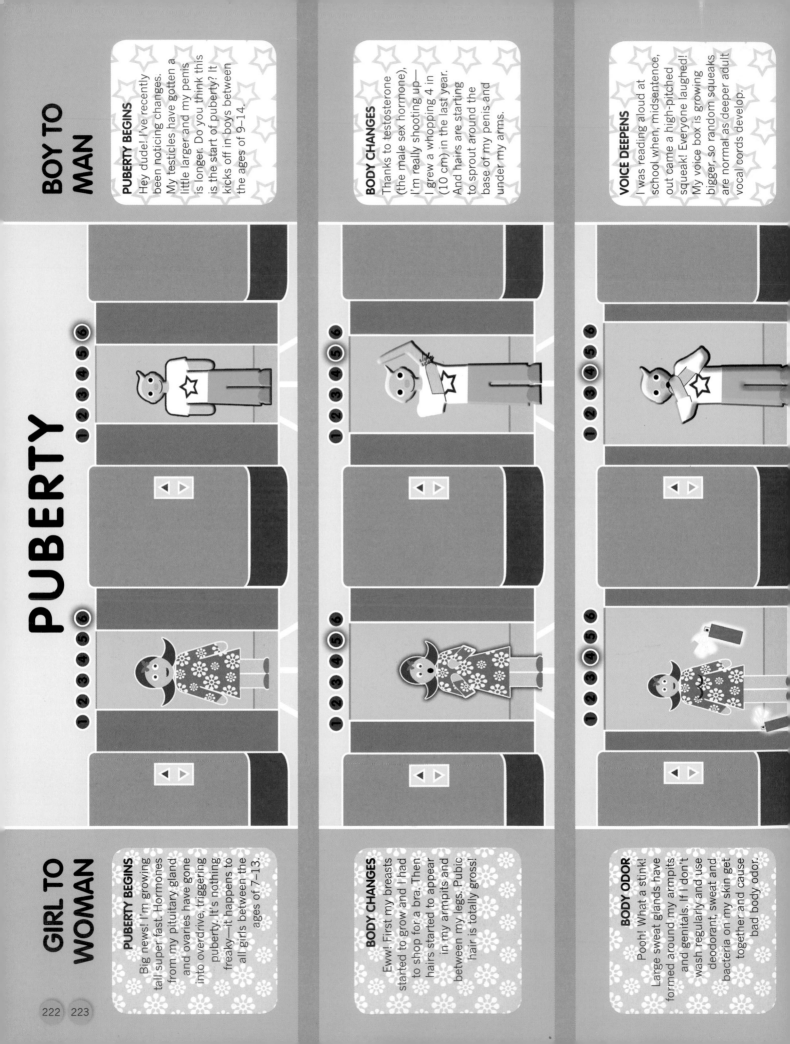

ERECTIONS

Hmm. This is awkward. My testes have started to produce sperm—almost 260 million a day. During an erection, blood makes my penis harden and semen ejaculates (spurts out). If only I could control when!

BODY HAIR

Hair is sprouting everywhere! My arm and leg hair is thicker and darker, and I've started to grow facial hair. I don't want a beard or mustache, so I shave. I've also got a few hairs on my chest.

MANHOOD

Phew! Made it through the zits, growth spurts, spontaneous erections, and voice breaking, and now I am a man. I can enjoy all the freedom and independence of being an adult. Whoa! Who's that beautiful woman in the pink dress? Think I'll just go over to say hello . . . .

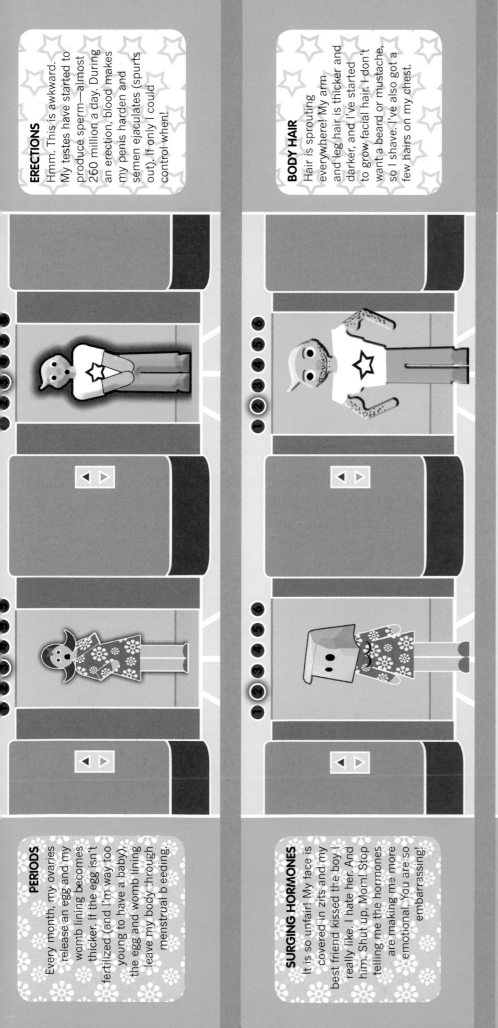

PERIODS

Every month, my ovaries release an egg and my womb lining becomes thicker. If the egg isn't fertilized (and I'm way too young to have a baby), the egg and womb lining leave my body through menstrual bleeding.

SURGING HORMONES

It is so unfair! My face is covered in zits and my best friend kissed the boy I really like. I hate her. And him. Shut up, Mom! Stop telling me the hormones are making me more emotional. You are so embarrassing!

WOMANHOOD

Check out my figure! Body fat has moved to my hips, buttocks, and thighs, but I like the new curvy me. The hormones have calmed down now (except around the time of my period!), and being an adult is pretty cool. I can stay out late, earn my own money, drive a car . . . Hey, he's cute!

BEING FEMALE

All human bodies work in the same way, but humans come in two distinct types—male and female. Your gender is determined by a pair of sex chromosomes, found in all your 100 trillion body cells. Sex chromosomes are shaped like the letters X and Y, and one chromosome is inherited from each parent. Two Xs and . . . Ta-dah! It's a girl! Here's what gives women girl power.

REPRODUCTIVE SYSTEM

A woman's main sex organs are tucked away inside her pelvis. Eggs are made in the two ovaries and are released one at a time into a fallopian tube. If the egg is fertilized by a male sperm after sexual intercourse, a fetus will develop into a baby in a hollow muscular organ called the uterus, or womb. The cervix, a small opening in the uterus, connects to the vagina. A man's penis enters the vagina during sexual intercourse, and the vagina opens wide when a baby is born. Women also have breasts, which can produce nutrient-rich milk for babies.

Fatty tissue

Milk gland

Milk ducts

Nipple

Areola

Muscle

Rib

Fallopian tube

Uterus (womb)

Ovary

Cervix

Vagina

BEHAVIOR

A woman's brain is smaller but is more compact than a man's—so women are just as intelligent!

The female brain is more densely packed with neurons, especially in the region responsible for language.

The female brain is hard-wired for empathy, so women are more sensitive to other people's emotions.

Women are more aware of facial expressions and better at decoding nonverbal communication.

Women are often better judges of character because they can pick up nuances from tone of voice.

Women tend to chat about problems and provide emotional support to others.

More likely to be indirectly aggressive, women will gossip or exclude others.

Multitasking is natural to women, who can juggle several jobs at the same time and conduct more than one conversation.

Relying more on landmarks than maps to navigate environments, women will also ask for directions if lost.

A lot of perceived "female" behavior is taught and culturally enforced.

Feeling secure is important to women, so they are less likely to take risks.

Naturally more sociable, women show a preference for working together and interacting in groups.

BODY SHAPE

Women have wider hips than men and tend to have more hip sway when they walk.

Estrogen—the female sex hormone—causes fat to be stored in the buttocks, thighs, and hips.

Women have two fleshy breasts on their chests.

Women usually have smaller noses and fuller lips than men.

On average, women are shorter than men and have smaller hands and feet.

Shorter vocal cords mean women have higher-pitched voices than men.

Women have a lower metabolic rate than men, so the female body converts more food into fat rather than muscle.

Women have smaller hearts and lungs, so the chest cavity is not as big as a man's.

Women are not as hairy as men because body-hair growth is triggered by the male sex hormone, testosterone.

WOMEN

BEING MALE

If a baby inherits one X sex chromosome and one Y sex chromosome, then . . . Congratulations! It's a boy! A powerful sex hormone called testosterone is what makes men so macho. Triggering the development of male reproductive organs before birth, testosterone is also busy at puberty, affecting growth and behavior. Here's what gives men the XY factor.

REPRODUCTIVE SYSTEM

Male sex organs mostly dangle outside the body. Sperm and testosterone are produced in the testes. Sperm mature in the epididymis and then travel along the ductus deferens tube to the prostate gland and seminal vesicles, where they mix with a fluid to create semen. This fluid is released from the body through the penis via the urethra during sexual intercourse.

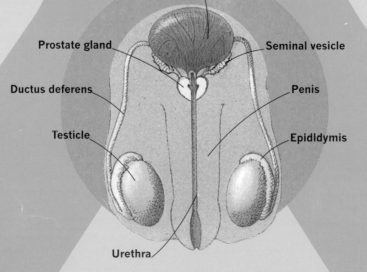

Bladder

Prostate gland

Seminal vesicle

Ductus deferens

Penis

Testicle

Epididymis

Urethra

BEHAVIOR

Men have bigger brains than women—but this doesn't make them more intelligent!

Male brains are hard-wired for analysing and understanding the world around them.

Men are less sensitive to the feelings of others and less likely to pick up on nonverbal communication.

Male communication is motivated by a search for answers rather than to give emotional support or share problems.

Men are more likely than women to act aggressively and display anger.

Men have more spatial awareness than women, so make better map readers.

Men are less likely to ask for help and directions if they are lost.

Men prefer to explore independently rather than in a group.

A lot of perceived "male" behavior is taught and culturally enforced.

Men are more likely to take risks than women, so are often more adventurous.

Men cannot multitask as well as women—they prefer to concentrate on one job at a time.

Constructing a 3-D model from a drawing is easier for men than women.

BODY SHAPE

Men have a V-shaped torso, with broad shoulders, expanded chest, narrow hips, and small buttocks.

Men have larger hearts and lungs, which is why they have bigger, broader chests.

There is hair pretty much everywhere on a man, including the face, chest, and genital region.

Men tend to have squarer jaws, larger noses, larger hands and feet, and more prominent brows than women.

Testosterone speeds up the metabolism, so men convert more food into muscle rather than fat. Any fat tends to deposit around the abdomen and waist.

Deeper voices are caused by the larger vocal cords and voice box, and this often gives men a prominent Adam's apple—a bump in the neck where the voice box sticks out.

MEN

MISSION: CONCEPTION

Attention. Intruder alert! Millions of male sperm released into the female vagina during sexual intercourse are now swimming toward the female egg. Their mission: to reach the egg, penetrate its outer covering, and fertilize it before the clock runs out. The task is daunting. Only a few hundred sperm will make it to the egg, and only one will eventually merge with its target. If the sperm fail to make contact within 48 hours, they will die. It is a race for survival—the survival of the human race. Let us observe.

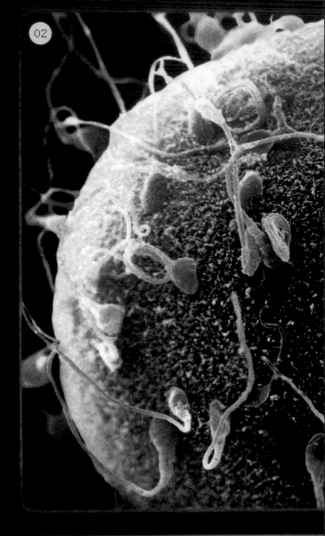

02

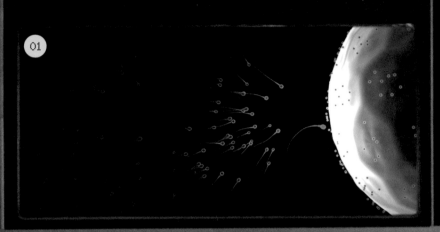

01

01: RACE TO THE EGG

As the egg waits in the far reaches of the uterus in one of two fallopian tubes, between 200 and 300 million sperm begin their mission. Each one whips its tail back and forth to swim toward the target. Fewer than 1,000 sperm eventually make it through the cervix to enter the uterus, and even fewer locate the egg.

02: SURROUNDING THE TARGET

Once the target is found, the sperm surround it. They move their tails to position their heads next to the egg. There they encounter another barrier—the egg is wrapped in a tough jellylike outer layer that is extremely difficult to penetrate. The clock is ticking, too, as the egg must be fertilized within one day of its release.

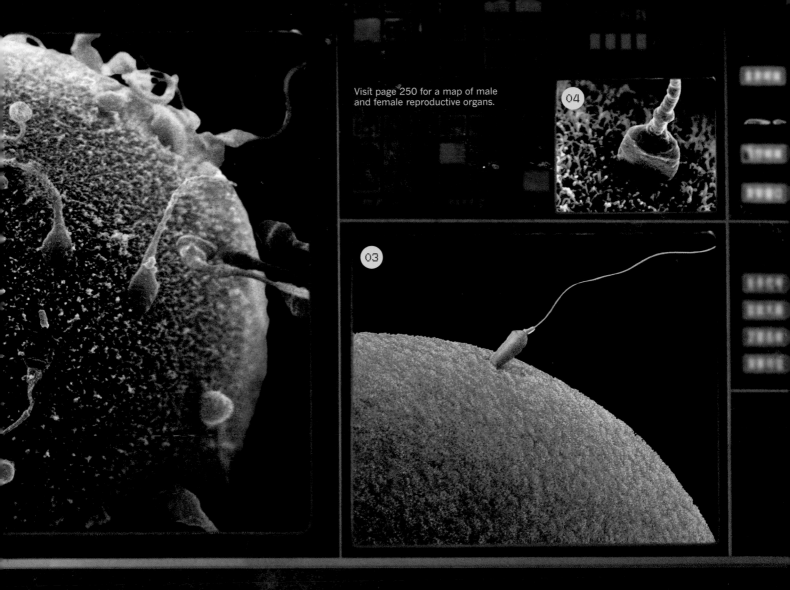

Visit page 250 for a map of male and female reproductive organs.

04

03

03: FIRST AMONG EQUALS

Now the sperm must use their heads. Each sperm releases enzymes from its head that can digest a pathway through the egg's outer barrier. As the wall begins to thin and break down, the sperm attempt to push their way through. One sperm will eventually break the barrier wall and bury its head into the egg. We have a winner!

04: FERTILIZATION

The winning sperm loses its tail as it burrows into the egg. The DNA (genetic material) in the sperm's head fuses with the egg's nucleus. Alert! We have fertilization. Once the successful sperm is inside the egg, a chemical reaction stops any more sperm penetrating. Mission accomplished! Well done, zygote (the name for a fertilized egg).

IN THE BEGINNING

The journey of a lifetime starts when the ripest female egg is swept into the fallopian tube. Within 24–36 hours after the egg and sperm unite, the fertilized egg divides into two identical cells. Now things begin to get really interesting!

A LUMPY BALL OF CELLS

Watch out, coming through! The two cells divide into four, eight, and then 16 cells as the fertilized egg travels all the way down the fallopian tube and toward the uterus. In around six days, this hollow ball of cells attaches itself to the lining of the uterus and pregnancy begins.

TAKING SHAPE

Four weeks after fertilization, the embryo is no longer just a blob of cells. In addition to a beating heart, it has a head, tail, backbone, and limb buds, which will eventually develop into the arms and legs. The placenta—the embryo's life-support system—is already formed and is attached to the uterus. It provides nourishment to the embryo and takes away waste via a tube called the umbilical cord.

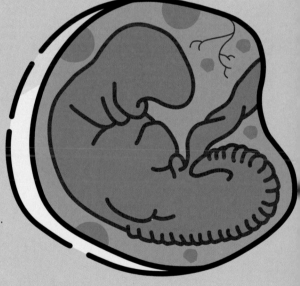

A TADPOLE WITH A HEART

Between five and six weeks after fertilization, the embryo appears unusually top heavy, with its oversize head resembling a tadpole rather than a human. Facial bones emerge, including the area under the eyes that forms the cheeks and sides of the upper lip. Some pigment can be detected in the eyes, the ears are forming, and taste buds are developing. Paddlelike hands and feet appear, and the intestines, liver, pancreas, and lungs can all be seen. The tiny heart beats up to an incredible 150 times a minute!

A BUNDLE OF ENERGY

Seven weeks after fertilization, this grape-size jumping bean is going crazy! There is no stopping this lively embryo as it shakes around in the uterus. Slightly webbed fingers and toes form, and under its paper-thin skin, veins are clearly visible. In one week, the embryo will start to develop its own unique fingerprints.

HI THERE, GOOD LOOKING

Nine weeks after fertilization, the embryo is called a fetus. One week later, it begins to look more human, although the head remains half the length of the body. The liver, kidneys, and brain are formed and functional. The fetus's galloping heartbeat can be heard, and hair and fingernails start to appear.

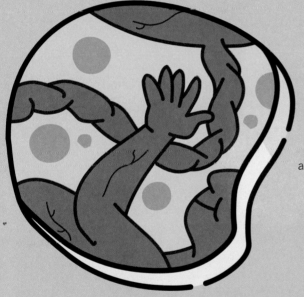

LEARNING NEW TRICKS

If the mother's abdomen is nudged 12 weeks after fertilization, the fetus responds by shifting and squirming like a big wiggly worm. The eyes move closer together, and the ears, which can now detect sound, are almost in position. The nerve cells in the brain are quickly multiplying, and the fetus moves around and flexes its growing limbs.

THAT'S SOME GOOD KICKING!

It is 20 weeks after fertilization and the mother can feel the fetus kick around inside her. A white fatty substance covers the fetus to protect it from the wrinkling effect of amniotic fluid. This liquid acts as a shock absorber, helps the lungs to develop, and provides a barrier against infection.

NOT LONG TO GO NOW

On the home stretch now, and 30 weeks after fertilization, the fetus's skin becomes pinker and smoother and its arms and legs fatter. It can open its eyes and blink. In around four weeks, its head will point downward. At 38 weeks, it is ready to enter the big, bright world. So let's get on with it!

BURP!

Who are you calling a crybaby? Listen, you. Getting to the age when I blow out my first birthday candle is no piece of cake. I have lots of growing and learning to do, and I need all the help I can get. So whenever I open up and say, "WaaaaaAAAUGH," you had better come running to figure out what I'm trying to say. Got it?

I already have the reflexes to help me find food—I can latch onto a nipple or bottle and suck. I'm going to need **feeding** a lot, around the clock, so that I double my weight in the first six months. Sometimes I swallow too much air when I feed, and that makes me gassy. Better pat my back to make me **BURP**—but not too hard, just in case what went down comes back up all over your shoulder.

WaaaaAAAUGH!

In my first few days, my **POO** is a sticky black mess with its own fancy name—meconium. I'm getting rid of all the stuff that I ingested in the womb, so it doesn't really smell and is just a trickle. But then I become a champion diaper filler, **peeing** around ten times a day and making several stinky poos. I hate wiggling around with a fully loaded diaper, so for crying out loud, come and change me already.

I had been hearing a muffled version of **Mom**'s voice for some time, and I recognize **Dad**'s voice, too. From one month old I can tell the difference between Mom's face and everyone else's. My parents even smell good to me, which is more than I can say for my diapers.

sick!

As I grow, I am learning all sorts of new tricks, and I want to PLAY! It'll be so much fun. (Well, by the time I am six weeks old you might get a gummy grin from me. The laughs come at around four months.) I like rolling from my back to my side and keeping my bobbing head steady. It isn't easy. My head can grow a whole centimeter in a month, so it isn't just my good looks making me big headed. When I am five months old I will grab for toys. And just wait until I'm seven months old— that's when I learn to BANG toys on the table.

When I am around four months old, I start drooling like crazy. Then I begin teething, which is when my little pearly whites emerge, and I am warning you—it can make me extremely cranky. I know it's a good thing, because teeth will enable me to chew so that I can start eating solid food later in my first year. But my first toothaches can be HOWLERS!

I need a whole lot of sleep—up to 20 hours a day at first. The hormones that help me grow are less active when I snooze, so getting enough shuteye helps regulate my development. When I'm awake, you need to take care of me, no matter if it's night or day. There are bound to be TEARS when we aren't on the same schedule, but in a couple of months, you'll probably get me around to your way of thinking.

Crying happens to be my only way of communicating at the moment. Most parents say a baby's different cries start to get distinctive at around two months old . . . But two whole months to train a parent to know what I want?! Sheesh.

Toot!

234
235

DIFFERENT FEATURES

The way you look depends on your genes. There are two copies of every gene, one inherited from each parent. Copies aren't always identical. This is really obvious where two varieties of a gene—called dominant and recessive—produce two distinct versions of one feature. Just having one bossy dominant gene is enough to produce its version, but it takes two shy, retiring recessive genes to produce theirs.

FRECKLES

A feature caused by a dominant gene, freckles are small patches of darker color in the skin created when some skin cells produce more brown melanin pigment than others. If you've got the freckly gene, your freckles will be more obvious if you have fair skin and when you're tan.

FREE EARLOBE

These are the soft fleshy parts at the bottom of your ears, ideal for attaching earrings. But take a look at people's earlobes and you'll notice a clear-cut difference. They're either free hanging and detached—thank you, dominant gene—or they're attached and joined to the head.

ROMAN NOSE

Noses come in all shapes and sizes, but there's one nosy feature that you have either got or you haven't. That's a Roman, or aquiline ("like an eagle's beak"), nose that curves outward. The alternative— a straight nose—needs two recessive straight-nose genes, one from each parent.

DARWIN'S EAR

Got a small bump on the outer fold of your ear? Then you're among ten percent of people to have Darwin's ear point, named after famous 19th-century scientist Charles Darwin, who first described it. A dominant gene produces a small bump in the ear's cartilage.

DIMPLES

Really cute in babies, these small dents in the cheeks appear when someone smiles. Like most of the features on view here, dimples are caused by a dominant gene. But just because the gene is dominant doesn't mean that many people carry it. That's why dimples are quite rare.

HITCHHIKER'S THUMB

Thumbs-up! Can you bend your thumb backward like this? If so, you've inherited two recessive genes for extreme thumb bending, one from each of your parents. But you'll be pleased to know that your curvy thumbs work just as well as the straight ones most people have.

TONGUE ROLLING

Can you, like the majority of people, roll your tongue into a tube shape? Or does your tongue just stay flat? Interestingly, tongue rolling is controlled not by one, but two different dominant genes, and you need both from your parents to be able to perform the feat.

CLEFT CHIN

If a fetus developing inside its mother has the dominant cleft-chin gene, this is what happens. The left and right sides of its lower jawbone don't completely fuse together. This leaves a dip in the chin, the shape of which is followed by the skin, producing a cleft chin.

BENT PINKIE

Get some friends together and try this out. Put your hands out in front of you and spread your fingers wide. Now inspect the little fingers, or pinkies. Most of you will have straight pinkies, but some may have bent pinkies that make an obvious curve toward the fourth finger.

TWINS

Many mammal mothers give birth to large litters, but in humans, multiple pregnancies are much less common. Gather together 80 pregnant women and statistically only one will be carrying twins. The odds for bigger broods are eggs-tremely small— one in 8,000 for triplets (three babies), one in 730,000 for quadruplets (four babies), and one in 50 million for quintuplets (five babies).

A single sperm fertilizes a single egg to form an embryo. This divides in two, creating identical twins.

We come from one fertilized egg, which split into two.

MIRROR IMAGE

Identical twins start off in the same way as a single baby—an egg is fertilized by a sperm to form an embryo. But this time the embryo divides in two, and each develops into a fetus. The twins share the same genes and look almost eggs-actly alike. They are always the same sex because each inherits the same sex chromosomes (XX for girls, XY for boys).

A single egg is fertilized by a single sperm and develops into a baby.

At the same time, a second egg is fertilized by a sperm and develops into a nonidentical twin baby.

WOMB FOR TWO

Sometimes a woman's ovaries release two eggs at the same time instead of the usual one. If both of these eggs are fertilized by separate sperm, nonidentical (fraternal) twins form. They can be the same sex or different sexes and are as genetically similar as any brother or sister.

We come from two separate fertilized eggs.

NATURE VS. NURTURE

Medical eggs-perts regularly recruit twins as research subjects to discover which characteristics are controlled by genes and which features are controlled by upbringing and environment. Scientists look at particular traits—such as intelligence, height, and food preferences—to see how identical twins compare to fraternal twins. If the identical twins, with their shared genes, show more similarity than the fraternal twins, that trait is likely to be genetic.

I've made an eggs-citing discovery.

Wow! I feel like I know you already!

STRANGE COINCIDENCES

There are eggs-traordinary stories of identical twins separated at births who meet much later and realize that they have led very similar lives. American twins James Arthur Springer and James Edward Lewis were adopted into different families as babies. When they were reunited 39 years later, they discovered that they had each married and divorced a woman named Linda and remarried a woman named Betty. They both had sons with the same name and both owned dogs named Toy. They had the same hobbies and interests and even had headaches at the same time of the day!

MULTIPLE BIRTHS

Fertility drugs have led to an increase in the number of large multiple pregnancies. The human womb doesn't have the room to accommodate lots of babies, so multiple sets are often born prematurely (early), and sadly, sometimes the babies are too small to survive. Births of sextuplets, septuplets, and octuplets are so rare that they make news around the world.

twins

triplets

quadruplets

quintuplets

sextuplets

septuplets

octuplets

nonuplets

decaplets

LIFETIME

After nine months developing inside its mother's womb, it's time for a baby to be born. The baby might greet its strange new world with a cry of alarm, but once a newborn clocks in, the hands of time start ticking, the sands of time start trickling, and the human life cycle begins. Time flies when you're having fun, but soon we'll all run out. At the end of the cycle, it's time for us to ring out the old, call it a day, and clock out.

▲ STAGE 1: BABY BELLS

Babies are completely dependent on their parents for their care, feeding, and transportation. Their brains develop and grow quickly, almost tripling in weight in the first year. Some of the skeleton is made of cartilage rather than bone—they have a lot of growing to do! By the age of one, a baby may have a few teeth and be able to walk.

▼ STAGE 4: ALARM BELLS

Adolescence (ages 11–18) can be a confusing time as young people cope with all kinds of changes. Puberty brings the onset of menstruation in girls and sperm production in boys. Through growth spurts, adolescents shoot up to their adult height, and hormone production can cause mood swings that change by the minute.

STAGE 3: SCHOOL BELLS ▶

Between the ages of 5–11, children become more independent. Many start school, where they learn practical as well as social skills. They take on new responsibilities as they learn about themselves. Physical and mental skills continue to sharpen as they develop. Baby teeth are gradually replaced by a permanent set.

▲ STAGE 2: LITTLE TINKER BELLS

In early childhood (1–5 years), children learn more about how to survive in the world. They become mobile, they speak in sentences, and they can take better care of themselves. Through play and daily activities, they develop a sense of identity as they figure out that their actions have consequences.

▼ STAGE 6: OLD-TIMERS

As the human body begins to age, the cells and tissues start to wear out. The effects of aging can include loss of hearing and vision, wrinkled skin, wear and tear on the body's moving parts, and a less efficient immune system. Good nutrition and a healthy lifestyle can slow the process, but time will eventually be called.

◀ STAGE 5: FAMILY TIME

In adulthood, the longest part of the human life cycle, most people reach their physical and cognitive (mental) peaks. Adults may choose to reproduce and have children of their own. Their social and personal qualities—such as personality, independence, and character—enable other people to see them as adults. From the mid-20s, a slow period of physical decline begins. The clock is ticking . . .

LIFE CYCLE

THE END

The final stage of the human life cycle is death. There can be any number of causes—infectious disease, heart attack, cancer, organ failure, fatal accident, or simply old age. Whatever the reason, the body's natural control systems break down, so its trillions of cells cannot survive.

Death begins when the **heart stops beating** and the **lungs stop breathing**. Blood no longer circulates, so **cells become starved of oxygen**.

Within ten seconds, **brain neurons**— the most oxygen-sensitive cells in the body—**cease working** properly and electrical activity is reduced.

Within four minutes, the **brain is irreversibly damaged**. The **pupils widen** and do not constrict (get smaller) when a light is shone in the eyes.

Over time, other body **cells and tissues die** and body temperature starts to cool.

Four to six hours after death, the body's **muscles stiffen** (rigor mortis). Body tissue breaks down, assisted by bacteria, and the body begins to **decompose**.

BODY PRESERVATION

So you've headed to the final checkout, paid your dues, and are ready to roll your cart to the big supermarket in the sky. What will you leave behind? Our bones and teeth are made of tough stuff, but soft tissue is vulnerable to decay after death. There are, however, methods to preserve a dead body. They may be accidental (for example, when weather conditions slow decay) or on purpose. Whichever way you make a mummy, you can be dead sure to find it here.

PETE MARSH, THE LINDOW MAN

Around 2,000 years ago in Cheshire, England, this 20-year-old was strangled, beaten, stabbed, and then pushed face first into a peat bog. The acidic conditions in the marsh preserved his skin, beard, teeth—and even the last meal in his stomach. Chemicals in the peat stained his skin a deep brown. Peat cutters discovered Pete by accident in 1984.

EGYPTIAN MUMMIES

The ancient Egyptians believed that they had to keep a dead person's body as lifelike and well preserved as possible to provide a home for the soul in the afterlife. They removed quick-to-spoil internal organs, dried out the body with salts, and painted the skin with oils and sticky resin before wrapping the body in linen bandages and tucking in a lucky amulet for eternal life. Charming.

ÖTZI THE ICEMAN

Just as food stays fresh for longer in your freezer, extremely cold temperatures can slow down the decay of a dead body. Ötzi the Iceman was found inside a glacier in the Italian-Austrian Alps. It was a chilling discovery: Ötzi had lost his outer layer of skin, but the rest of him (and his clothing, found nearby) had remained intact since his death sometime in 3300 B.C.

CHINESE MUMMIES

More than 100 naturally preserved mummies were found in burial sites in the Tian Shan Mountains of northwest China. Between 2,400 and 4,000 years old, the corpses still have bountiful hair, and many are dressed in colorful woolen clothes. A combination of icy cold air and salt-rich soil meant their bodies froze and dried out before they could decay.

CRYOPRESERVATION

In this high-tech process, an antifreeze-like fluid is added to the body to prevent damage to body cells. Then the body is cooled down to $-321°F$ ($-196°C$) so that it is impossible for decaying agents like bacteria to grow. Cryofolk hope their bodies can be revived in the future when there are cures for what has killed them, but they should just chill.

CATACOMBS OF PALERMO

The underground passageways beneath this Italian Capuchin monastery contain the preserved remains of some 8,000 bodies. In the 1500s, monks were mummified, and later on, local residents chose to have their dead loved ones air dried in the cool catacombs so that they could visit them, although the bodies never had much to say for themselves.

CHILE MUMMIES

The Chinchorros of Chile may have been the world's first mummy makers. They dismembered the body and stripped the flesh down to the bone, setting aside the skin. The skull was split, the brain drained and replaced with stuffing, and then the body was reassembled, stuffed with leaves or animal fur, and topped with the reserved skin.

EMBALMING

The goal of this process is to preserve a body for viewing at a funeral, or for transporting a body home for burial. Any remaining bodily fluids are drained away, and preservatives to replace them are injected into the body to keep it fresh. Then the corpse is dressed and groomed to provide a more "lifelike" appearance. Vladimir Lenin, a Russian revolutionary leader, was embalmed in 1924 and is still on display.

PLASTINATION

By replacing water and fat in a dead body with plastics, people can create modern mummies that are flexible, touchable (if you dare), and resistant to decomposition. Plastination of donated body parts is used to create models for anatomy students. German entrepreneur Gunther von Hagens exhibits plasticized bodies around the world.

BRAIN ENHANCERS

Tiny integrated circuits have been commonplace in computers for years, but now we can insert them into your brain to repair damage, enhance your memory and intelligence, and even let you speak a foreign language without having to learn it. ¡Magnífico!

BODY ORGANS

If an out-of-order organ is making life a misery, we can help. We'll extract some of your stem cells (the ones that can turn into any body tissue) and persuade them to grow into a replacement organ in a lab, creating a perfect match for your body. Fully guaranteed.

DESIGNER CHILDREN

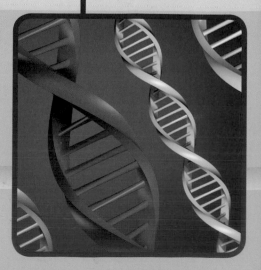

Want to avoid passing on an inherited disease to your children? Or would you like them to have red hair or be good at math? Leave it to us and we'll eliminate faulty genes from your fertilized egg and insert new genes to add your requested features. Your designer child will be just as you ordered.

DATELINE 2040: Advances in medicine and technology have made it feasible to repair and improve bodies in ways previously thought impossible. Try these innovations for yourself with our Body Parts 24-Hour Service. Delivery and installation are free! And check out our COMING SOON list to see what exotic enhancements the future may have in store.

ARTIFICIAL EYES

We stock and supply the greatest innovations that the mid-21st century can offer, such as amazing artificial eyes for people with impaired vision. The kit includes sophisticated light sensors that feed information to a brain implant, letting you see the world clearly and in full color.

BIONIC PARTS

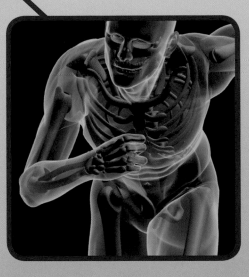

Have you ever wanted stronger arms or faster-moving legs? Forget the gym and go bionic. In development for 40 years, our replacement limbs are revolutionary. We'll fit the bionic limb and rewire your nerves so that your brain can tell a tiny lightweight computer in the limb to make it move.

NANOBOTS

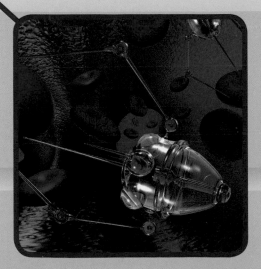

Marvel at these microscopic machines. Once injected into your bloodstream, nanobots look after themselves as they look after you. Self-propelled, responsive, and able to use their initiative, they detect, diagnose, and repair damaged tissues and organs. Have an injured artery? Don't worry, your nanobot will fix it.

COMING SOON!

✔ Life span increased to at least 200 years

✔ Extra-hard teeth that won't rot and are self-cleaning

✔ Automatically changing hair color to suit all occasions

✔ Improved oxygenation system for the lungs to boost their efficiency

✔ Ultrareceptive ears with an enhanced self-cleaning option

✔ Solar-protected skin with a range of different tones

✔ Fiber-optic channels in the spinal cord to speed up brain/body communication

✔ Facility to download information between computer and brain

BODY ENHANCEMENTS

SUPER SLACKERS

If future humans rely on gadgets and robots to do everything for them, they may lose the ability to get around on their own. Without exercise, they would have less muscle yet larger bodies, and their chins might recede if they eat more processed junk food that doesn't need to be chewed.

DESIGNER HUMANS

Through tinkering around with human genes, future parents could not only choose the sex of their child but also ensure they were beautiful, bright, talented social butterflies, able to live long and healthy lives. What parent could resist the opportunity to create a "perfect" child? (Would yours?)

NO CHANGE

One thing that might happen is nothing at all. Perhaps humans are fully evolved . . . Well, most of us. The things that drive evolution, like natural selection, are no longer so important because medicine and good nutrition have increased life expectancy, so it is less likely that a random genetic difference will give someone an edge.

The next step

You've made it to the end of the book, so you should know pretty much everything about how the human body works. Congratulations, you've evolved! What about the rest of the human race? It's clear that our bodies are not the same as our ancestors' were (turn back to pages 10–11 for the ugly truth), but what might future humans look like?

HAVES AND HAVE-NOTS

What happens if we end up with lots of designer children? Like the cool kids at school, these charmers will inevitably socialize with one another, and eventually they may get married and have perfect children of their own. Humanity might split into two groups: the attractive, intelligent, healthy, creative "haves" and the ugly, thick, dull-witted, boring "have-nots."

SPACE FACE

Say humans eventually set up colonies on far-flung planets throughout the solar system. Natural selection would come into play again, because certain human-body types are better suited for a life in space. With less gravity, for example, a race of tall, thin people with delicate limbs could emerge.

BIG BRAINS

Perhaps all the complicated stuff humans will need to deal with in the future will cause their brains to grow and their heads to expand. After all, examining prehistoric skulls shows that our brain size has increased in past generations in order to cope with more mental challenges. It's something to think about, anyway.

CYBORG

What if the evolutionary road takes us to a future world in which mechanical parts are built right into the body, or you upload your brain into a computer? A race of half-human, half-robot cyborgs could mark the ultimate in human achievement . . . But if the robot half decides to take over, it could also be the end of the evolutionary road for humans.

FUTURE EVOLUTION

MUSCULAR

Skeletal muscles contract (get shorter) to pull the bones, enabling the body to perform a wide range of movements. More than 640 layered muscles make up the skeletal system, which also shapes the body.

Frontalis wrinkles the forehead

Pectoralis major pulls the arm forward and toward the body

External oblique twists the trunk and bends it sideways

Quadriceps femoris straightens the leg at the knee and bends the thigh at the hip

Tibialis anterior lifts the foot upward and inward

Orbicularis oculi closes the eye

Deltoid raises arm away from body

Biceps brachii bends arm at elbow

Sartorius bends the thigh at the hip and rotates it outward

Gastrocnemius bends the foot downward

SKIN, HAIR, AND NAILS

The integumentary system—skin, hair, and nails—forms the body's protective covering. Skin provides a waterproof barrier that keeps out pathogens, helps regulate body temperature, and shields against harmful Sun rays.

Thick terminal hairs grow from scalp and protect top of the head

Fat layer under the skin insulates the body

Fingernails protect the ends of the fingers and thumbs

Brown melanin pigment in skin filters out harmful rays in sunlight

Eyebrows help shade, and direct sweat away from, the eyes

Skin forms a barrier between the body's interior and its surroundings

Fine vellus hairs grow from most areas of the skin

Toenails protect the ends of the toes

BODY SYSTEMS DATABASE

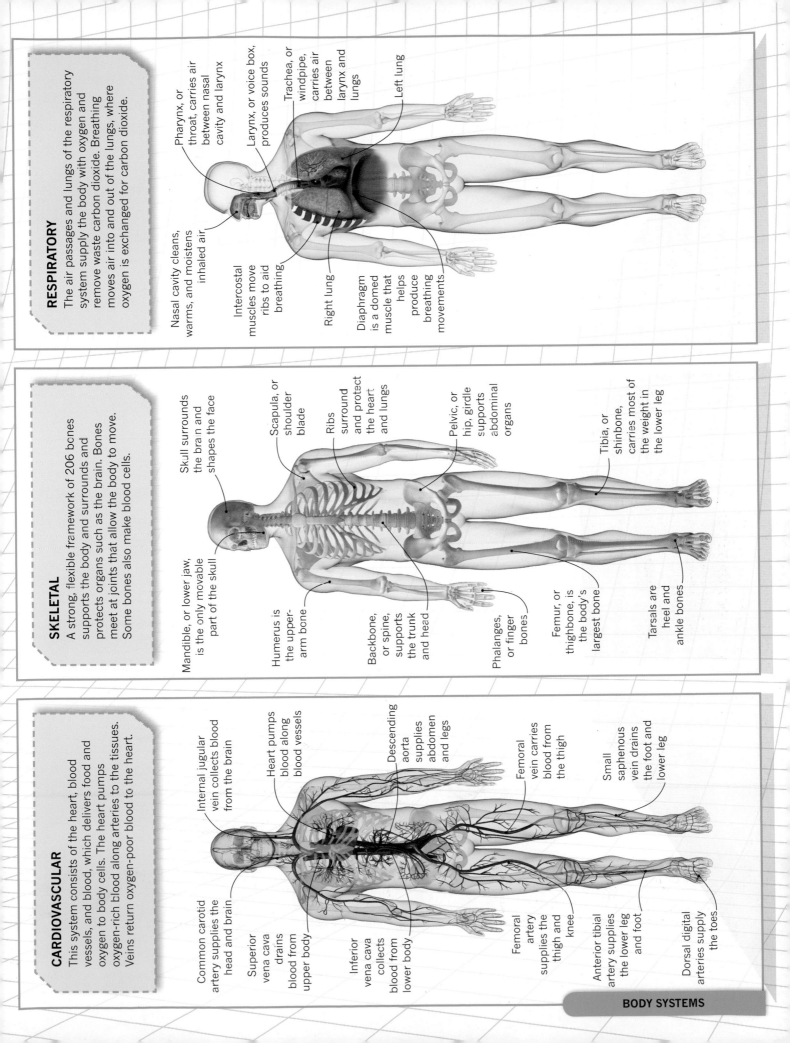

RESPIRATORY

The air passages and lungs of the respiratory system supply the body with oxygen and remove waste carbon dioxide. Breathing moves air into and out of the lungs, where oxygen is exchanged for carbon dioxide.

- Pharynx, or throat, carries air between nasal cavity and larynx
- Larynx, or voice box, produces sounds
- Trachea, or windpipe, carries air between larynx and lungs
- Left lung
- Nasal cavity cleans, warms, and moistens inhaled air
- Intercostal muscles move ribs to aid breathing
- Right lung
- Diaphragm is a domed muscle that helps produce breathing movements

SKELETAL

A strong, flexible framework of 206 bones supports the body and surrounds and protects organs such as the brain. Bones meet at joints that allow the body to move. Some bones also make blood cells.

- Skull surrounds the brain and shapes the face
- Scapula, or shoulder blade
- Ribs surround and protect the heart and lungs
- Pelvic, or hip, girdle supports abdominal organs
- Tibia, or shinbone, carries most of the weight in the lower leg
- Mandible, or lower jaw, is the only movable part of the skull
- Humerus is the upper-arm bone
- Backbone, or spine, supports the trunk and head
- Phalanges, or finger bones
- Femur, or thighbone, is the body's largest bone
- Tarsals are heel and ankle bones

CARDIOVASCULAR

This system consists of the heart, blood vessels, and blood, which delivers food and oxygen to body cells. The heart pumps oxygen-rich blood along arteries to the tissues. Veins return oxygen-poor blood to the heart.

- Internal jugular vein collects blood from the brain
- Heart pumps blood along blood vessels
- Descending aorta supplies abdomen and legs
- Femoral vein carries blood from the thigh
- Small saphenous vein drains the foot and lower leg
- Common carotid artery supplies the head and brain
- Superior vena cava drains blood from upper body
- Inferior vena cava collects blood from lower body
- Femoral artery supplies the thigh and knee
- Anterior tibial artery supplies the lower leg and foot
- Dorsal digital arteries supply the toes

REPRODUCTIVE

Female and male reproductive systems differ, but together they have the ability to create children. The female system produces ova (eggs), while the male system produces sperm. If a sperm fertilizes an ovum, a baby will result.

Fallopian tube carries ova from ovary to uterus

Uterus protects and nourishes the fetus during pregnancy

Prostate gland activates sperm

Penis delivers sperm to female's vagina

Testis produces sperm

Mammary glands inside breast produce milk to feed baby

Ovary produces and releases ova (eggs)

Vagina is passage through which baby is born

Seminal vesicle releases fluid that feeds sperm

Ductus deferens carries sperm from testis

Male

ENDOCRINE

The endocrine system helps control body processes. It consists of a collection of endocrine glands that release chemical messengers called hormones into the bloodstream that alter cell activities.

Hypothalamus controls the pituitary gland

Thyroid gland releases thyroxine, which increases metabolic rate

Pancreas releases hormones that control blood glucose levels

Intestines release hormones that stimulate the release of digestive enzymes

Pituitary gland controls many other endocrine glands

Thymus gland primes the body's defense cells

Adrenal glands release stress-controlling hormones

Ovaries (in women) release female sex hormones

DIGESTIVE

The digestive system extends from the mouth to the anus and includes the throat, esophagus, stomach, and intestines. It breaks down food into simple nutrients that provide the body with energy and building materials.

Salivary gland releases watery saliva into the mouth

Throat (pharynx) carries food to the esophagus

Esophagus pushes food to the stomach

Stomach stores, churns, and partially digests food

Small intestine is the major site of digestion and absorption of food

Teeth chop and crush food into small pieces

Tongue moves food between the teeth and toward throat

Liver processes absorbed food

Large intestine forms and transports feces

Rectum stores feces until it can be released

Anus opens to release feces (undigested waste)

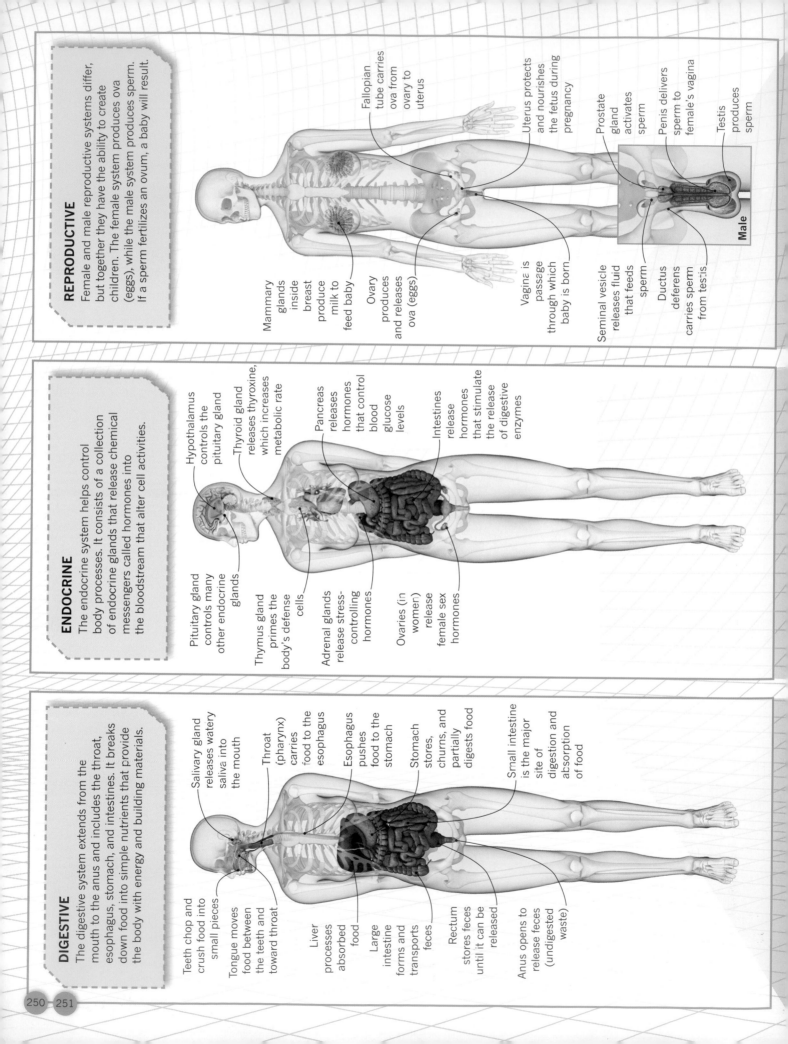

URINARY

The urinary system maintains the body's water content and removes wastes. Two kidneys process blood, removing wastes and excess water to make urine. Urine is stored in the bladder then eliminated from the body.

Left kidney opened to show internal structure

Renal artery carries blood into kidney to be processed

Bladder stores urine and releases it when convenient

Right kidney contains one million nephrons, or filtering units, that produce urine

Ureter carries urine from kidney to bladder

Urethra carries urine from bladder to outside

NERVOUS

Consisting of the brain, spinal cord, and nerves, the nervous system is the body's premier control system. The brain enables us to feel, think, and move. Nerves relay signals between brain and body.

Brain receives and processes signals from the body and sends out instructions

Spinal nerve, one of 31 pairs arising from the spinal cord

Spinal cord relays signals between brain and body

Sciatic nerve controls thigh muscles that bend the knee

Common peroneal nerve controls shin muscles that lift foot upward

Cranial nerve, one of 12 pairs arising from the brain

Intercostal nerve controls muscles between the ribs

Radial nerve controls muscles that bend the wrist and fingers

Tibial nerve supplies calf muscles that bend the foot downward

LYMPHATIC AND IMMUNE

A large network of vessels, the lymphatic system drains excess tissue fluid called lymph into the bloodstream. Lymph passes through lymph nodes, which contain cells called lymphocytes that destroy pathogens (germs).

Tonsils destroy eaten or inhaled pathogens

Left subclavian vein is a blood vessel that receives lymph

Spleen is largest lymph organ

Lymph node removes pathogens from lymph passing through it

Lymph capillary drains lymph (excess fluid) from tissues

Right lymphatic duct receives lymph from upper right side of body

Thymus gland processes lymphocytes

Thoracic duct empties lymph from body's lower and left side into left subclavian vein

Peyer's patches help protect the small intestine from pathogens

Lymph vessel carries lymph received from lymph capillaries

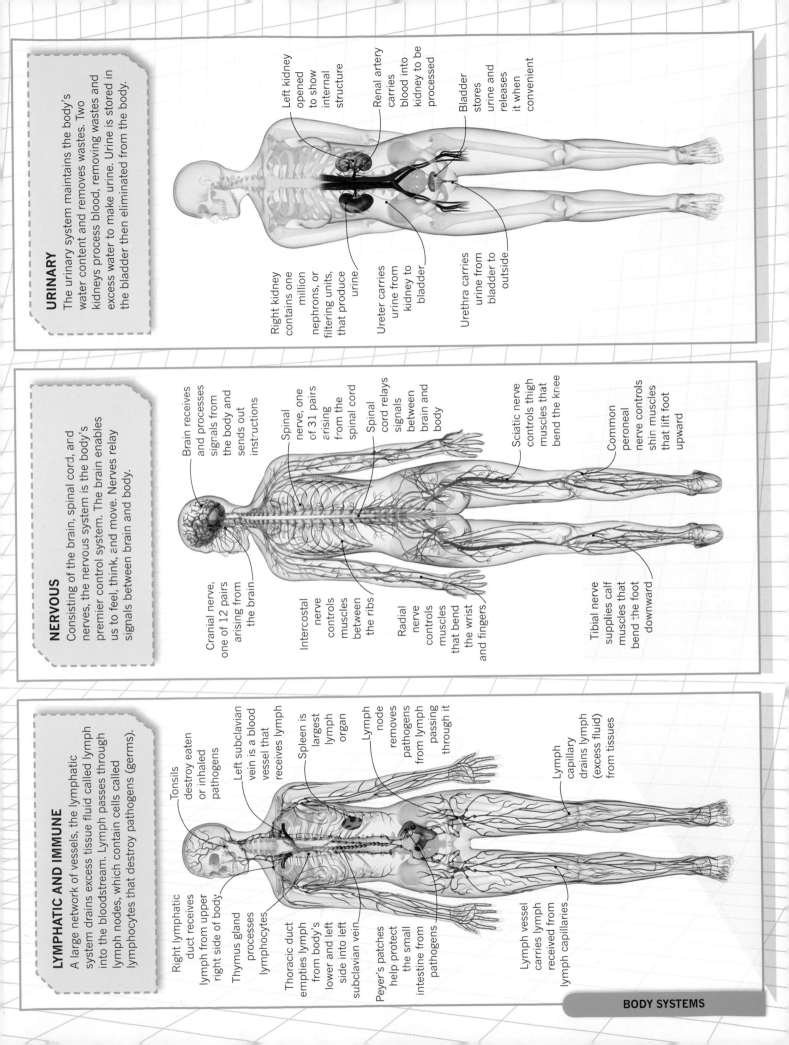

INDEX

ACKNOWLEDGMENTS

DK WOULD LIKE TO THANK:

Vladimir Aleksic, Darren Awuah, Balloon Art Studio, Seb Burnett, Ray and Corinne Burrows, Rich Cando, Jim Cohen, Chris Corr, Hunt Emerson, Martin Hargreaves, Rod Hunt, KJA-artists.com, Mark Longworth, Ed Merritt, Ali Pellatt, Pedro Penizzotto, Jason Pickersgill, Yuliya Somina, Alex Spiro, Ricardo Tercio, Denise Wilton, and Tina Zellmer for illustrations. Jenny Finch for knitting a DNA double helix. Twitter for use of their logo. Ali Gibbs for proofreading. Jackie Brind for preparing the index.

THE PUBLISHER WOULD LIKE TO THANK THE FOLLOWING FOR THEIR KIND PERMISSION TO REPRODUCE THEIR PHOTOGRAPHS:

Key: a-above; b-below/bottom; c-center; f-far; l-left; r-right; t-top

4 Science Photo Library: medicalrf.com (bl). 6 Getty Images: Dr. David M, Phillips (br). 8 Science Photo Library: medicalrf.com (br). 10 iStockphoto.com: inktycoon (br/rhino); ThomasVogel (br/paper tear). 10–11 Corbis: Alan Schein Photography (tc/crowd). Getty Images: Daiju Kitamura / Aflo (c/running track). iStockphoto.com: cyan22 (ca/foot prints). 11 Corbis: Bettmann (bc); Dimitri lundt/ TempSport (crb); Weatherstock (cr). 12 Corbis: Julie Habel (br); Ken Seet (cla). Getty Images: BLOOMimage (tl); Kevin Cooley (tr); Davis McCardie (ftl); Dana Neely (clb); Oliver Renck (cl). 13 Corbis: David P. Hall (br); Helen King (tl); Michael Prince (tl). Getty Images: Bob Carey (cra); ColorBlind Images (bl); Stuart Dee (tl); Galla Images (clb); Image Source (c); Andy Ryan (cr); Sabine Scheckel (tr). 16 The Bridgeman Art Library: Musee d'Histoire de la Medecine, Paris, France / Archives Charmet (fcl); Museo Real Academia de Medicina, Madrid, Spain / Index (cr); Private Collection / Ken Welsh (cl). Corbis: Bettmann (fcr); Peter Turnley (bl/podium). Getty Images: blue jean images (crb/ doctors body); Shuji Kobayashi (cb/Aurelius body). 16–17 Getty Images: Shuji Kobayashi (c/curtains). 17 The Bridgeman Art Library: Louvre, Paris, France / Giraudon (cr). Corbis: Bettmann (cl/Vesalius); DLILLC (tc); Wally McNamee (fcl); Peter Turnley (cb/podium). Getty Images: Jonathan Kirn (fbr). 18 akg-images: (cr). The Bridgeman Art Library: Bibliotheque des Arts Decoratifs, Paris, France / Archives Charmet (bc); Mauritshuis, The Hague, The Netherlands (br). Corbis: Bettmann (cb). Getty Images: The Bridgeman Art Library (clb). 18–19 Getty Images: The Bridgeman Art Library (c). 19 akg-images: (bl). The Bridgeman Art Library: Bibliotheque de la Faculte de Medecine, Paris, France / Archives Charmet (br). Corbis: Rune Hellestad (cr). iStockphoto.com: lucato (bl/easel). 20–21 Alamy Images: imagebroker (tc). iStockphoto.com: sneska (graph paper). 22 Corbis: Visuals Unlimited (cl). Science Photo Library: (c); Robert Chase (tr). 22–23 Science Photo Library: (c). 23 Science Photo Library: CNRI (bl); GJLP (cra/feet scans); Geoff Tompkinson (c). 24 Corbis: Digital Art (cl); image100 (bl). 25 Corbis: Arctic-Images (cr); George Steinmetz (br); Ken Weingart (tr); Jens Nieth / zefa (cla). Getty Images: Ted Kinsman (clb). 26 Science Photo Library: A. Dowsett / Health Protection Agency (cra). 30 Corbis: Imagemore Co., Ltd. (bc) (br) (fbr); Bob Krist (c). Getty Images: (ftr); AFP (tl); John Banagan (r). National Geographic Stock: Nicolas Reynard (bl). 31 Alamy Images: Will Dolder / vario images (cr). Corbis: Danny Lehman (ftr). Getty Images: (tl); Annabelle Breakey (fcr); Tim Graham (tl); David Sacks (tr); Paule Seux (cl). 34 Corbis: Fendis / zefa (tl). 34–35 iStockphoto.com: Tony Bonus (bc). 35 Alamy Images: Agripicture Images (crb). Corbis: Deddeda / Design Pics (br/elephant foot); Tom Grill (tr); Arthur Morris (cb/eagle talons). FLPA: Mike Lane (bc). Getty Images: Alex Cao (fbr). iStockphoto.com: Spiderstock (fcl). 37 Corbis: Austrian Archives (cla); L. Clarke (tr/twins); Visuals Unlimited (cl). 40 iStockphoto.com: gaffera (tr/lung background). 40– 41 iStockphoto.com: A-Digit (c/silhouettes); dlewis33 (c/gallery background). 41 iStockphoto.com: gaffera (tr/lung background). 42 Corbis: doc-stock (ca/chocolate box); Louie Psihoyos (bl/skull in box). 42–43 Corbis: Andy Aitchison (c/background shelves). 43 Corbis: Sean Justice (bc/box of labels). Science Photo Library: J ohn Bavosi (crb/appendix). 46 Science Photo Library: Steve Gschmeissner (b) (ca); Omikron (br). 47 Science Photo Library: (c); R. Bick, B. Poindexter / UT Medical School (tc); A. Dowsett / Health Protection Agency (bl); Eric Grave (br). 48–49 Getty Images: The Bridgeman Art Library (c). 50 Getty Images: Photosindia (c/scarf). Science Photo Library: (ca). 50–51 Corbis: Bettmann (ca/Watson &Crick). Getty Images: Thomas Northcut (c/sofa). iStockphoto.com: Maliketh (c/wallpaper); yasinguneysu (cb/floor). 51 Corbis: Bettmann (ca). 54–55 Getty Images: Laurence Griffiths (c). 56 Science Photo Library: CNRI (bl). 56–57 Science Photo Library: Lawrence Lawry (c). 57 Science Photo Library: James King-Holmes (tl) (br). 59 Corbis: Hulton-Deutsch Collection (crb). 60–61 Corbis: Pawel Libera (c). 62 Photolibrary: John Cadenhead (cla/crutches). 62–63 Photolibrary: BSIP Medical / Laurent Lisa (c/plaster cast). 64 Nobel Foundation: (br). 64–65 Corbis: Bettmann (c). 65 Corbis: Bettmann (fbr). Science Photo

Library: (crb). TopFoto.co.uk: (tc). 68 iStockphoto.com: aldra (tl/ dumbbells); Cimmerian (cl); ErickN (bl); Ultra Generic (tr). 68–69 iStockphoto.com: oblachko (c/background). 69 iStockphoto.com: aldra (tr/dumbbells); Cimmerian (cl); ErickN (crb/red dumbbells); kirstypargeter (br/weights). 70–71 NASA: (c/window). 71 NASA: (tc/ blue sky). 72 iStockphoto.com: A-Digit (bl); SchulteProductions (c/ poster background). 72–73 iStockphoto.com: moorsky (c). 73 Getty Images: Win Initiative (tl); Paul Ekman Group: (tr) (bl) (br) (cl) (clb) (crb) (tc). 74 Corbis: Randy Faris (tr); Photo Kishimoto / amanaimages (tr); Randy Lincks (bc); MedicalRF.com (cr); Nice One Productions (br); Marie Schmitt / Image Point FR (cla); Somos Images (tc); Herb Watson (clb). 74–75 Corbis: Redlink Production (c). 75 Corbis: Ted Levine / zefa (bl); Thinkstock (c). 78 Corbis: Hulton –Deutsch Collection (c). 78– 79 Photolibrary: Edmund Sumner (c/museum interior). 79 Association des Amis de Marey et des Musées de Baune: (cl/Étienne-Jules Marey images) (cr/man in bowler hat). Etienne-Jules MAREY, Etude chronophotographique de la locomotion humaine: 1. Marcher revêtu d'un costume blanc dont la jambe gauche teinte en noir devient invisible, chronophotographie sur plaque fixe, 2. Images successives d'un courer, chronophotographie géométrique partielle retouchée à la gouache, vers 1883, Musée Marey, Beaune, France. Photo: J.Cl. Couval. Corbis: Bettmann (cra/strongman); Hulton -Deutsch Collection (br/ man lifting weights); Sean Sexton Collection (cr/penny-farthing) (cra/ top-hatted man with woman) (tr/Edwardian woman). Getty Images: (crb/straw hat couple); Sasha (c/dancers); Edward Tracey (tr/stilts). Mary Evans Picture Library: (crb/acrobats). 80 Lebrecht Music and Arts: Fototeca / Leemage (cla/Ambroise Paré leg). Össur UK: (br/legs for athletes). Otto Bock HealthCare: (c/C-Leg) (cl/peg leg). Science & Society Picture Library: Science Museum (fcla/bronze leg). 81 Courtesy of the rehabilitation Institute of Chicago: (cla/bionic arm) (cra/hook hand). Science & Society Picture Library: Science Museum (ftr/von Berlichingen arm). 82 Getty Images: White Packert (cla). 83 Alamy Images: The London Art Archive (br). 86 Corbis: Danilio Calilung (br); Richard T. Nowitz (cl); Solus-Veer (fbl). 86–87 Corbis: Solus-Veer (c/book). 87 Science Photo Library: (br). 90 DK Images: British Museum (tc/banknotes); Stephen Oliver (fbl). 90 Getty Images: White Packert (bl). 90–91 DK Images: Andy Crawford / Ray Smith (tc); Jamie Marshall (ca); Museum of Moving Image (bc/maps and photographs). 91 DK Images: The British Library (bc); Musee du Louvre (cr/Mona Lisa). 94 Getty Images: Creative Crop (tl). 95 DK Images: John Chase / The Museum of London (clb/quill). Getty Images: Creative Crop (cra/ cup of tea); Davies and Starr (crb/drawing pins); Peter Landon (ftr). 98 Getty Images: C Squared Studios (c). 98–99 Corbis: Rob Matheson. 99 Getty Images: C Squared Studios (cl) (cr). 106–107 iStockphoto.com: fpm (c). 108–109 Getty Images: Yashuhide Fumoto (bc/speaker mesh). 109 Getty Images: Monty Rakusen (cb/green square buttons). 110 Alamy Images: The London Art Archive (cl/ painting details). 110–111 Alamy Images: The London Art Archive (cr). 116–117 Corbis: Images.com (c). 120 Getty Images: Ray Smith (tr). 120–121 Getty Images: Butch Martin (bc); Ray Smith (c). 121 Getty Images: Dorling Kindersley (bc); Butch Martin (tl); Ray Smith (tr). 122 iStockphoto.com: cscredon (crb/canvas behind squares) (crb/black squares). Science Photo Library: (bl). 122–123 iStockphoto.com: lisegagne (c/art gallery & man). 123 Science Photo Library: (crb). 124– 125 iStockphoto.com: tarras79 (c). 126–127 Corbis: Swim Ink 2, LLC (c). iStockphoto.com: Vik_Y (c/decorative borders). 137 akg-images: (tc). 138–139 Getty Images: Steve & Ghy Sampson (c). 139 iStockphoto.com: 4x6 (cl); filo (bl). 142–143 Getty Images: Jonathan Knowles (c). 144 Corbis: Matthias Kulka / zefa (bl); MedicalRF.com (cl); Visuals Unlimited (cl). 145 Corbis: MedicalRF.com (r). Getty Images: 3D4Medical.com (cl); Dr. Dennis Kunkel (c). 146 Science Photo Library: Tony McConnell (c). 147 Science Photo Library: Tony McConnell (c). 154 Alamy Images: Ace Stock Limited (cl); axel leschinski (cr). Corbis: Fancy / Veer (c). 154–155 Corbis: Jeremy Horner (c/train carriage). 155 Alamy Images: Ace Stock Limited (cl). Getty Images: PM Images (cr). Photolibrary: Javier Larrea (c). 156 Getty Images: Dr. David M, Phillips (cb). 157 Getty Images: Time & Life Pictures (cla). 161 Getty Images: Time & Life Pictures (cr). 163 Alamy Images: H. Mark Weidman Photography (br/heart model); Nucleus Medical Art, Inc. (fbl). DK Images: Combustion (c). Getty Images: 3D Clinic (cr/septum). Science Photo Library: (fcr). Wellcome Library, London: M. I. Walker (fbl). 164 Getty Images: Tim Robberts (cla). 164– 165 Getty Images: Clouds Hill Imaging Ltd. (bc). Getty Images: Yorgos Nikas (c/blood cells background). 165 Getty Images: Tim Robberts (bl) (tr). 168–169 Getty Images: 3D4Medical.com (c). 169 Getty Images: 3D4Medical.com (bl). 172 Science & Society Picture Library: Science Museum (cra/transfusion instrument). 172–173 Getty Images: Yorgos Nikas (blood cells). 173 Corbis: Richard T. Nowitz (cra/monkey). Getty Images: (cra/Karl Landsteiner); Tom Schierlitz (cra/blood bag). 174– 175 DK Images: Judith Miller / Feljoy Antiques (cr). 175 Getty Images: Oksana Struk (tl) (bl) (br) (tr). 176 DK Images: Geoff Brightling /

courtesy of Denoyer – Geppert Intl (cr/heart). iStockphoto.com: Pannonia (cl/border hearts); Rekinc1980 (tl/ribbon); tacojim (c/heart shaped box); ValentynVolkov (cr/ice-cubes). 176–177 iStockphoto.com: racnus (satin background). 177 Corbis: Bettmann (tc/Dr. Barnard). iStockphoto.com: aggressor (cr); katyakatya (cb/decorative dividers); whitemay (tc/envelope & card). 178 Alamy Images: Steven Widoff (cra). iStockphoto.com: tombaky (cb) (br/sun lounger). Photolibrary: Ricardo Funari (tr/sun lounger) (br/parasol); Henryk Tomasz Kaiser (tl). 178–179 Alamy Images: Russell Kord (c/water). Photolibrary: Ricardo Funari (c/pool edging); Jun Tsukuda (c/pool divider). 179 Getty Images: C Squared Studios (tr/drain & plug); Matthias Clamer (ca/child in armbands). iStockphoto.com: Spanishalex (cra/drinks). Photolibrary: Wilfried Beege (cb); Steve Chenn (cra/waiter & woman); Ricardo Funari (br/sun lounger); Henryk Tomasz Kaiser (tr/parasol). 182 Corbis: Mauritius, GMBH / MedNet (tl). Science Photo Library: CNRI (tr). 183 Science Photo Library: CNRI (bl); Steve Gschmeissner (tl). 184 Getty Images: rubberball (br); Eric Tucker (bl). Science Photo Library: CNRI (cr); Dr. Gopal Murti (cl). 184–185 Getty Images: Eric Tucker (background). 185 Corbis: Burke / Triolo Productions / Brand X (tc/paper on nail). Getty Images: rubberball (bl); Science VU / CDC (tl); Eric Tucker (br). Science Photo Library: A. Dowsett / Health Protection Agency (tc); Eye of Science (cr) (tr); Profs. P. M. Motta & F. M. Magliocca (cl). 190 iStockphoto.com: aamorim (tc); boris64 (cr); cyrop (c); designalldone (bc); k-libre (cb). 190–191 iStockphoto.com: penfold (c/background dots). 191 Science Photo Library: GJLP / CNRI (cr). 192 Science Photo Library: Clouds Hill Imaging Ltd. (cl); Eye of Science (cr) (bc); Steve Gschmeissner (ca); K. H. Kjeldsen (bl). 192–193 Corbis: Louise Gubb (guinea worm). 193 Corbis: Visuals Unlimited (cla). Science Photo Library: Eye of Science (bl) (cl); Steve Gschmeissner (crb); Andrew Syred (bc); Cath Wadforth (cr). 194 The Bridgeman Art Library: Museo Correr, Venice, Italy (bc); Fitzwilliam Museum, University of Cambridge, UK (cr). Mary Evans Picture Library: (tr) (cl/skull). Science & Society Picture Library: Science Museum (clb) (bl). Wellcome Library, London: (cl/ trepanning instruments) (br). 195 The Bridgeman Art Library: Courtesy of the Warden and Scholars of New College, Oxford (tr). Getty Images: Dimitri Vervitsiotis (cr). Science & Society Picture Library: Science Museum (tc) (bc). Wellcome Library, London: (bl/buttock cupping). 196 Corbis: PoodlesRock (cl). Wellcome Library, London: (bc). 196–197 Getty Images: The Bridgeman Art Library (cb) (ca). 197 Corbis: (tl); Karen Kasmauski (bc). Science Photo Library: CDC (c). 198–199 Science Photo Library: NIBSC (c). 200 Getty Images: (tr). Science Photo Library: (bl). Wellcome Library, London: (cl). 200–201 Corbis: Helen King (c/office). Wellcome Library, London: (c/map). 201 Corbis: Bettmann (cla); Hulton - Deutsch Collection (cr); Image Source (bc). Getty Images: (tl). Science Photo Library: (tr). 208 Getty Images: Neil Beckerman (cl); Wayne H. Chasan (br); Chad Ehlers (cra); Imagemore Co., Ltd. (clb); Caroline Schiff (fcl); Gregor Schuster (tl) (bc); Bruce T. Brown (tc); Kris Timken (cl); ZenShui (br). 210–211 Dreamstime.com : Gelpi (c/doctor holding clipboard). 212 Mary Evans Picture Library: (bc). 214 The Bridgeman Art Library: Royal College of Surgeons, London (c). 215 Corbis: Mauritius, GMBH / MedNet (c). 216 Corbis: MedicalRF.com (fcra/liver); Vo Trung Dung (bl) (br). Getty Images: 3D4Medical.com (cra/inner duodenum); Dorling Kindersley (fcr/stomach); Nucleus MedicalArt.com (cr/colon) (cb/ oesophagus). Science Photo Library: David M. Martin, MD (bc); Gastrolab (ca/capsule endoscope); Cordelia Molloy (ca/pill camera). 216–217 Getty Images: Pal Hermansen (c/whirlpool background). 217 Corbis: Ted Horowitz (cra); Pete Saloutos (cra/spinal column). Getty Images: 3D4Medical.com (c/shoulder muscles); SMC Images (c/knee x-ray); Steve Wisbauer (cla/endoscope). Science Photo Library: CNRI (bl); Brad Nelson / Custom Medical Stock Photo (cl). 221 Getty Images: Bruce Laurance (clb). 222–223 iStockphoto.com: kkonkle (c/all lift). 225 Getty Images: Gregor Schuster (cl). 227 Getty Images: Gregor Schuster (b). 228 Science Photo Library: medicalrf.com (cl). 228–229 Corbis: Roger Ressmeyer (c/men at monitor). Science Photo Library: D. Phillips. 229 Science Photo Library: Francis Leroy / Biocosmos (cr); D. Phillips (tr). 234 Corbis: Image Source (cr). Getty Images: Tariq Dajani (c); Siri Stafford (br). 234–235 Getty Images: James Woodson (cl/face with freckles). 235 Getty Images: ERproductions LTD (tl); Somos / Veer (c). 236–237 iStockphoto.com: Jamesbowyer (c/checked background). 237 Corbis: J. Garcia / photocuisine (tl) (tr). 238 Getty Images: Fred Morley (tr); H. Armstrong Roberts (bl/dancers). iStockphoto.com: hemul75 (tr/clock); muratsen (bl/clock); ODV (tl). 238–239 Getty Images: Warner Bros. (bc/ The Munsters). iStockphoto.com: asterix0597 (cb/clock); billnoll (wallpaper background); ScantyNebula (c/shelves). 239 The Advertising Archives: (tr/party). Alamy Images: The Print Collector (tl/nursery). The Bridgeman Art Library: The Fine Art Society,London / Private Collection (br/Elderly Couple). iStockphoto.com: anvodak (br/clock); Futter_97321 (tl/clocks); KarenMower (tr/clock). Photolibrary: Jerry Millevoi (ca/boys on beach). 240–241 Getty Images: Ryan McVay (c/screen). Science Photo Library: Daniel Sambraus (c/heart ECG). 244 iStockphoto.com: (cr); Kativ (br); luismmolina (c). Science Photo Library: Pasieka (ca). 244–245 iStockphoto.com: sunnygraphics (c/van). 245 iStockphoto.com: angelhell (cl); billyfoto (bl); BlackJack3D (br); Thirteen-Fifty (cla)

All other images © Dorling Kindersley
For further information see: www.dkimages.com